AGING
Volume 33

CENTRAL NERVOUS SYSTEM DISORDERS OF AGING
Clinical Intervention and Research

Aging Series

Aging
Volume 33

Central Nervous System Disorders
of Aging
Clinical Intervention and Research

Editors

Randy Strong, Ph.D.

*Geriatric Research, Education
  and Clinical Center
St. Louis Veterans Administration
  Medical Center, and
Departments of Pharmacology and
  Internal Medicine
St. Louis University School of Medicine
St. Louis, Missouri*

W. Gibson Wood, Ph.D.

*Geriatric Research, Education
  and Clinical Center
St. Louis Veterans Administration
  Medical Center, and
Departments of Neurology and
  Internal Medicine
St. Louis University School of Medicine
St. Louis, Missouri*

William J. Burke, M.D., Ph.D.

*Neurology Service
St. Louis Veterans Administration
  Medical Center, and
Department of Neurology
St. Louis University School of Medicine
St. Louis, Missouri*

Raven Press 🦫 New York

Raven Press, Ltd., 1185 Avenue of the Americas, New York, New York 10036

Made in the United States of America

Library of Congress Cataloging-in-Publication Data

Central nervous system disorders of aging.

  (Aging; v. 33)
  Based on a symposium held in St. Louis, Mo. in Sept.
1986 and sponsored by the St. Louis Veterans Administration
Geriatric Research, Education, and Clinical
Center.
  Includes bibliographies and index.
  1. Central nervous system—Diseases—Age factors—
Congresses. 2. Brain—Aging—Congresses.
3. Neuropsychiatry—Congresses. I. Strong, Randy.
II. Wood, W. Gibson, 1945-   . III. Burke,
William J. (William Joseph), 1940-   . IV. Geriatric
Research, Education, and Clinical Center (Saint Louis,
Mo.) V. Series. [DNLM: 1. Brain Diseases—in old age—
congresses. 2. Central Nervous System Diseases—in old
age—congresses. W1 AG342E v.33 / WL 348 C397 1986]
RC361.C45 1988   618.97'68   87-7148
ISBN 0-88167-354-4

9 8 7 6 5 4 3 2 1

This volume is dedicated to
Anthony P. Fletcher, M.D.,
Physician, Scientist, Colleague, and Friend
(1919–1987)

Preface

The upward shift in the median age of the population of industrialized nations has become a matter of concern for health care providers. As the group of persons 65 years of age and older increases in size, relative to other age groups, it is anticipated that health care services will be increasingly utilized. The elderly appear in outpatient facilities 50% more often than younger age groups, stay three times as long in acute care hospitals, and occupy more than 90% of the long-term care beds in the United States.

One group of disorders requiring utilization of health care services is neurological and behavioral dysfunctions. Aging is associated with an increased incidence of stroke, deterioration of motor function, depression, and dementia. The prevalence rate of Alzheimer's disease doubles in those over 60 years of age, increasing to around 40% by 90 years of age. The incidence of Parkinson's disease also increases dramatically after age 65. Furthermore, changes in the brain that occur as part of the normal aging process make the elderly more susceptible to drug side effects such as tardive dyskinesia.

This volume presents information on the current state of knowledge of age-related neuropsychiatric disorders, neurodegenerative diseases, stroke, and molecular and cellular changes in the aging brain. Rather than providing a general overview of disorders of the aging brain, selected topics in which significant advances have recently been made are examined in detail.

The first section addresses research and clinical intervention in neurodegenerative disorders. It includes chapters on the pathological criteria for diagnosis of neurodegenerative diseases, the mechanism of degeneration of neurons in Alzheimer's disease, the role of neurotrophic factors in neurodegenerative diseases, and clinical drug trials in the treatment of Alzheimer's disease.

The second section examines the diagnosis and treatment of selected central nervous system disorders during aging. Included are chapters on differential diagnosis of depressive dementia and Alzheimer's dementia, diagnosis and prevention of tardive dyskinesia, clinical research on sleep disorders in the elderly, diagnostic imaging of neurological disorders, strategies for intervention in stroke, and the use of family support systems in the treatment of progressive neurological disorders.

The final section addresses two emerging areas of research in which attempts have been made to establish the underlying causes of biological changes in the aging brain—changes that may predispose the elderly to certain age-related neurological disorders. These areas are (1) the role of gene expression in aging and age-related neurodegenerative disorders and (2) the role of membranes in age-associated changes in cellular function. This section includes chapters on the molecular biology of neuronal degeneration, the expression of genes coding for structural proteins in the brain, age changes in membrane fluidity and lipid composition, recent findings on membrane asymmetry, and effects of dolichol on membrane structure and function.

This volume examines recent advances in clinical intervention and research. It will serve as a clinical resource and a stimulus for new research. Clinicians, researchers, and students in neurology, psychiatry, neurobiology, pharmacology, and allied health professions will find this volume useful.

Randy Strong
W. Gibson Wood
William J. Burke

Acknowledgments

This volume is based in part on a symposium entitled "Central Nervous System Disorders of Aging: Strategies for Intervention" held in St. Louis, Missouri, in September 1986. This symposium was sponsored by the St. Louis Veterans Administration Geriatric Research, Education and Clinical Center (GRECC) (through a continuing education grant from the Veterans Administration Office of Academic Affairs via the Office of Geriatrics and Extended Care), the Veterans Administration South Central Regional Medical Education Center, the St. Louis College of Pharmacy, St. Louis University School of Medicine, and St. Louis University School of Nursing.

The editors would like to thank Sharon Smith of the St. Louis GRECC for her administrative support on all phases of this project. We would also like to express our appreciation to Sandy Melliere for her editorial and typing expertise in preparation of this volume. Sincere expressions of thanks are extended to Cheryl Mason for her invaluable support during this project and to Diane Palumbo for her creative efforts in preparation of symposium materials. The Editors are very thankful for the cooperation of the entire GRECC staff toward successful completion of this project. A final word of appreciation to the chapter authors and to the symposium participants for their contributions.

Contents

Neurodegenerative Diseases

Diagnosis and Clinical Intervention

Molecular Biology and Membrane Structure

Contributors

Stanley H. Appel, M.D.
Department of Neurology
Baylor College of Medicine
One Baylor Plaza
Houston, Texas 77030

J. Wesson Ashford, M.D., Ph.D.
Department of Psychiatry
Southern Illinois University School
of Medicine
P.O. Box 3926
Springfield, Illinois 62708

Harriet Baker, Ph.D.
Laboratory of Molecular Neurobiology
Cornell University Medical College
1300 York Avenue
New York, New York 10021

Leonard Berg, M.D.
Alzheimer's Disease Research Center
Department of Neurology and
Neurological Surgery
Washington University School
of Medicine
St. Louis, Missouri 63110

J. Robert Bostwick, Ph.D.
Department of Neurology
Baylor College of Medicine
One Baylor Plaza
Houston, Texas 77030

William J. Burke, M.D., Ph.D.
Neurology Service
Veterans Administration Medical
Center
St. Louis, Missouri 63125

Hyung D. Chung, M.D.
Laboratory Service
Veterans Administration Medical
Center
St. Louis, Missouri 63106

Edward F. Domino, M.D.
Department of Pharmacology
University of Michigan
Ann Arbor, Michigan 48109-0010

Rodger J. Elble, M.D., Ph.D.
Department of Internal Medicine
Southern Illinois University School of
Medicine
P.O. Box 3926
Springfield, Illinois 62708

James W. Fletcher, M.D.
Nuclear Medicine Service
Veterans Administration Medical
Center
St. Louis, Missouri 63106

Ezio Giacobini, M.D., Ph.D.
Department of Pharmacology
Southern Illinois University School of
Medicine
P.O. Box 3926
Springfield, Illinois 62708

Chris Gorka, M.S.
Geriatric Research, Education and
Clinical Center
Veterans Administration Medical
Center
St. Louis, Missouri 63125

George T. Grossberg, M.D.
Division of Geriatric Psychiatry
Department of Psychiatry and Human
Behavior
St. Louis University Medical Center
St. Louis, Missouri 63104

John H. Haring, M.D.
Department of Anatomy
St. Louis University School of
Medicine
St. Louis, Missouri 63104

Asao Hirano, M.D.
Bluestone Laboratory
Division of Neuropathology
Department of Pathology
Montefiore Medical Center
Bronx, New York 10467

Tong H. Joh, Ph.D.
Laboratory of Molecular Neurobiology
Cornell University Medical College
1300 York Avenue
New York, New York 10021

Vinod Kumar, M.D.
Department of Psychiatry
Southern Illinois University School
of Medicine
P.O. Box 3926
Springfield, Illinois 62708

Gary L. Marshall
Research and Development Service
Veterans Administration Medical
Center
St. Louis, Missouri 63125

Michael B. Mattammal, Ph.D.
Geriatric Research, Education and
Clinical Center
Veterans Administration Medical
Center
St. Louis, Missouri 63125

James L. McManaman, Ph.D.
Department of Neurology
Baylor College of Medicine
One Baylor Plaza
Houston, Texas 77030

John W. Murphy, M.D.
Department of Laboratory Medicine
Southern Illinois University School
of Medicine
P.O. Box 3926
Springfield, Illinois 62708

Raj Nakra, M.D.
Department of Psychiatry and Human
Behavior
St. Louis University Medical Center
St. Louis, Missouri 63104

Arlan Richardson, Ph.D.
Department of Chemistry
Illinois State University
Normal, Illinois 61761

Friedhelm Schroeder, Ph.D.
Department of Pharmacology and
Medicinal Chemistry
College of Pharmacy
University of Cincinnati Medical
Center
3223 Eden Avenue
Cincinnati, Ohio 45269-0004

John B. Selhorst, M.D.
Department of Neurology
St. Louis University School
of Medicine
St. Louis, Missouri 63110

John W. Shepard, Jr., M.D.
Geriatric Research, Education and
Clinical Center
Veterans Administration Medical
Center
St. Louis, Missouri 63125

Kathleen A. Sherman, Ph.D.
Department of Pharmacology
Southern Illinois University School
of Medicine
P.O. Box 3926
Springfield, Illinois 62708

R. Glenn Smith, Ph.D.
Department of Neurology
Baylor College of Medicine
One Baylor Plaza
Houston, Texas 77030

S. Scott Stewart, M.D.
Department of Neurology
Baylor College of Medicine
One Baylor Plaza
Houston, Texas 77030

Randy Strong, Ph.D.
*Geriatric Research, Education and
    Clinical Center
Veterans Administration Medical
    Center
St. Louis, Missouri 63125*

Albert Y. Sun, Ph.D.
*Sinclair Research Farm
and University of Missouri School of
    Medicine
Columbia, Missouri 65203*

Grace Y. Sun, Ph.D.
*Sinclair Research Farm
and University of Missouri School of
    Medicine
Columbia, Missouri 65203*

**Peggy A. Szwabo, R.N.,
    A.C.S.W., C-CS**
*Division of Geriatric Psychiatry
St. Louis University Medical Center
St. Louis, Missouri 63104*

Yasuko Tomozawa, Ph.D.
*Department of Neurology
Baylor College of Medicine
One Baylor Plaza
Houston, Texas 77030*

Lisa S. Williamson, B.S.
*School of Veterinary Medicine
University of Missouri
Columbia, Missouri 65203*

Carol T. Wismer
*Department of Chemistry
Illinois State University
Normal, Illinois 61761*

W. Gibson Wood, Ph.D.
*Geriatric Research, Education and
    Clinical Center
Veterans Administration Medical
    Center
St. Louis, Missouri 63125*

Mary Zibart
*Department of Chemistry
Illinois State University
Normal, Illinois 61761*

Central Nervous System Disorders of Aging:
Clinical Intervention and Research, edited by
Randy Strong et al. Raven Press, New York
© 1988.

THE AGING BRAIN

Leonard Berg

Alzheimer's Disease Research Center
Department of Neurology and Neurological Surgery (Neurology)
Washington University School of Medicine
St. Louis, Missouri 63110

This chapter is designed to provide a background for this volume on the neurologic and psychiatric disorders of the brain in aging. Because of well-known demographic changes, the absolute numbers and the prevalence of these disorders are increasing to proportions that threaten the well-being and economy of our nation. The urgency is illustrated by estimates from the National Institute on Aging regarding Alzheimer's disease (AD), one of the major age-related disorders. There are approximately two million people in the country who are now suffering from this disease, and that number is expected to double by the year 2030. Even now, the burden is staggering, since the current national cost of the illness is estimated at $40 billion annually! It behooves us to explore and extend our knowledge about why the aging brain is susceptible to these disorders, what are their causes and mechanisms, and how can they be better understood, treated and prevented.

We will review selected topics on the aging brain and its function to highlight subjects of current research interest, especially when relevant to discussions in the other chapters of this volume.

BEHAVIORAL CHANGES IN THE ELDERLY

The history of our understanding of the age-related declines in human brain function verifies that the more care taken to exclude the effects of disease, the less decline attributable to age itself can be found (30). That conclusion appears true not only for reported declines in intellectual function, loss of tendon reflexes and impaired sensation, but also for claims of aging effect on EEG (16), cerebral blood flow and metabolism, whether measured by older techniques or the increasingly popular positron emission tomography (PET).

Those of us who study human aging know that dementia and depression, though common, are not the norm for the elderly. While the advancing decades bring some decline in the intellectual and behavioral capabilities of the brain, the majority of individuals, even in their tenth decade, maintain good intellectual function that allows them to make proper decisions and cope with everyday intellectual problems. Data are still sparse on the mental health of the very old, but it appears that, even after the age of 100, serious intellectual decline is not the inevitable consequence of aging. "Senility" is the result of disease, not just age-induced decline.

Longitudinal studies have shown that younger adults who perform well on tests of intellectual function tend to perform well with advancing years. We still have too few data derived from combinations of cross-sectional and longitudinal investigations, but one can say that, of the multiple factors which characterize intellectual behavior, some can be shown to improve with age, some remain at the same level, and some decline. As an example, "fluid" intelligence tends to decline with aging, but "crystallized" intelligence remains well preserved. The former includes the perceptual-integrative skills for solving new kinds of problems and adapting to novel situations; the latter is based on learned skills and information such as vocabulary. Intuitively, we believe that if we continually challenge our brain throughout life by providing ourselves with tasks that require "fluid" intelligence, there would be less decline in those measures. That proposition, which touches on the plasticity of the aging brain, has never been rigorously examined.

One of the best established differences in psychometric results in the elderly, as compared with those of younger adults, is age-related decline in memory, whether tested by verbal or nonverbal means. These age differences have been demonstrated even during self-pacing when speed is ruled out as a factor. However, the more relevant the material is to everyday experience, the less evident are the differences between younger and older cohorts.

Even when pertinent diseases are excluded and an apparently healthy population in their eighties is studied, one finds at least mild impairment of motor and sensory function with aging (30). The changes include prolonged reaction times, slowness of movement, mildly stooped posture and impaired balance, decreased perception of vibration, and declines in the special senses of vision, smell, taste, and hearing.

Similar evidence of cognitive and motor impairment has been recognized in the relatively few studies on aged nonhuman primates (13) and in the plentiful investigations of lower animals (28), one example of which will be described later.

STRUCTURAL CHANGES IN OLD BRAINS

Age-induced changes in the gross structure of the brain include general shrinkage, long recognized both in humans and in many lower animals. Declines in brain weight, dilatation of the ventricles, shrinkage of the gyri, and widening of the sulci are well-documented by observations both at the time of autopsy and in recent years by computed tomography (CT) or magnetic resonance imaging (MRI) of the brain (6,60). Note, however, that the brain weights of old laboratory rats remain stable or even increase (15).

Number of Neurons

Several aspects of microscopic anatomy of the brain change with aging. Even though we recognize the considerable limitations of cell-counting techniques in an organ as complex as the human brain, it appears that there are age-related declines in numbers of large neurons. These are selective both with regard to brain region and cell type. Some regions of cerebral cortex seem to show no age-related loss of neurons. Certain brain stem nuclei, notably the inferior olive and the trochlear nucleus, retain their full complement of neurons, whereas, substantia nigra and locus ceruleus seem to show some loss. Sleep disorders in the elderly (Shepard, this volume) may be related to aging changes in locus ceruleus. The problems of estimating cell counts are exemplified by the fact that there is still dispute whether neurons diminish in number with age in the human nucleus basalis of Meynert, despite the attention that structure has received in the excitement over the brain's cholinergic system (44) in relation to age- and disease-related declines in memory.

Neuronal Shrinkage

Data are available indicating that the cell bodies of some classes of neurons shrink in size with advancing age even in the absence of disease. Whereas, some years ago it was taught that old neurons uniformly have shrinking dendritic arborization, more recent evidence points to preserved and even expanding dendritic trees with aging in some (9,11). Of course, it has not been possible to estimate dendritic surface in total, because of the lack of appropriate quantitative histological methods. Limited data on a biochemical approach to this problem suggest an overall decline in dendritic surface area in the aged human brain, since amounts of ganglioside sialic acid (a marker for neuronal membrane) per neuron have been estimated to be smaller in aged than in younger cortex (14). Evidence is conflicting (54) on the question of whether synaptic density declines or remains stable with aging (mainly in the rat).

The principle of regional neuronal selectivity is illustrated by the fact that granule cells of human parahippocampal gyrus show continuing elaboration of their dendritic trees into very advanced age, whereas, those in the dentate gyrus show regressive changes more uniformly (19). This regional selectivity, with respect to aging changes, reminds one of the exquisite selectivity of histological changes in the hippocampal formation in AD. Hyman and his colleagues (27) pointed out the susceptibility of the subiculum and CA1 in the hippocampus and layer II of the entorhinal cortex to the cell loss and neurofibrillary tangles of AD, whereas, adjacent regions and layers were spared. Does regional selectivity in aging contribute to susceptibility to Alzheimer changes or to their focal accentuation?

Examples of Neurochemical Changes

Chemical measures indicate that myelination of the white matter and cortex continues throughout the life span of the rat (15), whereas, the aged human brain tends to lose myelin. The principle of variability is underscored by the observation of DeKosky et al. (15). Cortical ganglioside and cerebroside correlates of aging vary between strains of rats even when other measures, such as neuron counts and synaptic densities in the hippocampus, remain stable in the two strains (54). Even sex differences are evident in aging effects on cholinergic markers in the rat (34).

Furthermore, observations that the numbers of basal forebrain cholinergic neurons remain the same in old rodents, despite reduction in forebrain cholinergic enzyme activity (34), suggest mechanisms other than cell loss are responsible for the declines in biochemical measures. Slowing of neuronal metabolism, decreased genomic activity, and impaired post-translational processing of proteins within the cells are all possible explanations.

Plaques and Tangles

Nondemented elderly persons accumulate neurofibrillary tangles (NFTs) within a few of their cortical neurons and sparse numbers of neuritic plaques in the cortex as the decades progress. As many as 90% of nondemented persons dying in the ninth or tenth decade are observed to have those changes which, when found in profusion, are the histological hallmarks of AD (31). It is noteworthy that these changes in the nondemented elderly affect hippocampus much more than other regions. Similarly, neuritic plaques have been demonstrated in the brains of old monkeys (48,59), and NFTs are found in old animals of various species (24).

It is not only the elderly who have neuritic plaques and NFTs in the absence of disease. Ulrich (63) found them in 38 of 51 brains of nondemented people who died between the ages of 55 and 64 years. The lesions were quite sparse and were largely confined to structures in the basal forebrain.

Plaques and tangles are also abundantly present in the brains of individuals with Down's syndrome (36) by the time they reach the age of 35. These may be pointed to as one of the evidences of precocious aging in Down's syndrome and of a probable link between Down's syndrome and AD.

A MODEL SYSTEM FOR THE NEUROBIOLOGY OF AGING

Just as a healthy 80-year-old man is no longer able to pull on his trousers while standing on one foot, old rats are impaired in their ability to cross a narrow plank in search of food. In a model approach to the multidisciplinary investigation of the aging nervous system, Rogers and colleagues (51-53) have studied cerebellar cortex in the aged rat. Purkinje cells are reduced in number; those surviving have altered rough endoplasmic reticulum as judged by reduction of Nissl staining. These neurons are better recognized by the presence of lipofuscin than by their properties shown with the Nissl technique. Some Purkinje cells have greatly reduced frequencies of spontaneous firing, whereas, others retain a normal rate. Even those with slow rates of firing continue to respond normally to stimulatory volleys arriving from the climbing fibers. Conduction of impulses is slowed in the parallel fibers of aged cortex as compared with those of young adults.

Shrinkage of the dendritic trees of the Purkinje cells and decreases in their spine densities (42) have been demonstrated and provide an explanation for the failure of some of these cells to respond to stimulation by parallel fiber volleys. Older rat Purkinje cells also tend to lose the normal enhancement of their responses to afferent stimulation that results from application of norepinephrine (5). Here is a good example of both structural and functional abnormalities in an aging neuronal system that helps us understand normal age-related decline in human brain function.

AGING AND THE DEEP CEREBRAL WHITE MATTER

Although the cortex and the deep nuclei deserve the lion's share of the attention in aging and the age-related disorders of the brain, the cerebral white matter cannot be ignored. Abnormal appearance of the white matter on CT and MRI of the brain has been increasingly reported in older subjects, especially when demented. These abnormal images are relevant both to strokes (Selhorst, this volume) and degenerative dementing disease (Fletcher, this volume). The first connection was that periventricular lucency (PVL) was considered part of the picture of normal pressure hydrocephalus in which ventricular fluid was said to exit via the periventricular white matter as a means of absorption. Then there was the postulate that periventricular lesions were evidence of ischemia resulting from disease of small penetrating arterioles that supply these regions. It was proposed that in more severe form these PVLs represented Binswanger's subcortical arteriosclerotic encephalopathy (SAE). However, Brun and Englund (8) recently reported that loss of myelin and axons is frequently evident in the periventricular white matter of patients who have the autopsy findings of AD without Binswanger's SAE.

The technique of MRI shows these white matter lesions more clearly and to a greater extent than does CT. We now have evidence that thin regions of periventricular hyperintensity (PVH) on MRI scans are seen in nondemented and apparently healthy elderly persons (7). Furthermore, our group at Washington University (50) has presented evidence that PVLs on CT scans of patients with autopsy-proven AD do not represent areas of infarction or evidence for the multi-infarct state. Rather, they are regions of partial loss of myelin and axons around ventricles which resemble the lesions that Brun and Englund (8) demonstrated in their studies of AD patients. Clearly, one must be conservative in concluding that PVL and/or PVH are evidence of clinically significant disease in the elderly or that they establish the cause of a dementia. They are seen more frequently in the impaired elderly and in those with cardiovascular risk factors than in the healthy elderly (23). These white matter changes may have an ischemic origin, but far more data are needed for clinicopathologic correlation.

AGING AND THE CATECHOLAMINES

Cognitive Function

Although most discussions of age- and disease-related declines in intellectual function have centered on the cholinergic hypothesis (44), Burke (this volume) reminds us that the adrenergic system cannot be ignored. Among other investigators, Gottfries (25) has reported that aged human brains have reduced concentrations of dopa decarboxylase, dopamine, homovanillic acid, norepinephrine and serotonin (5-HT). Tyrosine hydroxylase activity, the rate-limiting step in the synthesis of dopamine, is also decreased in the aged brain. On the other hand, levels of monoamine oxidase B (MAO-B) activity are increased, another reason for catecholamine depletion.

Reduced α_2-adrenergic function probably plays a role in the decline of working memory in aged Rhesus monkeys, since clonidine, a receptor agonist in that transmitter system, improves their performance on delayed-response tasks via an effect in the principal sulcus region of their prefrontal cortex (1).

Cholinergic systems are largely spared in the dementia of progressive supranuclear palsy (33), another neurodegenerative disorder of the elderly. The data thus far suggest a role of dopamine deficiency in striatum (especially caudate) and parolfactory cortex to help explain the dementia.

Depression

Depression in the elderly and its relation to dementia are discussed later in this monograph by Grossberg. There is the well-known hypothesis that depression may be related to a deficiency of catecholamines (especially norepinephrine) at functionally important central adrenergic receptors. A depletion of serotonin (5-HT) has also been postulated. It is tempting to reflect that the prevalence of cognitive impairment with depression in the elderly may be related to catecholamine as well as acetylcholine depletion in their brains.

Motor Dysfunction and Tardive Dyskinesia

Are age-related changes in the structure and function of the basal ganglia responsible for the increased susceptibility of older patients to tardive dyskinesia (Domino, this volume)? The burgeoning investigations of receptor binding with auto-radiography and PET (41,58) are providing additional evidence of age-related changes in neurotransmitter systems of the basal ganglia (29,37,40,55). However, the complexities of neuro-pharmacology (e.g., up- and down-regulation, modulation, second messengers) are such that one must be skeptical of simplistic explanations of clinical phenomena based on limited laboratory approaches. The relevant issues of altered pharmacokinetics and pharmacodynamics in the elderly were discussed in a previous volume in the Raven Press Aging series (67).

Parkinson's Disease

Parkinson's disease (PD) is another neurodegenerative disorder of the elderly. The age-specific incidence rates may be related to the decline in numbers of neurons in the substantia nigra and depletion of dopaminergic markers which have been documented in the human brain with aging (37). The most exciting recent development in PD has been the recognition that the toxin N-methyl-4-phenyltetrahydropyridine (MPTP) selectively destroys dopaminergic neurons in the substantia nigra (57). A faithful animal model for the disease has been produced in which MPTP toxicity is age-related, being more marked in older animals. The MPTP is not directly toxic, but must be oxidized by glial MAO-B to the N-methyl-4-phenylpyridinium ion (MPP$^+$) which enters and destroys the nigral neurons. The neurotoxicity can be prevented by the use of MAO inhibitors.

Since pyridines are widespread in nature and in man-made products, there is reason to suppose that such neurotoxicity may underlie PD as well as "aging" of the extrapyramidal system. Aging and neurotoxicity may well be additive. For that reason, scientists are closely watching the future course of those individuals who have as yet no parkinsonian signs after exposure to MPTP, but who have been shown by PET to have decreased dopamine (6-fluorodopa) pools in their basal ganglia.

It is reasonable to believe that clinical manifestations of AD and PD become evident only when the anatomic, physiologic and chemical abnormalities reach a certain threshold level. Effects of brain aging may well contribute to that movement toward the critical level and account for the susceptibility of the elderly to both diseases. The threshold phenomenon seems applicable to both AD and PD since one recognizes subclinical changes of each in the brains of unaffected elderly persons. Furthermore, the subclinical neuronal and biochemical lesions of each are sufficiently prevalent in the elderly to account for varying degrees of dementia in PD and extrapyramidal signs in dementia of the Alzheimer type (49).

OTHER THEMES OF CURRENT INTEREST

Focus on Calcium

Many subcellular, cellular and tissue investigations suggest that a major role for the related system of the calcium ion (Ca^{2+}) and the calcium-binding, calcium-modulated proteins is maintenance of neuronal function and interneuronal communication (32). Both Ca^{2+} and cyclic AMP are second messengers for neurons (12); calmodulin is one of the links between Ca^{2+} and cyclic AMP. Lynch and Baudry (35) have hypothesized a specific role in the mechanism of memory for the calcium-activated proteinase, calpain, which irreversibly increases receptors for glutamate in the forebrain.

A case can be made that the regulation of cytoplasmic Ca^{2+} levels is central to transmitter synthesis, energy metabolism, cross-linkage of proteins, axonal transport (see Richardson, this volume), aging and cell death. For instance, several proteolytic enzymes are sensitive to Ca^{2+} concentrations (3) and are activated by excessive cytosolic Ca^{2+}. Furthermore, it has been proposed that a disturbance in the homeostasis of Ca^{2+}, resultant activation of phospholipases, and accumulation of free fatty acids can act as a common mechanism of cell death from a wide variety of precipitating factors that affect energy homeostasis within the cell. These hypotheses may have relevance to the selective vulnerability of certain large neurons in neocortex and of pyramidal cells in the hippocampus to hypoxia, ischemia and the pathological changes associated with AD and aging (32).

Pyruvate dehydrogenase complex (PDHC), a pivotal mitochondrial enzyme system in the regulation of energy metabolism, has been linked to the critical function of sequestration of Ca^{2+} by mitochondria and to regulation of the cholinergic system. PDHC activity has been found to be markedly reduced in brain samples from AD patients at autopsy (56). These observations have led to investigations of oxidative enzyme activity and calcium metabolism in non-neural tissues of AD patients (46) in a search for non-neural markers of the disorder. Furthermore, 4-aminopyridine and 3,4-diaminopyridine are being studied as a means to improve abnormalities in these Ca^{2+}-related systems in both aging and disease (47).

Aluminum, Tangles and Plaques

Whereas, the initial enthusiasm about a special role for aluminum (Al^{3+}) in AD has waned, there are still the important observations that it accumulates selectively in tangle-bearing neurons (43) and that the Al^{3+} content of aged brains is greater than that found in brains of younger individuals. An exciting observation is that environmental deficiency of Ca^{2+} and Mg^{2+} promotes the development of Al^{3+}-laden tangle-bearing neurons in persons on Western Pacific islands where Guamanian parkinsonism-dementia and amyotrophic lateral sclerosis are prevalent. Now there is the observation that Al^{3+} and silicon are found together in the center of the amyloid cores of neuritic plaques in AD (10,45). They occur in the form of aluminosilicates, compounds that have the extremely interesting properties of assuming fibrillary forms, being self-replicating, and showing catalytic (e.g., proteolytic) actions.

Neurotrophic Factors

Another topic of considerable interest is that of trophic factors (Stewart, this volume). They may well play a role in maintenance of normal neuronal function and in the mechanisms of disease, in addition to their known actions in development of nerve cells and in neuronal responses to injury. Increasing evidence has been adduced to support a role of one such agent, nerve growth factor (NGF), in the central nervous system (61). Receptors for NGF have been demonstrated selectively on cholinergic neurons of the human basal forebrain (26). No doubt there will be increasing attention given to trophic factors (2) in relation to brain aging.

Membranes

There is evidence that cellular membranes become more rigid or lose their fluidity with increasing age. That point has

been made for neurons as well as for other cells. It may well
be that changes in intracellular membranes, those of
cytoskeletal components or mitochondria, for instance, are as
important as those in neuronal surface membranes. Obviously,
these changes could have important consequences for the function
of neurons in normal aging as well as in disease (see
individual chapters by Wood, Schroeder and Sun, this volume),
but the clinical application of these laboratory clues has yet
to be demonstrated.

Plasticity

Not long ago, it was held that damage to adult brain resulted
only in degenerative changes. One of the illuminating
developments in neurobiology has been the recognition that the
adult mammalian brain responds to injury with dynamic neural
phenomena, such as rerouting of axons, collateral sprouting and
reactive synaptogenesis (18,39). While these examples of
neuronal reorganization have been best studied following acute
injuries to the brain, there is reason to believe that more
chronic or slowly developing injuries, such as those which
might occur with normal aging, can also be followed by similar
signs of reorganization.

Similarly, early reports on neuronal dendrites in the aged
suggested that the dendritic trees were lost progressively,
whereas, now there is evidence that, at least in healthy aging,
the dendritic arborization of many neurons continues to expand
(11,19). That expansion in adult life can be promoted by
sensory stimulation, as documented in the rat. We have
commented earlier on the variability of the human dendritic
sprouting into old age according to regional specificity.

Investigators (22) have been studying plasticity of the
brain for some years and recently demonstrated signs of
hippocampal neuronal reorganization in patients with AD. In
the molecular layer of the dentate gyrus, they found expansion
of the kainic acid-binding sites (increased receptor field for
amino acid transmitters) and enhanced acetylcholinesterase
activity. The latter suggests aberrant sprouting from septal,
commissural and associational afferents in response to
cholinergic denervation of hippocampal gyrus. The findings
were analogous to the plasticity demonstrable in rat
hippocampus after entorhinal lesions. Note that sprouting may
well increase vulnerability of cells to excitotoxic activity of
neurotransmitter amino acids such as glutamate.

Neuronal reorganization after injury ("neuroplasticity") has
been assumed to subserve recovery of behavioral function after
brain damage. As Finger and Almli (18) have pointed out,
however, there is good evidence that aberrant neural circuitry
has also been associated with neurological dysfunction. These
authors find little reason to believe that these reorganiza-
tional events represent recovery or healing mechanisms. They

may be better interpreted as processes of growth and
development triggered by cell loss or injury. Among the many
avenues waiting to be explored is the manipulation of neuronal
plasticity to promote improvement in neuronal function and,
therefore, in disordered behavior.

Transplantation

All of us have been excited by observations that improvement
in age-related impairment of learning and movement can follow
transplantation of fetal brain tissue into older animals (20).
An important recent symposium (21) highlighted the promises,
progress and problems attendant upon brain transplantation. As
an example, the insertion of cholinergic grafts of fetal rat
septal region into the hippocampus of learning-impaired old
rats improved both the cholinergic deficits and the impaired
performance. While there are enormous technical, moral, ethical
and legal issues to be dealt with in a reasoned way, one cannot
help but speculate upon the potential for future therapy of
neurodegenerative illnesses and stroke when appropriate tissues
can be implanted to improve or restore function.

COMPARISON OF AGING AND ALZHEIMER'S DISEASE

In a recent review (4), I discussed the many ways in which
the clinical, neuropsychological, pathological, chemical, and
physiological changes in AD could be viewed as an exaggeration
of those changes seen in normal aging. In that sense, AD might
represent an acceleration of the normal aging process. For
instance, in AD one finds greater shrinkage of the brain,
greater loss of neurons from cortex and the nucleus basalis of
Meynert, greater deficits in chemical markers of the
cholinergic system, and more prevalent neuritic plaques and
NFTs. It is not clear whether there is a sharp separation
between the greater numbers of plaques found in the demented
elderly and those in the nondemented elderly, especially if one
studies subjects close to age 90 and beyond. Terry and
colleagues (62) believe that very old, but truly "normal",
individuals who make no errors on mental status examinations,
can be shown to have brains without the plaques, tangles and
neurochemical markers of decline that characterize the brains
of the mildly impaired elderly.
Some important points that suggest AD does not represent
exaggerated aging include:
1) Moderate numbers of NFTs are found in increasingly
greater percentages of control brains with advancing age until
the tenth decade when the percentages begin to decline (31).
2) The incidence and prevalence of AD increase with
advancing age until the tenth decade; then they appear to
decline or at least to stabilize.

3) Changes of AD have not been seen in the brains of the few progeric individuals studied.

4) Lipofuscin, the aging pigment which is recognized as the most consistent histologic abnormality in aging tissues, does not appear in excessive amounts in AD brains as compared with age-matched control brains.

5) Dendritic sprouting continues in hippocampal neurons of the nondemented elderly, but not in AD neurons (9).

6) Younger patients with AD are found to have far greater depletion of neurons (36) and of cholinergic and other neurochemical markers than do older patients with the disease. On the assumption that early and late onset AD represent the same disorder, this finding suggests that aging and AD are different phenomena. One can, however, easily defend the position that early and late onset AD represent different disorders, with late onset AD being more closely akin to exaggerated aging.

PROMISE AND PROBLEMS

There has literally been an explosion of research related to aging of the brain and AD, the prime example of a common neurodegenerative disorder. One measure of that increase is the comparison of the $7 million that represented the support of AD-related research by National Institutes of Health (NIH) in 1978 with the $56 million spent by NIH for that purpose in fiscal year 1986. Another indicator is the mention of 118 clinical trials (!) of the effect of vasopressin on memory at a recent symposium (65) on drug research in senile dementia of the Alzheimer's type.

Literally all of the clues reported are accompanied by assertions that much more work is needed to obtain more convincing answers. The problems of AD are being confronted along many avenues. Similarities and differences between cytoskeletal components (24) in AD neurons and their healthy counterparts are being explored (Hirano, this volume). Newly discovered proteins (66), hardly present in normal brain but found abundantly in AD brain both in tangle-bearing neurons and in apparently unaffected neurons, should be pursued. Efforts are already underway to clone the gene that expresses itself in the synthesis of that protein.

Following some years of recognizing possible links between scrapie and AD, a gene has been identified whose expression is increased in scrapie (64). Furthermore, the complementary DNA which corresponded to that gene appeared to hybridize preferentially and focally to cells in the brains of scrapie animals. What is challenging is the further observation that the same cloned DNA was shown to hybridize to neuritic plaques in tissue sections of three out of three patients with confirmed AD, but not to the NFTs or to brain tissue of three control subjects who had no plaques. Wietgrefe et al. (64)

suggested there may be an increased expression of certain cellular RNAs common to both "degenerative changes in the aging human brain best exemplified by Alzheimer's disease" and to spongiform encephalopathies resulting from infection with unconventional agents (see Joh, this volume).

In fact, the term "neurodegenerative disorder" should be abandoned! It implies that we understand the cause(s) and/or the mechanism(s), whereas, we use the term only for disorders whose basis is as yet unknown. Wilson's disease was a "degenerative disorder" until the role of copper was discovered, followed quickly by curative chelation therapy. Perhaps AD and PD should be labeled "diseases of (as yet) unknown cause."

Progress in AD research is limited by the relatively small number of brains examined from persons who have been studied longitudinally during life (both those with AD and those who are aging normally as control subjects). Particularly scarce are examinations of brain tissue from subjects who only have mild AD. Note that in England important observations (38) have been made from biopsies of presenile subjects with AD performed when the disease is only mild or moderate. Should biopsies for research purposes be resurrected in this country?

Despite numerous clues regarding the identity of the various culprits, we do not seem close to having answers to the important major questions: 1) What are the causes and mechanisms of brain aging and age-related declines in brain function? 2) What are the causes and mechanisms of AD (62) and its dementia? 3) Is the aged brain more susceptible to an environmental cause of AD, or does the disease appear only many years after the first exposure? 4) How do genetic and environmental factors interact?

Finch (17) pointed out the likelihood that supporting the resources required for a serious attack on the problems of AD would very likely benefit the basic neurosciences in the same way that funding for cancer research has promoted the advancement of knowledge in many areas of molecular, cell and developmental biology. It is probable that research on AD will shed light on one of the great mysteries in neurobiology, the nature and mechanism of thinking.

We should recognize that our greatest problem at the moment and the greatest threat to continued progress toward the goal of finding the cause, cure and prevention of AD is the current cutback in Federal funds available to support research in both AD and the neurobiology of aging. Following the lead of lay people in Alzheimer's Disease and Related Disorders Association, scientists should be protesting these cutbacks and stressing the obvious need for directed research in this disorder which currently is costing the nation $40 billion annually, a figure which dwarfs the $56 million recently spent in one year by NIH on related research.

This crisis in funding must be addressed immediately.

CONCLUSION

Aging of the brain and the age-related neurologic and psychiatric disorders have been brought "out of the closet." We must lobby for increased funding to find better answers as we continually improve the quality of our research in order to justify the dollar amounts we request.

ACKNOWLEDGMENT

Supported in part by grant #P50 AG05681 from the National Institute on Aging and by the Norman J. Stupp Foundation.

REFERENCES

1. Arnsten, A.F.T., and Goldman-Rakic, P.S. (1985): Science, 230:1273-1276.
2. Atterwill, C.K., and Bowen, D.M. (1986): Acta Neuropathol. (Berl.), 69:341-342.
3. Baudry, M., DuBrin, R., Beasley, M.L., and Lynch, G. (1986): Neurobiol. Aging, 7:255-258.
4. Berg, L. (1985): Arch. Neurol., 42:737-739.
5. Bickford, P.C., Hoffer, B.J., and Freedman, R. (1985): Neurobiol. Aging, 6:89-94.
6. Bird, J.M., Levy, R., and Jacoby, R.J. (1986): Br. J. Psychiatry, 148:80-85.
7. Brant-Zawadzki, M., Fein, G., Van Dyke, C., Kiernan, R., Davenport, L., and de Groot, J. (1985): AJNR, 6:675-682.
8. Brun, A., and Englund, E. (1986): Ann. Neurol., 19:253-262.
9. Buell, S.J., and Coleman, P.D. (1981): Brain Res., 214:23-41.
10. Candy, J.M., Klinowski, J., Perry, R.H., Perry, E.K., Fairbairn, A., Oakley, A.E., Carpenter, T.A., Atack, J.R., Blessed, G., and Edwardson, J.A. (1986): Lancet, 1:354-357.
11. Coleman, P.D., Buell, S.J., Magagna, L., Flood, D.G., and Curcio, C.A. (1986): Neurobiol. Aging, 7:101-105.
12. Cooper, J.R., Bloom, F.E., and Roth, R.H. (1986): The Biochemical Basis of Neuropharmacology, pp. 109-121. Oxford University Press, New York.
13. Davis, R.T., and Leathers, C.W., editors (1985): Behavior and Pathology of Aging in Rhesus Monkeys. Alan R. Liss, Inc., New York.
14. DeKosky, S.T., and Bass, N.H. (1982): Neurology, 32: 1227-1233.
15. DeKosky, S.T., Scheff, S.W., Hackney, C.G., and Bass, N.H. (1985): Neurobiol. Aging, 6:277-286.
16. Duffy, F.H., Albert, M.S., McAnulty, G., and Garvey, A.J. (1984): Ann. Neurol., 16:430-438.
17. Finch, C.E. (1985): Science, 230:1109.

18. Finger, S., and Almli, C.R. (1985): Brain Res. Rev., 10: 177-186.
19. Flood, D.G., Buell, S.J., Defiore, C.H., Horwitz, G.J., and Coleman, P.D. (1985): Brain Res., 345:366-368.
20. Gage, F.H., Dunnett, S.B., Stenevi, V., and Bjorklund, A. (1984): Science, 221:966-969.
21. Gash, D.M., Collier, T.J., and Sladek, Jr., J.R. (1985): Neurobiol. Aging, 6:131-150.
22. Geddes, J.W., Monaghan, D.T., Cotman, C.W., Lott, I.T., Kim, R.C., and Chui, H.C. (1985): Science, 230:1179-1181.
23. Gerard, G., and Weisberg, L.A. (1986): Neurology, 36: 998-1001.
24. Goldman, J.E., and Yen, S.-H. (1986): Ann. Neurol., 19: 209-223.
25. Gottfries, C.G. (1985): Psychopharm. (Berl.), 86:245-252.
26. Hefti, F., Hartikka, J., Salvatierra, A., Weiner, W.J., and Mash, D.C. (1986): Neurosci. Lett., 69:37-41.
27. Hyman, B.T., Van Hoesen, G.W., Damasio, A.R., and Barnes, C.L. (1984): Science, 225:1168-1170.
28. Ingram, D.K. (1985): Ann. NY Acad. Sci., 444:312-331.
29. Joyce, J.N., Loeschen, S.K., Sapp, D.W., and Marshall, J.F. (1986): Brain Res., 378:158-163.
30. Katzman, R., and Terry, R. (1983): The Neurology of Aging. F.A. Davis Company, Philadelphia.
31. Kemper, T. (1984): In: Clinical Neurology of Aging, edited by M.L. Albert, pp. 9-52. Oxford University Press, New York.
32. Khachaturian, Z.S. (1984): In: Handbook of Studies on Psychiatry and Old Age, edited by D.W. Kay and G.D. Burrows, pp. 7-30. Elsevier Science Publishers B.V., New York.
33. Kish, S.J., Chang, L.J., Mirchandani, L., Shannak, K., and Hornykiewicz, O. (1985): Ann. Neurol., 18:530-536.
34. Luine, V.N., Renner, K.J., Heady, S., and Jones, K.J. (1986): Neurobiol. Aging, 7:193-198.
35. Lynch, G., and Baudry, M. (1986): Science, 224:1057-1063.
36. Mann, D.M.A., Yates, P.O., and Marcyniuck, B. (1985): J. Neurol. Sci., 69:139-159.
37. McGeer, P.L., McGeer, E.G., and Suzuki, J.S. (1977): Arch. Neurol., 34:33-35.
38. Neary, D., Snowden, J.S., Mann, D.M.A., Bowen, D.M., Sims, N.R., Northen, B., Yates, P.O., and Davison, A.N. (1986): J. Neurol. Neurosurg. Psychiatry, 49:229-237.
39. Nottebohm, F., editor (1985): Hope for a New Neurology (Ann. NY Acad. Sci., 457). New York Academy of Sciences, New York.
40. O'Boyle, K.M., and Waddington, J.L. (1986): Neurobiol. Aging, 7:265-267.
41. Palacios, J.M., Probst, A., and Cortes, R. (1986): Trends Neurosci., 9:284-289.
42. Pentney, R.J. (1986): Neurobiol. Aging, 7:241-248.

43. Perl, D.P. (1985): Environ. Health Perspect., 63:149-153.
44. Perry, E.K. (1986): Br. Med. Bull., 42:63-69.
45. Perry, E.K., and Perry, R.H. (1985): Trends Neurosci., 8:301-303.
46. Peterson, C., and Goldman, J.E. (1986): Proc. Natl. Acad. Sci. USA, 83:2758-2762.
47. Peterson, C., Nicholls, D.G., and Gibson, G.E. (1985): Neurobiol. Aging, 6:297-304.
48. Price, D.L., Cork, L.C., Struble, R.G., Kitt, C.A., Price, Jr., D.L., Lehmann, J., and Hedreen, J.C. (1985): In: Behavior and Pathology of Aging in Rhesus Monkeys, edited by R.T. Davis and C.W. Leathers, pp. 113-135. Alan R. Liss, Inc., New York.
49. Quinn, N.P., Rossor, M.N., and Marsden, C.D. (1986): Br. Med. Bull., 42:86-90.
50. Rezek, D.L., Morris, J.C., Fulling, K.H., and Gado, M. (1986): Neurology, 36(Suppl. 1):263-264.
51. Rogers, J., Silver, M.A., Shoemaker, W.J., and Bloom, F.E. (1980): Neurobiol. Aging, 1:3-11.
52. Rogers, J., Zornetzer, S.F., and Bloom, F.E. (1981): Neurobiol. Aging, 2:15-25.
53. Rogers, J., Zornetzer, S.F., and Mervis, R.E. (1984): Brain Res., 292:23-32.
54. Scheff, S.W., Anderson, K.J., and DeKosky, S.T. (1985): Neurobiol. Aging, 6:29-34.
55. Severson, J.A., Marcusson, J., Winblad, B., and Finch, C.E. (1982): J. Neurochem., 39:1623-1631.
56. Sheu, K.-F.R., Kim, Y.-T., Blass, J.P., and Weksler, M.E. (1985): Ann. Neurol., 17:444-449.
57. Snyder, S.H., and D'Amato, R.J. (1986): Neurology, 36: 250-258.
58. Stahl, S.M., Leenders, K.L., and Bowery, N.G. (1986): Trends Neurosci., 9:241-245.
59. Struble, R.G., Price, Jr., D.L., Cork, L.C., and Price, D.L. (1985): Brain Res., 361:267-275.
60. Takeda, S., and Matsuzawa, T. (1984): J. Am. Geriatr. Soc., 32:520-524.
61. Taniuchi, M., Schweitzer, J.B., and Johnson, Jr., E.M. (1986): Proc. Natl. Acad. Sci. USA, 83:1950-1954.
62. Terry, R.D. (1985): Dan. Med. Bull., 32(Suppl. 1):22-24.
63. Ulrich, J. (1986): Ann. Neurol., 17:273-277.
64. Wietgrefe, S., Zupancic, M., Haase, A., Chesebro, B., Race, R., Frey, II, W., Rustan, T., and Friedman, R.L. (1985): Science, 230:1177-1179.
65. Wilson, J. (1986): Neurobiol. Aging, 7:219-222.
66. Wolozin, B.L., Pruchniki, A., Dickson, D.W., and Davies, P. (1986): Science, 232:648-650.
67. Wood, W.G., and Strong, R., editors (1986): Geriatric Clinical Pharmacology. Raven Press, New York.

Central Nervous System Disorders of Aging:
Clinical Intervention and Research, edited by
Randy Strong et al. Raven Press, New York
© 1988.

CERTAIN ASPECTS OF THE PATHOLOGY OF DEGENERATIVE

DISEASES OF THE CENTRAL NERVOUS SYSTEM

Asao Hirano

Bluestone Laboratory, Division of Neuropathology,
Department of Pathology, Montefiore Medical Center;
Albert Einstein College of Medicine,
Bronx, New York 10467

For this chapter, I have chosen to discuss three of the
most prevalent neurodegenerative disorders with which I have
worked. These include Alzheimer's disease (AD), Parkinson's
disease (PD), and amyotrophic lateral sclerosis (ALS). For
the purposes of this review, I shall present the data in the
manner in which I confronted it, i.e., from a historical
perspective.

THE CLASSICAL VIEW

Most conventional textbooks of neuropathology described AD,
PD, and ALS in rather simple terms. AD was characterized by
generalized, bilateral involvement of the cerebral cortex with
a certain degree of predilection for the temporal and frontal
lobes and relative sparing of the motor and sensory cortices.
The histological hallmarks were loss of cortical neurons and
the appearance of Alzheimer neurofibrillary tangles and senile
plaques.
PD, on the other hand, was known to primarily affect the
subcortical and brain stem nuclei, especially the substantia
nigra, locus ceruleus and the substantia innominata among
other areas. The histological findings were neuronal loss
associated with Lewy bodies.
ALS was described primarily as a disease of the motor
system involving the anterior horn cells of the spinal cord,
the lower motor cranial nerve nuclei in the brain stem as well
as the Betz cells in the motor cortex. Histologically,
neuronal loss of the large motor neurons was seen as well as
degeneration in the anterolateral column of the spinal column,

17

especially both the crossed and uncrossed pyramidal tracts. Surviving large motor neurons did not display specific changes but showed atrophy and accumulation of lipofuscin.

This was the approximate state of knowledge at the time I was introduced to the field, which coincided with the beginning of the application of electron microscopy to neuropathology. The advent of this new technique allowed more detailed description of some of the histological hallmarks connected with neurodegenerative disorders (7).

The Advent of Electron Microscopy

Perhaps the earliest of histological hallmarks that was examined by electron microscopy was the neurofibrillary tangle. This technology made possible the discovery of the nature of Alzheimer's neurofibrillary tangles (17,28). Sections through these tangles in material from patients with AD revealed the presence of fibrils with characteristic, periodic constrictions. At their widest, the fibrils measure about 25 nm and narrow to about 10 nm at 80 nm intervals.

The senile plaques were shown to be composed of aggregates of swollen neuronal processes filled with various organelles, including mitochondria, neurofilaments, synaptic vesicles, Alzheimer's neurofibrillary tangles, and lysosomes among others. These processes often surrounded a core of amyloid filaments. In addition to neuronal processes, astrocytic processes are invariably present and, often, microglia as well.

Lewy bodies seen in the brains of Parkinson's patients were shown to consist of a core of densely tangled 10 nm filaments, thicker linear structures and electron-dense granular material (3). Often, minute membrane-bound vesicles were interspersed among the filaments. No limiting membrane separates the Lewy body from the neuronal cytoplasm. Instead, there is a less dense halo of radiating filaments which extends from the core and penetrates the surrounding cytoplasm. The interior of the core may contain larger lamellated or homogeneous electron-dense material in addition to the discrete filaments and other structures.

ALS and Parkinsonism-Dementia Complex on Guam

While much of the pioneering work in the fine structure of neuropathologic alterations was occurring, I was sent to Guam to study the native Chamorro population which displayed an extraordinarily high incidence of fatal neurological diseases. Previous workers had shown that approximately 10% of adult deaths were the result of ALS. My clinical impression confirmed these findings. Detailed neuropathologic study, however, revealed some surprising findings.

Malamud et al. (20) noted that in addition to the typical changes characteristic of ALS, there were relatively large

numbers of Alzheimer neurofibrillary tangles in patients dying
with ALS. These initial observations were subsequently
confirmed (20). The tangles were widely distributed in the
central nervous system and were especially common in the
cerebral cortex. These tangles were most common in the
temporal lobe including the pyramidal neurons of Sommer's
sector and adjacent areas, in the glomerular formation of the
parahippocampal gyrus, the amygdaloid nucleus, the substantia
innominata [nucleus basalis of Meynert (nbM)], various
hypothalamic nuclei, the substantia nigra, the locus ceruleus,
the periaqueductal gray, the dorsal raphe nucleus, and the
reticular formation of the brain stem (15). Granulovacuolar
bodies and Hirano bodies were almost always present in Ammon's
horn. Senile plaques were most often not present in these
patients.

In addition to ALS, there appeared to be an equally common
neurological disorder among the same population. Clinically,
this was characterized by Parkinsonian symptoms, but was also
frequently accompanied by progressive dementia and, in some
patients, both ALS and parkinsonism-dementia complex (PDC)
were found in the same patient (9). Neuropathologic studies
of patients with PDC revealed severe neuronal loss in the
expected areas, namely, the substantia nigra, locus ceruleus
and the other brain stem nuclei, nbM, and the hypothalamic
nuclei usually affected in PD. In the Chamorro population on
Guam, however, the neuronal loss is especially severe and,
more surprisingly, the hallmark of PD; Lewy bodies were
usually absent. Instead, extraordinarily high numbers of
Alzheimer neurofibrillary tangles were present in the
remaining neurons (13). These tangles were found in all those
areas in which they were seen in the ALS patients. That is,
they involved the cerebral cortex, especially the temporal
lobe, in addition to the subcortical and brain stem nuclei.
In those cases of PDC in which a few Lewy bodies were found
(approximately 10%), Alzheimer neurofibrillary tangles were
always found nearby (12). Again, no senile plaques were found
in the majority of the PDC cases regardless of the number of
tangles. Furthermore, when senile plaques were present, their
distribution did not necessarily correspond to those areas
which were the usual sites of predilection for tangles in
PDC. For example, the substantia nigra and locus ceruleus
were consistent targets of tangle formation but were always
free of senile plaques. As in ALS on Guam, granulovacuolar
bodies and Hirano bodies were commonly found in Sommer's
sector and in adjacent areas of Ammon's horn.

Subsequent to these studies, we realized that to be able to
speculate meaningfully on the significance of Alzheimer's
neurofibrillary tangles among the ALS and PDC patients on
Guam, we had to undertake a more comprehensive study of these
structures in Chamorro patients dying of non-neurological
disease and of these same structures in a non-Chamorro

population (15). Surprisingly, neurofibrillary tangles are relatively frequent in Chamorro patients who die of non-neurological disease (11,12). As in other populations, they are found more commonly in aged individuals, but they are also seen at unexpected ages in patients in other populations. When tangles are found in the control Chamorro group, they are distributed in ALS and PDC patterns. Their numbers, however, are usually much less than in PDC, but are equivalent to those seen in ALS cases with relatively few tangles.

The significance of these findings is difficult to assess. Could it be that the Chamorro population is simply prone to neurofibrillary changes and tend to show them at a relatively young age compared to other populations? If so, how does one explain the fact that one half of the control Chamorro group did not show the tangles, even some at relatively advanced age? Another possibility is that given the high incidence of ALS and PDC on Guam, the apparent "control" group included large numbers of incipient cases of PDC.

Our study of Alzheimer's neurofibrillary tangles in non-Chamorro populations also showed their increased presence in aged individuals in a distribution corresponding to that of ALS and PDC on Guam, although their numbers are much less than among the Chamorro population. In addition, tangles have not been observed in various parts of the central nervous system in a variety of disorders (7). Incidentally, structures identical to the Alzheimer's neurofibrillary tangles have not, so far, been identified in any animal, including aged primates, although some fibrillary configurations have been described (10).

During our study of the distribution and incidence of Alzheimer's neurofibrillary tangles in different conditions and in different populations, we managed to gain some insight into the natural history of these structures. Apparently, the early neurofibrillary tangles which may be found in seemingly intact neurons are hematoxylinophilic, strongly argentophilic, congophilic, and intensely fluorescent when stained with thioflavine. These are confined to the perinuclear area and generally appear as a single peripheral bundle. As tangle formation progresses, multiple bundles appear, fill the perikaryon, and penetrate into the proximal portions of the dendrites. Finally, the nucleus is lost, and the entire cell body comes to consist of nothing but tangles permeated by gliotic astrocytic processes. The tangles lose their hematoxylinophilia and become eosinophilic. The argentophilia is markedly diminished, and thioflavine staining yields only a faint fluorescence. Fine structural studies tend to confirm a progressive change. The earlier intracellular tangles are usually composed of the constricted profiles described above. The older tangles tend to have a much larger complement of apparently nonconstricted filaments approximately 15 nm in diameter (11).

RECENT ADVANCES

Since those relatively early times, investigations have continued into the nature and etiology of AD, PD, and ALS. The etiologies of these conditions remain obscure, but some important advances have been made.

AD has been shown to be associated with severe loss of cholinergic activity in the cerebral cortex. To some extent, at least, this has been related to substantial neuronal loss in the nbM, the major source of cholinergic processes to the cerebrum (29). In addition to neuronal loss, fine structural study of neurofibrillary tangles in the nbM has revealed the presence of both constricted and straight forms of the fibrils identical to those seen in cortical and brain stem neurons (22,25).

In addition to the cholinergic system, both the noradrenergic and the serotonergic systems are affected in AD. This observation leads one to suspect that the locus ceruleus and the dorsal raphe nucleus are also involved in AD. Morphological study has revealed that, indeed, these areas are selective sites of cell loss and neurofibrillary tangles in AD (32), just as they are in PDC (31).

Senile plaques in the cerebellar cortex in AD have not received great attention until recently. It has now been shown, however, that plaques occur in the cerebellar cortex in a large fraction of patients with AD. Fine structural study of these plaques has revealed the presence of all features of senile plaques found in the cerebral cortex with the exception of neurofibrillary tangles. Interestingly, Hirano bodies are present just as they are in senile plaques in the cerebral cortex. This difference in the presence of neurofibrillary tangles within senile plaques between the two areas may be a reflection of the source of the neurites participating in the formation of the plaques. Presumably, Purkinje cell processes form part of the cerebellar plaques. These cells are not known to form Alzheimer neurofibrillary tangles, but they sometimes contain Hirano bodies in both their cell bodies and dendrites (30).

Studies of PD have been guided by the clinically observed effects of L-dopa which seemed originally to confirm the theory that PD represented a dopamine deficiency. Recent studies of the effects of 1-methyl-4-phenyl-1,2,3,6-tetrahydro-pyridine (MPTP) reveal that there is selective neuronal loss in the substantia nigra and Parkinson-like symptoms. The substantia nigra is a dopaminergic area. This synthetic drug does not seem, so far, to result in the formation of Lewy bodies in either man or monkey, and the area of involvement is not as wide as in PD (19). Otherwise, this drug would be a promising candidate as an experimental model for PD. Proper dosage or chronicity may result in a closer correlation between the experimental system and the natural disease (5).

This is a good time to point out a particular puzzle regarding the effects of neuronal loss in the nbM. As previously mentioned, the formation of neurofibrillary tangles, senile plaque formation, and loss of cholinergic activity in the cerebrum in AD has been attributed to the neuronal loss in the nbM. Indeed, some workers have suggested that the dementia in AD is related to the same process. On the other hand, studies of the nbM in some cases of PD also show significant cell loss; and some investigators now consider dementia to be a part of PD even in non-Chamorro patients. However, no consistent correlation between the degree of neuronal loss in the nbM and either neurofibrillary tangle or senile plaque formation in the cerebral cortex has been found (4,24). One can find instances of severe neuronal loss in the nbM and virtual absence of either neurofibrillary tangles or senile plaques in the cerebral cortex of Parkinsonian patients. Among Chamorro PDC patients, senile plaques are also generally absent despite severe neuronal loss in the nbM (23).

A fine structural study of the nbM in a case of diffuse Lewy body disease, which showed Parkinsonism features and dementia, revealed the presence of Lewy bodies as expected. Interestingly, however, the Lewy bodies in the nbM in this case showed a mixture of morphological details of Lewy bodies which are usually characteristic of those seen in cerebral cortical neurons, in the substantia nigra or in the autonomic nervous system (21).

Upon reflection of all the morphological data on ALS accumulated during my stay on Guam, I realized that, aside from the obvious cell loss, relatively little attention has been paid to the single most important target of this disease, namely, the anterior horn cells. The question arose as to what were the earliest signs of this degenerative process. Certainly, it was not the formation of Alzheimer's neurofibrillary tangles which are only rarely observed in anterior horn cells even among the Chamorro population. On the other hand, when we examined familial ALS outside of Guam with posterior column and spinocerebellar tract involvement, we became aware of the presence of argentophilic structures reminiscent of Lewy bodies in both the neurites and soma of the surviving anterior horn cells. Fine structural studies revealed that in the soma, these structures were composed of focal masses of 10 nm neurofilaments, arranged at random and intermingled with thick linear structures and some granular material (14). In the axons, the argentophilic structures consisted of 10 nm filaments neatly arranged parallel to each other and to the long axis of the axon. The involved portions of the axon, which were confined to the anterior horns and sometimes to the intramedullary portion of the anterior roots, were enormously enlarged and filled with the neurofilaments.

Carpenter (2) pointed out the existence of "spheroids" in the axons of the anterior horns of sporadic ALS patients. These were focal accumulations and reached diameters of over 20 microns. His fine structural studies showed that the spheroids, too, were composed of 10 nm neurofilaments. Subsequently, we confirmed his findings in our own cases of sporadic ALS and found that, unlike the axonal filamentous accumulations we had seen in our study of familial ALS, these filaments were arranged in intertwining bundles of parallel filaments (8). On occasion, the soma contained structures similar to those seen in familial ALS.

Another structure seen in the anterior horn cells of sporadic ALS are Bunina bodies, first reported by Bunina (7). These are small, single or multiple eosinophilic granules confined to the soma or proximal portions of the dendrites. Fine structural study of these structures revealed accumulations of dense, granular material surrounded by vesicular profiles. Often, the center of the dense, granular zone contained a pale region with 10 nm neurofilaments. It is not yet clear whether these structures are confined to ALS (18).

In addition, the normal anatomy of the processes of human anterior horn cells and the changes seen in ALS have not been adequately explored. Information gained so far indicates an atrophy of the cell processes accompanying ALS. These studies rest mainly on silver impregnation (26) and Golgi-Cox techniques (16).

CONCLUSIONS

When one compares our present state of knowledge with that which was available 25 years ago, one must be pleased with the progress. On the other hand, we still have not determined the etiology of any of these degenerative disorders with the possible exception of PD. We must conclude, therefore, that our work is by no means done and we must continue to explore these diseases with every means at our disposal (1,6,27).

REFERENCES

1. Appel, S.H. (1981): Ann. Neurol., 10:499-505.
2. Carpenter, S. (1968): Neurology, 18:841-851.
3. Duffy, P.O., and Tennyson, V.M. (1965): J. Neuropathol. Exp. Neurol., 24:398-414.
4. Ezrin-Waters, C., and Resch, L. (1986): Can. J. Neurol. Sci., 13:8-14.
5. Forno, L.S., Langston, J.W., DeLanney, L.E., Irwin, I., and Ricaurte, G.A. (1987): Ann. Neurol. (in press).
6. Gajdusek, D.C. (1985): N. Engl. J. Med., 312:714-719.
7. Hirano, A. (1981): A Guide to Neuropathology, Igaku-Shoin, New York.

8. Hirano, A., Donnenfeld, H., Sasaki, S., and Nakano, I. (1984): J. Neuropathol. Exp. Neurol., 43:461-470.
9. Hirano, A., Kurland, L.T., Krooth, R.S., and Lessell, S. (1961): Brain, 84:642-661.
10. Hirano, A., and Llena, J.F. (1983): In: The Clinical Neurosciences, Vol. 3, edited by R.N. Rosenberg, pp. 285-324. Churchill Livingstone, New York.
11. Hirano, A., and Llena, J. (1986): In: Progress in Neuropathology, Vol. 6, edited by H.M. Zimmerman, pp. 17-31. Raven Press, New York.
12. Hirano, A., Malamud, N., Elizan, T.S., and Kurland, L.T. (1966): Arch. Neurol., 15:31-51.
13. Hirano, A., Malamud, N., and Kurland, L.T. (1961): Brain, 84:662-679.
14. Hirano, A., Nakano, I., Kurland, L.T., Mulder, D.W., Holley, P.W., and Saccomanno, G. (1984): J. Neuropathol. Exp. Neurol., 43:471-480.
15. Hirano, A., and Zimmerman, H.M. (1962): Arch. Neurol., 7:227-242.
16. Kato, T., and Hirano, A. (1986): VI International Congress on Neuromuscular Diseases, p. 102. (Abstract)
17. Kidd, M. (1964): Brain, 87:307-320.
18. Kusaka, H., and Hirano, A. (1985): J. Neuropathol. Exp. Neurol., 44:430-438.
19. Langston, J.W., Ballard, P.A., Tetrud, J.W., and Irwin, I. (1983): Science, 219:979-980.
20. Malamud, N., Hirano, A., and Kurland, L.T. (1961): Arch. Neurol., 5:401-415.
21. Morimura, Y., and Hirano, A. (1986): Neurol. Med. Chir. (Tokyo), 24:370-378.
22. Morimura, Y., Hirano, A., and Llena, J.F. (1985): Acta Neuropathol. (Berl.), 68:130-137.
23. Nakano, I., and Hirano, A. (1983): Ann. Neurol., 13:87-91.
24. Nakano, I., and Hirano, A. (1984): Ann. Neurol., 15:415-418.
25. Nakano, I., and Hirano, A. (1984): Neurol. Med. Chir. (Tokyo), 20:264-276.
26. Nakano, I., and Hirano, A. (1987): J. Neuropathol. Exp. Neurol. (in press).
27. Rowland, L.P. (1984): N. Engl. J. Med., 311:979-981.
28. Terry, R.D. (1983): J. Neuropathol. Exp. Neurol., 22:629-642.
29. Whitehouse, P.J., Price, D.L., Clark, A.W., Coyle, J.T., and DeLong, M.R. (1981): Ann. Neurol., 10:122-126.
30. Yamamoto, T., and Hirano, A. (1985): Acta Neuropathol. (Berl.), 67:167-169.
31. Yamamoto, T., and Hirano, A. (1985): Acta Neuropathol. (Berl.), 67:296-299.
32. Yamamoto, T., and Hirano, A. (1985): Ann. Neurol., 17:573-577.

Central Nervous System Disorders of Aging: Clinical Intervention and Research, edited by Randy Strong et al. Raven Press, New York © 1988.

THE ROLE OF NEUROTROPHIC FACTORS IN THE

PATHOGENESIS OF NEUROLOGIC DISEASE

S. Scott Stewart, James L. McManaman, R. Glenn Smith, Yasuko Tomozawa, J. Robert Bostwick, and Stanley H. Appel

Department of Neurology
Baylor College of Medicine
Houston, Texas 77030

Neurobiologists since the time of Santiago Ramon y Cajal have suspected that target organs play an important role in the development of innervating neurons (94). A great deal of interest has developed in one potential mechanism for this interaction, namely, through hormone-like neurotrophic factors which are produced in the target and act on the neuron in a retrograde manner. Neurotrophic factors appear to influence survival, growth and differentiation in many neuronal systems during development, and may play a role in the regeneration process in the adult nervous system.

It is the thesis of our laboratory that functional impairment of neurotrophic factors may underlie the neuronal degeneration seen in several system-specific neurologic diseases in humans. If a target-derived factor is required for the maintenance of a neuron, then interference within this system will result in death of the neuron. Primary target pathology, genetic abnormalities, or alteration of post-translational processing or secretion may prevent the production of adequate quantities of trophic factors or lead to the synthesis of a functionally inactive form. After secretion, a target-derived trophic factor must be transported to the nerve cell body. This process can be interrupted by immune attack in the synaptic cleft, by alteration in receptor function, by abnormalities in retrograde axoplasmic transport, or by any necessary post-transport processing.

Striking examples of human disease produced by similar mechanisms can be found within the endocrine system. In type I diabetes mellitus, an immune attack on islet cells leads to a decrease in production of insulin, a trophic substance (32).

Similarly, antibodies to a trophic factor receptor, the thyroid stimulating hormone receptor, are intimately involved in the pathophysiology of Graves' hyperthyroidism (95).

Before the question of mechanism can be addressed, though, the presence of specific target-derived trophic factors which retrogradely affect the survival of innervating neurons must be confirmed. This chapter will review the evidence for these factors in several neuronal systems and relate this to the pathophysiology of relevant disorders.

FAMILIAL DYSAUTONOMIA

In 1951, Levi-Montalcini and Hamburger (71) first published data showing that a murine sarcoma implanted into chicken embryos grew and was innervated by sensory and sympathetic neurons. Of particular interest was their observation that these embryos had hypertrophied dorsal root ganglia (DRG) and sympathetic ganglia. Soluble extracts of the tumor produced similar effects both in vivo and in vitro, and caused extensive neurite outgrowth from explanted DRG. Eventually, the substance responsible for these phenomena, nerve growth factor (NGF), was isolated (21) and found to regulate survival, growth, differentiation, and neurite orientation of target neurons (45,70).

NGF acts on neural crest-derived neurons after retrograde transport from receptor sites in the periphery (30) and is absolutely required for the survival of sympathetic and some sensory neurons. In immature animals, NGF antiserum destroys sympathetic and spinal sensory neurons (41,89). Administration of exogenous NGF during the period of naturally occurring cell death rescues sensory and sympathetic neurons destined to die (63,120) and can partially prevent the effects of axotomy (45).

Certain features of neonatal animals treated with anti-NGF antibodies resemble the familial dysautonomia (FD) syndrome first detailed by Riley et al. in 1949 (96). This syndrome, also called type III hereditary sensory neuropathy, is an autosomal recessive disorder carried predominantly by Ashkenazi Jewish populations (88). Afflicted infants have prominent disturbances of autonomic functions, behavior, and sensation. Lack of overflow tears, absence of the fungiform papillae on the tongue, diminished deep tendon reflexes, pupillary hypersensitivity to methacholine, and loss of the histamine flare response are important diagnostically (7).

Pathologically, patients with FD have a dramatic loss of neurons in the cervical and thoracic sympathetic ganglia (88). Sympathetic preganglionic neurons in the intermediolateral cell column are also affected, but these cells are probably only indirectly involved (86). The parasympathetic sphenopalatine ganglia are severely involved, while other parasympathetics show little or no change. DRG neurons are also affected and continue to degenerate throughout the life of the patient. In the sural nerve, small myelinated and unmyelinated axons are depleted (2), while larger axons are less severely affected. No consistent central nervous system (CNS) changes have been identified, but this determination is made more difficult by the repeated anoxic insults often associated with this disease.

The similarity of clinicopathologic features of FD to those of transplacental transfer of maternal antibodies to NGF are striking (42,89). Patients and experimental animals both show a dramatic loss of sympathetic and DRG neurons, loss of spinal cord substance P, cataracts and chronic aspiration. In addition, several studies have indicated that there may be elevated levels of NGF by radioimmunoassay (RIA) but no change in functional NGF (e.g., by bioassay or by binding assay), suggesting that an abnormal, nonfunctional form of NGF is present (14,104,105). Fibroblasts of patients produce normal amounts of β-NGF cross-reacting material, but by bioassay it is only one-tenth as potent (100). The hypothesis that a mutation-based, nonfunctional form of NGF is produced is attractive, because it neatly ties many pathologic features of the disease into a single genetic abnormality, as would be expected from the autosomal recessive inheritance. However, there are a number of problems with this theory. Breakefield et al. (15) have shown that the gene for human NGF is normal in FD, suggesting that, if NGF is involved, the abnormalities must be in processing, in transport, or in receptors. Also, dramatic loss of sphenopalatine ganglion cells is a prominent feature of FD, while fetal NGF deprivation by anti-NGF antibody treatment has no effect on this parasympathetic ganglion experimentally (89). The absence of fungiform papillae in FD contrasts with normal tongue morphology (89) and normal quantitative behavioral responses to bitter taste (9) in anti-NGF treated rat or guinea pig fetuses.

Techniques for the measurement of NGF levels in FD have been controversial. Large variations in reported serum NGF levels may be related to assay type. Original reports that β-NGF cross-reacting material was elevated in FD may be an artifact of nonspecific serum binding of radiolabeled antigen, which falsely elevates the apparent serum NGF levels (115). Alternatively, it is possible that high levels of β-NGF cross-reactivity are due to α-NGF, γ-NGF, or mouse IgG contamination (8). Of great concern is the report (8) that purified human β-NGF does not cross-react with antibodies to murine β-NGF, either in a typical two-site RIA or in a functional bioassay, suggesting that studies using competitive antibody binding of mouse β-NGF to determine levels of human β-NGF are erroneous. In any respect, it is important to note that RIA for β-NGF in human serum is fraught with hazard. Functional assays such as neurite outgrowth or binding assays (105), survival (106), or extrusion of $^{22}Na^+$ from DRG neurons (106) all show normal levels of functional NGF in FD sera, although these assays are working at the lower limits of their sensitivities.

The remarkable similarities between immunosympathectomy and FD continue to be the strongest evidence for the involvement of NGF in the pathogenesis of the disease. Although this alone is far from convincing, it is more than sufficient evidence that further study in the processing and uptake of NGF in FD may provide an understanding of the molecular basis of this disorder.

ALZHEIMER'S DISEASE

It is estimated that 1 out of every 6 persons over 65 years of age is afflicted with moderate dementia (3), the most frequent cause of which is the neurodegenerative disorder, Alzheimer's disease. The clinical presentation consists of a diffuse deterioration of intellectual function, primarily in thought and memory processes, and secondarily in social aptitude and emotional processes (3). Pathologically, the disease is characterized by senile plaques (spherical masses of degenerating neurites and reactive cells around a core of amyloid) and by neurofibrillary tangles, which consist of large intraneuronal accumulations of paired helical filaments (119). Since senile plaques and neurofibrillary tangles are also common in elderly, undemented individuals, only the excessive frequency of these structures indicates the presence of Alzheimer's disease (11). In addition, intracellular cytoplasmic inclusions such as Hirano bodies are often present, primarily in the hippocampus. Granulovacuolar degeneration of neurons is widespread.

One of the most striking aspects of Alzheimer histopathology is the widespread, but nonuniform, loss of large neurons. In the cerebral cortex, neurons larger than 90 μm^2 are markedly depleted (118) predominantly in the hippocampus and association areas of the cortex, while other areas such as the occipital poles are less involved. There is a marked loss of subcortical neurons which project to the cortex, most notably in the amygdala (53), the ventral tegmentum (75), the locus ceruleus (77), and the cholinergic basal forebrain nuclei (i.e., the medial septal nucleus, the nucleus basalis, and the nucleus of the diagonal band) (125). As might be expected, neurotransmitter systems associated with these neurons are also depleted. For example, choline acetyltransferase (CAT) activity (24), serotonin uptake (13), and norepinephrine concentration (1) all appear to be decreased in Alzheimer's cortex compared with age-matched controls. Cortical interneurons are also impaired; and one prominent neuropeptide constituent of such cells, somatostatin, is also depleted (25).

One of the key questions about the pathogenesis of Alzheimer's disease is whether primary cortical pathology leads to retrograde losses of subcortical neurons, or if subcortical pathology is the primary cause of neuronal loss. Although definitive proof is not available, the weight of evidence would seem to favor a primary cortical pathology, since only those subcortical neurons projecting to the cortex are affected in Alzheimer's disease. Subcortical neurons from the locus ceruleus, for example, may project either to the cortex or to the spinal cord, basal ganglia, and cerebellum. Those locus ceruleus neurons which project cortically are heavily affected in Alzheimer's disease, but the others are not (76,77). In addition, cells in the locus ceruleus which project to the occipital cortex, which is less involved than other cortical areas in Alzheimer's disease, are less compromised (76). Similar topographic arrangement of neuronal loss can be seen in the nucleus basalis (5). Furthermore, dopaminergic neurons from the substantia nigra, which primarily project to the striatum, are less affected than cortically projecting dopaminergic neurons from the ventral tegmentum (75). It is difficult to conceive a pathologic process primarily affecting specific sections of multiple subcortical nuclei which then results in widespread cortical pathology. It seems more likely that trophic factors produced in the cortex are necessary for the survival of subcortical neurons, and cortical pathology interfering with these factors causes death of subcortical neurons.

A great deal of evidence has accumulated that CNS neurons can, indeed, be influenced by endogenous trophic factors. NGF, for example, was initially thought to be active only in the peripheral nervous system (10,64,69). However, early studies showed that sympathetic fibers which innervate arteries on the surface of the brain send sprouts to the hippocampus after lesions of the septo-hippocampal pathway (23,72-74,112). These effects can be mimicked by intracerebral NGF inoculation (70), suggesting that the deafferentation-induced ingrowth is mediated by NGF. In fact, denervation of the hippocampus by this type of lesion does cause a transient increase in hippocampal NGF levels (65,113,126). Furthermore, messenger RNA for NGF has been found in the hippocampus, suggesting that NGF is actively synthesized within the CNS (103). These observations raise the question of why NGF is present in the hippocampus. NGF is specifically transported from hippocampus to basal forebrain cholinergic neurons (99,101), and intraventricular injections of NGF enhance CAT activity in the septal region, the hippocampus, and the cortex (38) both in neonatal and adult rats. There are also specific NGF binding sites within the brain which are developmentally regulated, suggesting that NGF plays a role in ontogenesis (34,35,116,117,127). Further, Honegger and Lenoir (59) have described a stimulatory effect of NGF on cultured cholinergic telencephalic neurons at concentrations comparable to those having physiologic effects in the sympathetic nervous system.

It has been postulated that the selective loss of cholinergic cells in Alzheimer's disease reflects a relative or absolute deficiency of trophic support in the form of NGF, resulting from reduced production of NGF by target cells or by decreased responsiveness of cholinergic neurons to NGF (3,47). However, a number of studies argue against this possibility. Transplacental transfer of maternal anti-NGF antibodies decimates the fetal sympathetic nervous system (89), but has only a mild (or possibly no) effect on cognitive tasks (9). Anti-NGF antibodies injected intraventricularly do not reduce CAT activity in the forebrain (38,48), though some preliminary data dispute this (87). Hefti et al. (49) demonstrated that while NGF enhances CAT activity in dissociated septal neurons, their survival and neurite outgrowth were not affected by the treatment. Furthermore, NGF mRNA levels in Alzheimer brains are normal (40).

NGF is not, however, the only hippocampal trophic factor which affects basal forebrain neurons. Ojika and Appel (85) showed that acetylcholine synthesis and CAT activity were increased in medial septal nucleus explants by hippocampus extracts. This cholinergic enhancement was not duplicated by NGF or blocked by antibodies to NGF. Our laboratory has identified and partially purified a peptide (C-CTF) in these extracts which enhances acetylcholine synthesis and, to a lesser extent, CAT activity in the culture system (12). At optimal concentrations, NGF also stimulates CAT activity, but not acetylcholine synthesis; and maximal effects of C-CTF and NGF are additive. The ability of C-CTF to enhance acetylcholine synthesis appears to be related to its ability to couple high-affinity choline uptake to acetylation of choline, an index of maturation of neurons in this system (102).

Although most work has been done on basal forebrain cholinergic neurons, other neurons affected in Alzheimer's disease may also be influenced by trophic factors. Dopaminergic trophic factors have been documented; circumstantial evidence suggests the existence of noradrenergic and serotonergic factors. Furthermore, basic fibroblast growth factor enhances the survival and neurite extension of hippocampal (123) and cortical (82) neurons in culture. Other defined growth factors may also demonstrate trophic effects on neurons (81).

As in FD, the evidence that trophic factors are involved in the pathophysiology of Alzheimer's disease is circumstantial, but provocative. Studies of trophic factors in Alzheimer's disease are not yet available. Nevertheless, the importance of trophic factors in preventing retrograde degeneration in animal models suggests that the loss of subcortical neurons is related to primary cortical pathology which results in a functional loss of central trophic factors. While it is unlikely that abnormalities in the biology of a single trophic factor could explain the entire spectrum of abnormalities seen in Alzheimer's disease, further insight into these mechanisms may lead to new avenues for effective therapy (3,50).

PARKINSONISM

The pathologic hallmark of Parkinson's disease is a loss of dopaminergic neurons in the pars compacta of the substantia nigra which project to the striatum, leading to a distinctive clinical syndrome consisting of a stereotyped, "pill-rolling" tremor, bradykinesia, rigidity, and loss of postural reflexes (for reviews, see 18 and 98). Like Alzheimer's disease, however, many other neuronal groups are also affected, including other monoaminergic brain stem neurons (31), hypothalamic nuclei (67), nucleus basalis (124), and anterior pituitary lactotrophic cells (68). Correlating with the loss of dopaminergic neurons is the loss of dopamine-synthesizing enzymes and total dopamine content of the brain (19). Effective compensation for a loss of up to 70% of substantia nigra neurons is provided by enhancement of dopamine receptors (78,91). However, further neuronal loss leads to symptomatic parkinsonism.

There is increasing evidence that survival and differen-tiation of neurons in the substantia nigra are affected by target neurons. Initial studies of striatal and nigral neurons in vitro indicated that co-culture induces dopaminergic neurite outgrowth (28,51) and stimulates the development of dopaminergic cells as measured by dopamine uptake and dopamine fluorescence (66,92). Although at least part of this effect is due to membrane bound constituents (93), and medium conditioned by striatal cultures could not reproduce the effects of co-culture, our laboratory has found that soluble striatal extracts can increase dopamine uptake in fetal rat mesencephalic explants (3). A partially purified, trypsin-sensitive fraction from striatal extract causes significant increases in the number of dopaminergic neurons in dissociated embryonic rat midbrain cultures, as well as increasing dopamine uptake and the length of dopamine-containing neurites (121).

A great deal of interest has developed in the role of toxins in idiopathic parkinsonism because of the recent demonstration that methyl-4-phenyltetrahydropyridine (MPTP) can specifically destroy nigral neurons in humans and lead to parkinsonism (111). Specific trophic factors which enhance the survival of dopaminergic neurons under adverse conditions such as exposure to toxic agents might be a useful adjunction to therapy. Alternatively, primary striatal pathology interfering with one or more of these factors would lead to the loss of nigral neurons.

MOTOR NEURON DISEASES

Amyotrophic lateral sclerosis (ALS) is a devastating, lethal degenerative disorder of the motor system. It has a prevalence of 5-7/100,000, afflicts males twice as often as females, and has a mean age of onset of 57, although patients can range from 20 to over 80 years of age (4). Because intellect is not affected, the patient finds himself a helpless observer while his muscles, strength and stamina gradually deteriorate over several years until death results from respiratory compromise and intercurrent infection.

The majority of patients with ALS have manifestations both of upper and lower motor neuron dysfunction. Pathologic changes are present in the motor cortex, cranial motor neurons, and anterior horn cells (56). Chromatolysis may be evident; spheroids and neurofilamentous changes have been described in axons as well as in the cell bodies (20,26) and eosinophilic inclusions called Bunina bodies are frequently found (61).

Although NGF is not active in the motor system, variations in the supply of other target-derived neurotrophic factors may play roles in the pathogenesis of motor system diseases. During development, manipulation of target size by limb bud extirpation (44) or implantation (58) alters the survival of motor neurons (increasing target size increases survival; decreasing target size decreases survival). Similarly, pharmacologic alteration of target activity (e.g., curare or carbachol treatment) during development also alters naturally occurring motor neuron death (90). In addition to these in vivo studies, it is apparent that motor neurons in vitro are profoundly affected by muscle. Co-culture of skeletal myotubes with spinal cord cells enhances CAT activity (36,37). Skeletal muscle extracts (54,55,107) and media conditioned with myotubes (16,29,39,52) can reproduce this effect. Skeletal muscle extract also stimulates the development of other cholinergic markers such as acetylcholinesterase, sodium-dependent high-affinity choline uptake, and acetylcholine synthesis in spinal cord cultures (79).

Unfortunately, in vitro studies of the effects of skeletal muscle proteins on spinal cord neurons have been limited by the unavailability of purified factors. Until a neurotrophic factor can be purified, its biologic characterization is difficult or impossible. Consequently, our laboratory has concentrated efforts on purification of neurotrophic factors from skeletal muscle extracts. We have found at least four separable protein or peptide factors which influence cultured motor neurons in different ways, and are regulated differently during development and with denervation (80,108-110). However, purification to homogeneity has not been accomplished to date.

Motor neurotrophic factors may be important in the maintenance of adult neurons as well as during development. Brown et al. (17) have hypothesized that terminal sprouting is under the control of a diffusible factor produced by denervated muscle. The response of motor neurons to axotomy may be related, in part, to the loss of materials transported retrogradely, suggesting that trophic factors from the periphery may be involved (22). Further, amputation of a limb in an adult human leads to the progressive loss of the innervating anterior horn cells suggesting that the survival of adult motor neurons, like developing motor neurons, is dependent on target-derived factors (62).

At present, only two substances which have been broadly considered to be "trophic" factors have been studied in ALS. Gurney and colleagues (43) presented evidence that antibodies to a 56,000 dalton protein secreted from denervated muscle decreased sprouting of motor neurons in botulinum toxin-treated mice. Sera from a few ALS patients reacted with a 56,000 dalton species by immunoblot analysis, and such sera also inhibited botulinum toxin-induced sprouting in mice (43). Replication of the immunoblot analysis with ALS sera has not confirmed these results, either in our own laboratory (unpublished) or in others (46,60). Furthermore, it is difficult to reconcile the importance of antibodies which appear to decrease sprouting with the widespread sprouting seen as a prominent compensatory feature in ALS.

The second putative motor neurotrophic factor implicated in ALS has been thyrotropin-releasing hormone (TRH). Interest in the role of TRH in ALS originated with demonstrations that the drug is present in neurons synapsing on lower motor neurons (57), and appears to exert a neuromodulatory effect on motor neurons with slow time course, subthreshold depolarizations, but increased overall excitability (83,84). This neuromodulatory effect has also been shown in innervated muscle cultures (6) and in vivo (27). The possibility that TRH might exhibit a long-term trophic effect on motor neurons has also been suggested (97), although the evidence for this is far from convincing. Early clinical trials of TRH demonstrated a short-term increase in the strength of ALS patients (33). However, the results of subsequent trials have been controversial (114). Furthermore, recent data suggests that TRH can be virtually eliminated from rat spinal cords in vivo by intraventricular injection of 5,7-dihydroxytryptamine, a serotonergic neurotoxin; 11 weeks after treatment, no motor deficits can be found, motor neuron counts are normal, and gastrocnemius muscles are not denervated (122).

There is little information which directly addresses the contribution of neurotrophic factors to motor neuron diseases. As with Alzheimer's disease, it is unlikely that a pathologic process interfering with a single neurotrophic factor would explain all the manifestations of ALS. On the other hand, a neurotrophic factor which, like NGF in the sympathetic nervous system, allows motor neuron survival under adverse conditions might be a useful adjunction to therapy.

REFERENCES

1. Adolfsson, R., Gottfries, C.G., Oreland, L., Roos, B.E., and Winblad, B. (1978): In: Alzheimer's Disease: Senile Dementia and Related Disorders, Vol. 7, edited by R. Katzman, R.D. Terry, and C.L. Bick, pp. 441-451. Raven Press, New York.
2. Aguayo, A.J., Nair, C.P.V., and Bray, G.M. (1971): Arch. Neurol., 24:106-116.
3. Appel, S.H. (1981): Ann. Neurol., 10:499-505.
4. Appel, S.H., Stockton-Appel, V., Stewart, S.S., and Kerman, R.H. (1986): Arch. Neurol., 43:234-238.
5. Arendt, T., Bigl, V., Tennstedt, A., and Arendt, A. (1985): Neuroscience, 14:1-14.
6. Askanas, V., Engel, W.K., and Kobayashi, T. (1985): Ann. Neurol., 18:716-719.
7. Axelrod, F.B., Cash, R., and Pearson, J. (1982): J. Pediatr., 103:60-64.
8. Beck, C.E., and Perez-Polo, J.R. (1982): J. Neurosci. Res., 8:137-152.
9. Bell, J., Gruenthal, M., Finger, S., Lundberg, P., and Johnson, E. (1982): Brain Res., 234:409-421.
10. Bjorkland, A., Bjerre, B., and Wiklund, L. (1975): In: Proceedings of the VIth International Congress of Pharmacology, edited by J. Toumisto and M. Passones, pp. 259-274. Pergamon Press, New York.
11. Blessed, G., Tomlinson, B.E., and Roth, M. (1968): Br. J. Psychiatry, 114:797-811.
12. Bostwick, J.R., Appel, S.H., and Perez-Polo, J. (1987): Brain Res. (in press).
13. Bowen, D.M. (1983): In: Biological Aspects of Alzheimer's Disease, Banbury Report 15, edited by R. Katzman, p. 219. Cold Spring Harbor Press, New York.
14. Breakefield, X.O. (1981): Neurosci. Commentaries, 1:28-32.
15. Breakefield, X.O., Orloff, G., Castiglione, C., Coussens, L., Axelrod, F.B., and Ullrich, A. (1984): Proc. Natl. Acad. Sci. USA, 81:4213-4216.
16. Brookes, N., Burt, D., Goldberg, A., and Bierkemper, G. (1980): Brain, 186:474-479.
17. Brown, M., Holland, R., and Hopkins, W. (1981): Annu. Rev. Neurosci., 4:17-42.
18. Burke, R.E., and Fahn, S. (1981): In: Current Neurology, Vol. 3, edited by S.H. Appel, pp. 92-137. John Wiley and Sons, New York.
19. Calne, D.B., Kebabian, J., Silbergeld, E., and Evarts, E. (1979): Ann. Intern. Med., 90:219-229.
20. Carpenter, S. (1968): Neurology, 18:841-851.
21. Cohen, J., and Levi-Montalcini, R. (1956): Proc. Natl. Acad. Sci. USA, 42:571-574.
22. Cragg, B. (1970): Brain Res., 23:1-21.

23. Crutcher, K.A., Brothers, L., and Davis, J.N. (1981): Brain Res., 210:115-128.
24. Davies, P., Katzman, R., and Terry, R.D. (1980): Nature, 288:279-280.
25. Davies, P., and Maloney, A.J.F. (1976): Lancet, 2:1403.
26. Delisle, M.B., and Carpenter, S. (1984): J. Neurol. Sci., 63:241-250.
27. Delwide, P.J., Schoenen, J., and Dubois, V. (1984): Neurology, 34(Suppl. 1):284.
28. Denis-Donini, S., Glowinski, J., and Prochiantz, A. (1983): J. Neurosci., 3:2292-2299.
29. Dribin, L., and Barrett, J. (1980): Dev. Biol., 74:184-195.
30. Dumas, M., Schwab, M.E., and Thoenen, H. (1979): J. Neurobiol., 10:179-197.
31. Eadie, M.J. (1962): Brain, 86:781-792.
32. Eisenbarth, G.S. (1986): N. Engl. J. Med., 314:1360-1368.
33. Engel, W.K., Siddique, T., and Nicoloff, J.T. (1983): Lancet, 2:73-75.
34. Frazier, W.A., Boyd, L.F., Pulliam, M.W., Szutowicz, A., and Bradshaw, R.A. (1974): J. Biol. Chem., 249:5918-5923.
35. Frazier, W.A., Boyd, L.F., Szutowicz, A., Pulliam, M.W., and Bradshaw, R.A. (1974): Biochem. Biophys. Res. Commun., 57:1096-1103.
36. Giller, E., Neale, J., Bullock, P., Schrier, B., and Nelson, P. (1977): J. Cell Biol., 74:16-29.
37. Giller, E., Schrier, B., Shaumberg, A., Fisk, H., and Nelson, P. (1973): Science, 182:588-589.
38. Gnahn, H., Hefti, F., Heumann, R., Schwab, M.E., and Thoenen, H. (1983): Dev. Brain Res., 9:45-52.
39. Godfrey, E., Schrier, B., and Nelson, P. (1980): Dev. Biol., 77:403-418.
40. Goedert, M., Fine, A., Hunt, S.P., and Ullrich, A. (1986): Brain Res., 387:85-92.
41. Goedert, M., Otten, U., Hunt, S.P., Bond, A., Chapman, D., Schlumpf, M., and Lichtensteiger, W. (1984): Proc. Natl. Acad. Sci. USA, 81:1580-1584.
42. Gorin, P.D., and Johnson, E.M. (1979): Proc. Natl. Acad. Sci. USA, 76:5382-5386.
43. Gurney, M.E., Belton, A.C., Cashman, N., and Antel, J.P. (1984): N. Engl. J. Med., 311:933-939.
44. Hamburger, V., and Keefe, E. (1944): J. Exp. Zool., 96:223-242.
45. Harper, G.P., and Thoenen, H. (1941): Annu. Rev. Pharmacol. Toxicol., 21:205-229.
46. Hauser, S.L., Henderson, C.E., Lyon-Caen, O., and Changeaux, J.P. (1985): Neurology, 35(Suppl. 1):250-251.
47. Hefti, F. (1983): Ann. Neurol., 13:109-110.
48. Hefti, F., Dravid, A., and Hartikka, J. (1984): Brain Res., 293:305-311.

49. Hefti, F., Hartikka, J., Eckenstein, F., Gnahn, H., Heumann, R., and Schwab, M. (1985): Neuroscience, 14:55-68.
50. Hefti, F., and Weiner, W.J. (1986): Ann. Neurol., 20:275-281.
51. Hemmendinger, L.M., Garber, B.B., Hoffmann, P.C., and Heller, A. (1981): Proc. Natl. Acad. Sci. USA, 78:1264-1268.
52. Henderson, C., Huchet, M., and Changeaux, J. (1981): Proc. Natl. Acad. Sci. USA, 78:2625-2629.
53. Herzog, A.G., and Kemper, T.L. (1980): Arch. Neurol., 37:625-629.
54. Hill, M., and Bennett, M. (1982): Neurosci. Lett., (Suppl), 8:s54.
55. Hill, M., Stratford, J., Nurcombe, V., and Bennett, M. (1981): Proc. Aust. Phys. Pharmacol. Soc., 12:160P.
56. Hirano, A. (1965): In: Slow, Latent and Temperate Virus Infections, edited by D.C. Gadjusek, C.G. Gibbs, and M. Alpers, pp. 23-37. NIH, Washington, D.C.
57. Hokfelt, T., Fuxe, K., and Johansson, D. (1975): Neurosci. Lett., 1:133-139.
58. Hollyday, M., and Hamburger, V. (1976): J. Comp. Neurol., 170:311-320.
59. Honegger, P., and Lenoir, D. (1982): Dev. Brain Res., 3:229-238.
60. Ingvar-Maeder, M., Steck, A.J., Figlewicz, D.A., and Regli, F. (1986): Muscle Nerve, 9(Suppl.):101.
61. Iwata, M., and Hirano, A. (1979): Prog. Neuropathol., 4:277-298.
62. Kawamura, Y., and Dyck, P.J. (1981): J. Neuropathol. Exp. Neurol., 40:658-666.
63. Kessler, J.A., and Black, I.B. (1980): Brain Res., 189:157-168.
64. Konkol, R.J., Mailman, R.B., Bendeich, E.G., Garrison, A.M., Mueller, R.A., and Breese, G.R. (1978): Brain Res., 144:277-285.
65. Korsching, S., Heumann, R., Thoenen, H., and Hefti, F. (1986): Neurosci. Lett., 66:175-180.
66. Kotake, C., Hoffmann, P.C., and Heller, A. (1982): J. Neurosci., 2:1307-1315.
67. Langston, J.W., and Forno, L.S. (1978): Ann. Neurol., 3:129-133.
68. Lawton, N.F., and MacDermot, J. (1980): J. Neurol. Neurosurg. Psychiatry, 43:1012-1015.
69. Levi-Montalcini, R. (1975): In: Proceedings of the VIth International Congress of Pharmacology, edited by J. Toumisto and M. Passones, pp. 221-230. Pergamon Press, New York.
70. Levi-Montalcini, R., and Angeletti, P.V. (1968): Physiol. Rev., 48:534-569.

71. Levi-Montalcini, R., and Hamburger, V. (1951): J. Exp. Zool., 116:321-362.
72. Loy, R., Milner, T., and Moore, R.Y. (1980): Exp. Neurol., 67:399-411.
73. Loy, R., and Moore, R.Y. (1977): Exp. Neurol., 57:645-650.
74. Loy, R., and Moore, R.Y. (1979): In: Catecholamines: Basic and Clinical Frontiers, edited by E. Usdin, E.J. Kopin, and J. Barchas, pp. 1336-1338. Pergamon Press, New York.
75. Mann, D.M.A., Yates, P.O., and Marcyniuk, B. (1987): J. Neurol. Neurosurg. Psychiatry (in press).
76. Marcyniuk, B., Mann, D.M.A., and Yates, P.O. (1986): J. Neurol. Sci., 76:335-345.
77. Marcyniuk, B., Mann, D.M.A., and Yates, P.O. (1986): Neurosci. Lett., 64:247-252.
78. McGeer, P.L., McGeer, E.G., and Suzuki, J.S. (1977): Arch. Neurol., 334:33-35.
79. McManaman, J.L., Haverkamp, L.J., and Appel, S.H. (1987): Dev. Biol. (submitted for publication).
80. McManaman, J.L., Smith, R.G., and Appel, S.H. (1985): Dev. Biol., 112:248-252.
81. Mill, J.F., Chao, M.V., and Ishii, D.M. (1985): Proc. Natl. Acad. Sci. USA, 82:7126-7130.
82. Morrison, R.S., Sharma, A., DeVellis, J., and Bradshaw, R.A. (1986): Proc. Natl. Acad. Sci. USA, 83:7537-7541.
83. Nicoll, R.A. (1978): J. Pharmacol. Exp. Ther., 207:817-824.
84. Nicoll, R.A. (1980): Proc. R. Soc. Lond. [Biol.], 210:133-149.
85. Ojika, K., and Appel, S.H. (1984): Proc. Natl. Acad. Sci. USA, 81:2567-2571.
86. Oppenheim, R.W., Maderdrut, J.L., and Wells, D.J. (1982): J. Comp. Neurol., 210:174-189.
87. Otten, U., Weskamp, G., Schlumpf, M., Lichtensteiger, W., and Mobley, W.C. (1985): Soc. Neurosci. Abst., 11:661.
88. Pearson, J. (1979): J. Auton. Nerv. Syst., 1:119-126.
89. Pearson, J., Johnson, E.M., and Brandeis, L. (1983): Dev. Biol., 96:32-36.
90. Pitman, R., and Oppenheim, R. (1979): J. Comp. Neurol., 187:425-446.
91. Poirier, L.J., Sourkes, T.L., Bouvier, G., Boucher, R., and Carabin, S. (1966): Brain, 89:37-52.
92. Prochiantz, A., Daguet, M-C., Herbet, A., and Glowinski, J. (1981): Nature, 293:570-573.
93. Prochiantz, A., DiPorzio, U., Kato, A., Berger, B., and Glowinski, J. (1979): Proc. Natl. Acad. Sci. USA, 76: 5387-5391.
94. Ramon y Cajal, S. (1928): Degeneration and Regeneration of the Nervous System, transl. R.M. May. Hafner Publishing Co., New York, 1959.

95. Rees-Smith, B., Creagh, F.M., Hashin, F.A., Howells, R.D., Davies-Jones, E., Kajita, Y., Buckland, P.R., and Petersen, V.B. (1985): Arzneimittelforsch, 35:1943-1948.
96. Riley, C.M., Day, R.L., Greeley, D., and Langford, W.S. (1949): Pediatrics, 3:468-477.
97. Schmidt-Achert, K.M., Askanas, V., and Engel, W.K. (1984): J. Neurochem., 43:586-589.
98. Schultz, W. (1984): Life Sci., 34:2213-2223.
99. Schwab, M.E., Otten, U., Agid, Y., and Thoenen, H. (1979): Brain Res., 168:473-483.
100. Schwartz, J.P., and Breakefield, X.O. (1980): Proc. Natl. Acad. Sci. USA, 77:1154-1158.
101. Seiler, M., and Schwab, M.E. (1984): Brain Res., 300:33-39.
102. Shelton, D.L., Nadler, J.V., and Cotman, C.W. (1979): Brain Res., 163:263-275.
103. Shelton, D.F., and Reichardt, L.F. (1986): Proc. Natl. Acad. Sci. USA, 83:2714-2718.
104. Siggers, D.C. (1976): Proc. Soc. Exp. Biol. Med., 69: 183-184.
105. Siggers, D.C., Rodgers, J.G., Boyer, S.H., Margolet, L., Dorkin, H., Bannerjee, S.P., and Shooter, E.M. (1976): N. Engl. J. Med., 295:629-634.
106. Skaper, S.D., and Varon, S. (1982): Exp. Neurol., 76: 655-665.
107. Slack, J., and Pockett, S. (1982): Brain Res., 247:138-140.
108. Smith, R., and Appel, S. (1983): Science, 219:1079-1080.
109. Smith, R.G., McManaman, J., and Appel, S.H. (1985): J. Cell Biol., 101:1608-1621.
110. Smith, R.G., Vaca, K., McManaman, J., and Appel, S.H. (1986): J. Neurosci., 6:439-447.
111. Snyder, S.H., and D'Amato, R.J. (1985): Neurology, 36: 250-258.
112. Stenevi, U., and Bjorklund, A. (1978): Neurosci. Lett., 7:219-224.
113. Stewart, G.R., Fredrickson, C.J., Howell, G.A., and Gage, F.H. (1984): Brain Res., 290:43-51.
114. Stewart, S.S., and Appel, S.H. (1986): Curr. Neurol. (in press).
115. Suda, K., Barde, Y.A., and Thoenen, H. (1978): Proc. Natl. Acad. Sci. USA, 75:4042-4046.
116. Szutowicz, A., Frazier, W.A., and Bradshaw, R.A. (1976): J. Biol. Chem., 251:1516-1528.
117. Taniuchi, M., Schweitzer, J.B., and Johnson, E.M. (1986): Proc. Natl. Acad. Sci. USA, 83:1950-1954.
118. Terry, R.D. (1981): Ann. Neurol., 10:184-192.
119. Terry, R.D., and Davies, P. (1980): Annu. Rev. Neurosci., 3:77-95.

120. Thoenen, H., Angeletti, P.U., Levi-Montalcini, R., and Kettler, R. (1971): Proc. Natl. Acad. Sci. USA, 68:1598-1602.
121. Tomozawa, Y., and Appel, S.H. (1987): Brain Res. (in press).
122. Van den Bergh, P., Kelly, J.J., Adelman, L., and Munsat, T. (1986): Neurology, 36(Suppl. 1):139.
123. Walicke, P., Cowan, W.M., and Ueno, N. (1986): Proc. Natl. Acad. Sci. USA, 83:3012-3016.
124. Whitehouse, P.J., Hedreen, J.C., and White, C. (1983): Ann. Neurol., 13:243-248.
125. Whitehouse, P.J., Price, D.L., Clark, A.W., Coyle, J.T., and DeLong, M.R. (1981): Ann. Neurol., 10:122-126.
126. Yoshida, K., Kohsaka, S., Idei, T., Nii, S., Otani, M., Toya, S., and Tsukada, Y. (1986): Neurosci. Lett., 66:181-186.
127. Zimmerman, A., Sutter, A., Samuelson, J., and Shooter, E.M. (1978): J. Supramol. Struct. Cell Biochem., 9:351-361.

Central Nervous System Disorders of Aging: Clinical Intervention and Research, edited by Randy Strong et al. Raven Press, New York © 1988.

MECHANISM OF DEGENERATION OF EPINEPHRINE

NEURONS IN ALZHEIMER'S DISEASE

William J. Burke,*† Hyung D. Chung,*†
Randy Strong,*† Michael B. Mattammal,*
Gary L. Marshall,* Raj Nakra,†
George T. Grossberg,† John H. Haring,†
and Tong H. Joh**

*Veterans Administration Medical Center and
† St. Louis University School of Medicine,
St. Louis, Missouri 63125; and
**Cornell University Medical College,
New York, New York 10021

Alzheimer's disease (AD) is a progressive dementing disorder of gradual onset usually occurring in mid or late life. A diagnosis of probable AD can be made if typical deficits in higher cortical function (memory loss, aphasia, apraxia, agnosia) are of insidious onset, progressive and cannot be explained by other systemic or brain disorders (47). The diagnosis of definite AD requires histopathologic analysis of the brain. The pathological diagnosis of AD depends on the finding of plaques in the neocortex or hippocampus (37,58). The plaques consist of an amyloid core surrounded by glial cells, degenerating axons and dendrites and appear to represent, in part, degenerating cortical neurons (36). In AD, the plaques are found in large numbers in hippocampus, amygdala and prefrontal cortex (36) regions of brain associated with memory (55), mood and behavior (23). In contrast, plaques are rare in cerebellum or motor cortex, areas of brain unaffected by AD (36). Because plaques increase during normal aging, the number of plaques required to diagnose AD increases with age (37). However, with a positive clinical history of AD, the number required may be revised downward (37).

Large numbers of neurons appear to be lost in various brain regions in AD (58); yet, little is known about the mechanisms underlying neuronal degeneration and death. In this chapter, we will describe studies on the brain epinephrine (Epi) system which provide evidence that transsynaptic retrograde degeneration plays a role in neuronal degeneration in AD. We will also suggest a mechanism for transsynaptic retrograde degeneration. Finally, we will discuss how clinical symptoms could be caused by secondary neuronal degeneration and suggest future therapeutic strategies which may prove useful in the treatment of AD.

THE NEUROTRANSMITTER DEFICITS IN ALZHEIMER'S DISEASE

Evidence Required for Identifying a Deficit in a Specific Transmitter System

One research strategy in AD has been to look for deficits in specific neurotransmitter systems in AD brains so that specific replacement therapies can be developed (48). This research may also give important clues to mechanisms underlying neuronal degeneration, the basic cause of the disease (13,49). Although deficits in a number of neurotransmitter systems have been postulated (20,21,26), only a few are documented with markers that are both stable in postmortem tissue and specific for a single neurotransmitter system (13,21). For instance, the peptide neuromodulator, somatostatin, may be co-localized with several neurotransmitters (31) and, therefore, does not identify a single type of neuron. Most other transmitters are poor markers for their neuronal systems because they are metabolized postmortem (61); therefore, enzymes in their biosynthetic pathways are used as markers for these neuro-transmitter systems. For example, the terminal enzyme in the synthesis of acetylcholine, choline acetyltransferase (CAT), is a stable (50) enzyme found only in cholinergic neurons and, hence, it is a specific marker for this neurotransmitter system. Other enzymes, however, have proven too vulnerable to pre- and postmortem factors to be measured accurately in postmortem brain, e.g., tryptophan hydroxylase (46), tyrosine hydroxylase (45), and glutamic acid decarboxylase (45,50). Finally, the activity of some enzymes cannot be used as specific markers because the enzyme is found in more than one type of neuron. For instance, aromatic L-amino acid decarboxylase (AADC) is found in both dopamine and serotonin neurons (18). And, dopamine β-hydroxylase (DBH), the enzyme which synthesizes norepinephrine (NE) in neurons whose numbers are decreased in AD (8), is also found in Epi neurons (Fig. 1). Therefore, AADC and DBH activity do not identify a specific type of neuron.

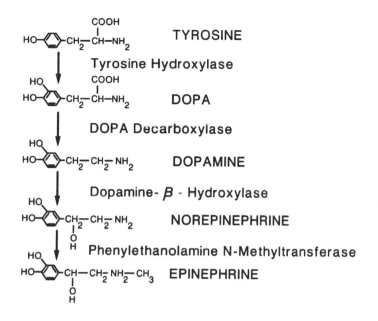

FIG. 1. The catecholamine biosynthetic pathway.

TABLE 1. Effect of pre- and postmortem factors on PNMT
activity in control brain

Factor	Length of time (mean ± SE)	Correlation with LC PNMT (correlation coefficient)
Age (yrs)	63.4 ± 3.5	-0.206
Coma (hrs)	33.7 ± 23.5	-0.793[a]
Death–Refrig (min)	97.6 ± 18.5	-0.426
Death–Autopsy (hrs)	16.1 ± 1.8	-0.054
Autopsy–Assay (days)	53.5 ± 13.4	-0.536

[a] $p < 0.05$

Correlation coefficients were determined in 10 control brains between various pre- and postmortem factors and PNMT activity in the LC.

Advantages of Studying the Epinephrine System· in Alzheimer's Disease

Study of the Epi system in AD has at least seven advantages:

1. Phenylethanolamine N-methyltransferase (PNMT), the enzyme which synthesizes Epi from NE, is the terminal enzyme in the catecholamine biosynthetic pathway (Fig. 1); hence, it is found only in Epi neurons and, therefore, is a specific marker for these neurons.

2. We have studied a variety of factors which occur during the dying process and between the time of death and assay of PNMT which could affect the measurement of enzyme activity. The enzyme is stable to most of these pre- and postmortem factors (13) (Table 1) and can be studied in postmortem brain.

3. The location of the neuronal cell bodies in the C-1 and C-2 regions of brain stem as well as the subcortical projections of this neurotransmitter system is well-documented (38). Further description of this neurotransmitter system was recently made possible by a highly sensitive assay for PNMT developed in our laboratory. Using this assay, we have demonstrated the Epi system in cortex as well (16). That the cortical Epi system also originates from brain stem C-1 and C-2 neurons is supported by the following evidence. No other Epi neurons have been described, and the adjacent NE neurons in A-1 and A-2 project to cortex (38). In addition, we have shown that a large lesion in the rat medial forebrain bundle, which contains axons going from brain stem to cortex (Fig. 2), reduces brain stem and hippocampal PNMT to the same extent (> 80%), indicating that these systems are connected. In contrast, PNMT in cerebellum whose connections to C-1 and C-2 neurons would not be interrupted by the lesion was not decreased (Table 2).

4. A further advantage of the Epi system is that it is simple both in terms of a relatively small cell population (23,000 neurons in C-1 and 7,600 neurons in C-2) and lack of topographical complexity (only two well-defined nuclei), simplifying cell counting. By contrast, there are 400,000 neurons in the topographically diffuse nucleus basalis portion of the cholinergic system alone (62).

5. The Epi system projects to the locus ceruleus (LC), another simple transmitter system whose NE neurons have been completely counted (60) and are known to be affected in AD (8). This allows, for the first time, an accurate analysis of the interaction between neuronal systems affected in AD.

6. Additionally, since PNMT is rate limiting in Epi synthesis (25), it may be used as a direct index of Epi itself. Because Epi itself is metabolized postmortem, this is a distinct advantage over systems where the biosynthetic enzyme is not rate limiting in neurotransmitter synthesis.

7. Finally, there are known replacement therapies for the catecholamine (CA) system (23).

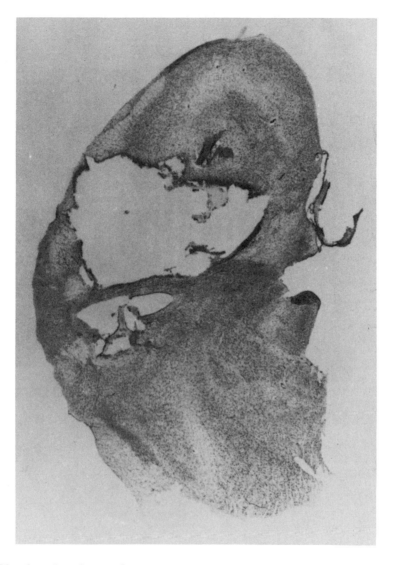

FIG. 2. <u>An electrolytic lesion in the right medial forebrain bundle at the level of the hypothalamus in an adult rat.</u>

TABLE 2. Effect on an electrolytic lesion of medial forebrain
          bundle on PNMT projections from C-1 and C-2 Epi
          brain stem neurons to hippocampus and cerebellum

| | PNMT activity (Units/g wet wt) | | |
Side	Hippocampus	Brain stem	Cerebellum
Control	59.3 ± 3.2	89.0 ± 0.67	9.7 ± 0.45
Lesioned	9.9 ± 1.3[a]	11.4 ± 0.66[b]	9.8 ± 1.7

[a]$p < 0.002$ [b]$p < 0.001$

An electrolytic lesion was made in the right hypothalamus
of an adult rat interrupting projections in the medial
forebrain bundle from brain stem neurons to cerebral cortex.
The left medial forebrain bundle was not lesioned. PNMT
activity was measured in the hippocampus, brain stem, and
cerebellum 14 days after the lesion.

EVIDENCE FOR AN EPINEPHRINE NEUROTRANSMITTER
DEFICIT IN ALZHEIMER'S DEMENTIA

Effect of Pre- and Postmortem Factors
on Measurement of PNMT

Control brain samples were obtained at autopsy from five
individuals who had no gross or histological evidence of brain
pathology at autopsy; the mean age at death was 70.8 ± 2.7
years and the postmortem interval 16.4 ± 1.2 hours. The
causes of death in this group were cardiac arrest, pulmonary
embolism, and upper gastrointestinal hemorrhage. On the basis
of the clinical history of dementia and histopathological
identification of neuritic plaques, the diagnosis of AD was
established in five cases with a mean age at death of
72.8 ± 3.1 years and postmortem interval of 18.4 ± 2.6 hours
(Table 4). The causes of death in this group were cardiac
arrest and pneumonia. We have previously shown that the cause
of death, including prolonged hypoxia, does not affect PNMT
levels (12). A variety of pre- and postmortem factors have
been described which may affect measurement of enzyme activity
in postmortem tissue (9,10,43,44,50). Table 1 shows the effect
of a variety of pre- and postmortem factors on measurement of
PNMT in human LC. Of these factors only prolonged coma prior
to death affected PNMT levels. There was no significant
difference in any of these pre- or postmortem factors between
control and AD groups (Table 3). In particular, the average
length of coma in the AD cases was not longer than in
controls. In addition to the above-mentioned premortem
factors, we examined the medications taken by each group
within one month of death (Table 5). AD cases were not taking

TABLE 3. Pre- and postmortem characteristics of control and Alzheimer patients

Group	Age (yrs)	Coma (hrs)	Death-Refrig. (hrs)	Death-Autopsy (hrs)	Autopsy-Assay (days)
Control	70.8 ± 2.7 (61-79)	58.3 ± 39.0 (0.16-228)	1.56 ± 0.39 (0.75-3.0)	16.4 ± 1.2 (13.2-20.2)	78 ± 19.6 (13-137)
Alzheimer	72.8 ± 3.1 (64-81)	13.4 ± 10.6 (0.5-61)	4.69 ± 1.35 (2.33-10.6)	18.4 ± 2.6 (14.8-30.0)	112 ± 78.9 (4-463)

A number of pre- and postmortem factors which could alter PNMT activity were determined for five control and five Alzheimer cases. Values shown are the mean ± S.E. The range is in parentheses.

TABLE 4.   Pathological criteria for diagnosing Alzheimer's in
                        brains from demented patients

Case	Age	Plaques/mm^2
AD-1	81	14.3 ± 0.74 (12–16)
AD-2	81	17.2 ± 0.65 (16–19)
AD-3	68	25.5 ± 0.90 (32–35)
AD-4	70	30.0 ± 0.93 (28–33)
AD-5	64	106.7 ± 1.98 (100–110)

   The average number of plaques in neocortex (AD-2 to AD-5) or
subiculum (AD-1) was determined from four fields. Each value
represents the mean ± S.E.   The range of counts is in
parentheses.

TABLE 5.   Drugs used to treat control and Alzheimer patients

Class of Drug	Control	Alzheimer
Antibiotic	Penicillin Ampicillin Gentamycin Clindamycin	Ampicillin Nafcillin Trimethoprim Sulfamethoxazole
Antihistamine	Hydroxyzine	Hydroxyzine
Antihypertensive	Prazosin Apresoline	Propanolol Apresoline
Benzodiazepine	Diazepam	Diazepam Flurazepam Temazepam
Bronchodilator	Theophylline Metaproferenol	
Cardiac Glycoside	Digoxin	
Dopamine Agonist	Dopamine	Sinnemet Amantadine
Dopamine Antagonist	Metoclopramide Prochlorperazine	Metoclopramide Prochlorperazine Thioridazine
Histamine (H-2) Receptor Antagonist	Cimetidine	Cimetidine
Membrane Stabilizer	Lidocaine	
Narcotic	Demerol	Demerol
Steroids	Prednisone	Betamethasone

   Drugs listed were taken by patients within one month of their
death.

TABLE 6. PNMT activity in brain regions from control and Alzheimer cases

Group	PNMT activity (Units/g wet wt)				
	LC	HIP	AMY	MF	CBL
Control	285.0 ± 30.5	31.5 ± 3.7	43.4 ± 5.9	36.3 ± 3.6	35.8 ± 5.1
Alzheimer	180.4 ± 27.5[a]	18.1 ± 2.9[b]	23.0 ± 4.1[b]	18.7 ± 4.0[c]	30.9 ± 4.7

[a]$p < 0.05$ [b]$p < 0.025$ [c]$p < 0.02$

PNMT activity in various brain regions from control and Alzheimer cases was measured in dialyzed supernatants as outlined in the text. Regions measured include: locus ceruleus (LC), hippocampus (HIP), amygdala (AMY), midfrontal (MF), cerebellum (CBL). One unit corresponds to formation of 1 pmol [^{3}H] Epi/h. Values shown are the mean ± S.E. of five control and five Alzheimer cases (taken from Burke et al., Ann. Neurol., in press, 1987).

any class of drug not also taken by controls. Of these medications, only steroids have been shown to affect PNMT (59,64). However, analysis of LC PNMT in control cases showed no change in enzyme activity in those treated with steroids. Similarly, those classes of drugs taken only by controls did not produce an increase in PNMT.

PNMT is Decreased in Alzheimer's Disease

PNMT activity in AD cases when compared to controls was significantly decreased in several areas of brain where there is neuronal loss in AD (8,36): LC (37%), hippocampus (42%), amygdala (47%), midfrontal cortex (48%) but not in cerebellum, an area of brain unaffected by AD (63) (Table 6). Likewise, in the motor cortex, another area where there is little neuronal loss in AD (36), there was no decrease in PNMT (Table 7). This decrease in PNMT was not due to a nonspecific effect of dementia since cases with multiple infarcts, another cause of dementia, did not have a further reduction in PNMT compared to the five AD cases analyzed here (Table 8). To determine whether the decrease in enzyme activity was due to a decrease in enzyme protein, antibody was prepared (35) and used to titrate (14) the amount of enzyme in soluble extracts from a control and an AD patient. To a constant volume of PNMT antibody an increasing amount of soluble extract from the LC was added. The equivalence point was shifted from 1.35 µl for the control to 3.4 µl for the AD case. This 60% decrease in PNMT protein agrees with the 65% loss of PNMT activity in the same extracts (376 units/g for the control vs. 130 units/g for AD) and indicates that the entire loss of PNMT was due to a decrease in the amount of enzyme protein (12).

TABLE 7. PNMT activity in motor cortex of control and Alzheimer cases

Group	PNMT activity (Units/g wet wt)
Control	12.9 ± 4.2
Alzheimer	15.3 ± 1.6

PNMT activity in motor cortex from three control and five Alzheimer brains was measured in dialyzed supernatants as outlined in the text. Values shown are the mean ± S.E.

Several pieces of evidence suggest that the decrease in PNMT in AD may be clinically significant. The deficit in PNMT occurs only in brain areas known to be affected in AD (36) (LC, hippocampus, amygdala, prefrontal cortex). These areas of brain are known to be important in regulation of attention, memory and behavioral functions which are deficient in AD (1).

TABLE 8. Effect of infarcts on PNMT activity in brain regions from Alzheimer cases

PNMT activity
(Units/g wet wt)

Group	LC	HIP	AMY	MF	CBL
Alzheimer	180.4 ± 27.5	18.1 ± 2.9	23.0 ± 4.1	18.7 ± 4.0	30.9 ± 4.7
Alzheimer + Infarct	163.5 ± 47	16.6 ± 5.2	17.4 ± 5.3	20.7 ± 6.9	33.2 ± 7.6

PNMT activity in various brain regions from Alzheimer cases with and without infarcts was measured in dialyzed supernatant as outlined in the text. Regions measured include: locus ceruleus (LC), hippocampus (HIP), amygdala (AMY), midfrontal (MF), cerebellum (CBL). Values shown are the mean ± S.E. of five cases without and two cases with infarcts.

In addition, experiments indicate that Epi may affect higher brain functions of memory (42), mood and behavior (23). Further, the clinical degree of dementia, as measured by the Blessed dementia scale of behaviorial impairment (6,66), is highly correlated to the loss of hippocampal PNMT (Fig. 3). These results suggest that the loss of PNMT which is the specific marker for Epi neurons and rate limiting in the synthesis of the neurotransmitter Epi, may contribute, in part, to the loss of brain function in AD.

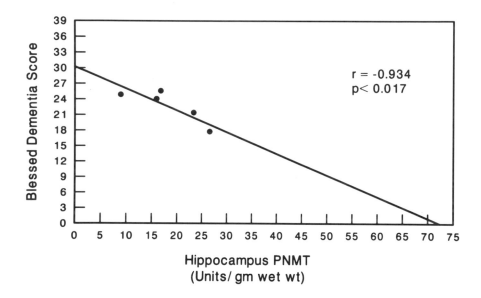

FIG. 3. Correlation between degree of dementia and PNMT activity in hippocampus. Scores on the Blessed dementia scale of behavioral impairment and hippocampal PNMT activity were determined in each of the five AD cases as described in the text.

THE MECHANISM OF DEGENERATION OF EPINEPHRINE NEURONS

Transsynaptic Retrograde Neuronal Degeneration

Although large numbers of neurons appear to be lost in AD brains (36), little is known about mechanisms underlying neuronal degeneration and death. An understanding of these mechanisms will lead to an understanding of the pathophysiology of the disease and may lead to new forms of therapy based on preventing neuronal death. One cause of neuronal death which has received little attention in AD is secondary retrograde transneuronal degeneration (13,49). Retrograde transneuronal degeneration has been defined as those atrophic and degenerative changes leading to neuronal death in second or third order neurons which occur not due to any direct injury to the neuron but secondary to loss of postsynaptic neurons in the projection field (17). On theoretical grounds alone, it seems likely that this process occurs in brains of victims of AD. There is widespread neuronal loss in AD not only in limbic systems but in cortical and subcortical regions as well (8,36). Thus, some of the postsynaptic connections of neurons may be effectively lesioned. Several of the subcortical nuclei whose neurons are affected in AD [nucleus basalis (49,62), LC (8), raphe nucleus (19,65), C-1 and C-2 neurons (13)] have large projections to the hippocampus and amygdala, regions which have significant cell loss in AD (36). Another factor affecting the degree of retrograde degeneration, namely, duration of the lesion (17), is also present in AD, a process which lasts for many years. It was, therefore, of interest to determine if this was the process affecting Epi neurons.

To determine whether the decrease in PNMT protein in Epi projection areas was due to loss of Epi neurons or to changes in the amount of PNMT in each neuron, the C-1 and C-2 Epi neurons were located in human brain using immunohistochemical staining with antibody to PNMT (13). These regions were then stained with haematoxylin eosin, and the total number and density of neurons in the C-1 and C-2 regions from the five control and five AD cases were determined. Although up to 25% of the neurons in AD cases were atrophic, there was no decrease in number or density of Epi neurons in AD compared to control cases (Table 9). These results indicate that the decrease in PNMT in the projection areas precedes cell death and is due to a decrease in PNMT protein in each neuron.

In contrast, however, there was a loss of postsynaptic neurons onto which Epi neurons project in AD. This was manifested by an increase in plaque counts in hippocampus and neocortex (Table 4), and by the decrease of 49% in the number and 50% in the density of LC neurons (Table 10). We have previously demonstrated that these LC neurons are innervated by Epi neurons in human brain (13). In addition, as we noted earlier, the decrease in PNMT occurs only in regions of AD brain where there is loss of postsynaptic neurons (Tables 6 and 7). Finally, the decrease in PNMT was highly correlated with the degree of postsynaptic neuronal loss in the hippocampus H-2 region (Fig. 4) and in the LC (Fig. 5). This data indicates that the atrophic changes and decreased amounts of PNMT protein in Epi neurons are due to transsynaptic changes caused by the loss of postsynaptic neurons. Furthermore, the decrease in LC neurons correlated significantly with the loss of hippocampal neurons in H-1 as manifested by the number of plaques (Fig. 6). Marcyniuk et al. (40,41) has recently reported a loss of LC neurons which project to areas of brain

affected by AD with little change in LC neurons projecting to
relatively uninvolved areas. We found no loss of neurons in
C-1 and C-2, the major afferent to the LC (3) in AD. Therefore,
in contrast to anterograde transsynaptic degeneration which
appears to be due to the loss of inhibitor afferent neurons
(53), the NE LC neurons also seem to be affected by retrograde
degeneration.

TABLE 9. Number and density of C-1 and C-2 neurons in control
                        and Alzheimer brain

Group	Total number of neurons		Cell density (neurons/field)	
	C-1	C-2	C-1	C-2
Control	22988 ± 1345	7649 ± 579	53.8 ± 3.2	19.2 ± 1.6
Alzheimer	21241 ± 769	7429 ± 328	48.2 ± 1.2	18.8 ± 0.9
	(0-20%)	(0-25%)		

The C-1 and C-2 regions were sectioned at 30 μ intervals,
stained and examined at a magnification of 125X. All neurons
containing nuclei were counted. The number of neurons in C-1
was determined in 5 to 10 sections and in C-2 in 5 to 8
sections. The total number of neurons in each case was
determined from the length of the nucleus and the thickness of
each section and was corrected for split cell error using
Abercrombie's formula. The cell density is the average number
of neurons in all sections examined from each case. Values are
the mean ± S.E. of five control and five Alzheimer cases. The
range of the percent of atrophic neurons in Alzheimer cases is
given in parentheses.

TABLE 10. Number and density of LC neurons in control
                        and Alzheimer brain

Group	Total number of neurons	Cell density (neurons/field)
	LC	LC
Control	25888.5 ± 1132.1	93.5 ± 2.2
Alzheimer	13058.7 ± 4271.9[a]	46.9 ± 15.5[a]

[a]$p < 0.02$

The LC was sectioned at 30 μ intervals, stained and examined
at a magnification of 125X. All neurons containing nuclei were
counted. The number of neurons was determined in 7 to 17
sections. The total number of neurons in each case was
determined from the length of the nucleus and the thickness of
each section and was corrected for split cell error using
Abercrombie's formula. The cell density is the average number
of neurons in all sections examined from each case. Values are
the mean ± S.E. of five control and five Alzheimer cases.

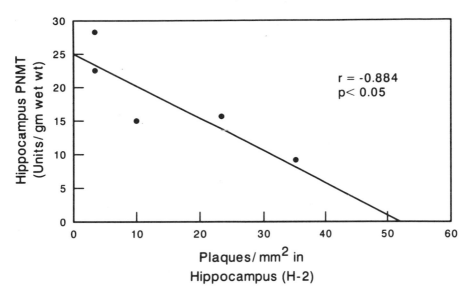

FIG. 4. Correlation between hippocampal PNMT activity and number of plaques in H-2 region of hippocampus. Hippocampal PNMT and plaque counts in each of five AD cases were determined as described in the text.

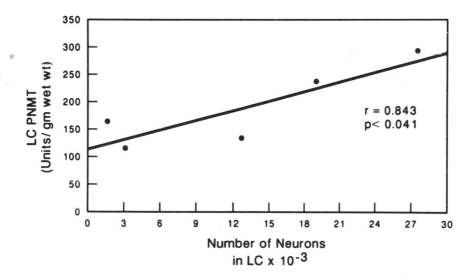

FIG. 5. Correlation between LC PNMT activity and the number of neurons in LC. LC PNMT activity and neuronal number were determined in each of five AD cases as described in the text.

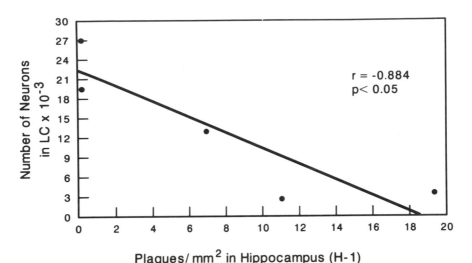

FIG. 6.　Correlation between the number of LC neurons and the number of plaques in H-1 region of hippocampus.　The number of LC neurons and plaque counts in hippocampus were determined in each of five AD cases as described in the text.

A Molecular Mechanism for Retrograde
Transsynaptic Degeneration

The previous data indicates that the loss of the postsynaptic neuron leads to degeneration of the presynaptic Epi neuron. Recently, results of Hirano and others (30,34) have led Gajdusek to postulate that interference with axonal transport may play a role in AD (24).　In addition, an accumulation of catecholamine enzyme protein has been noted by Ross et al. (52) during experimental retrograde reaction.　To determine whether reduced axonal transport may play a role in retrograde degeneration, we examined the distribution of PNMT within the neuron.　Despite the fact that PNMT was decreased in axonal projection areas (Table 6), there was no decrease in PNMT in the C-1 and C-2 neuronal cell bodies from these AD cases (Table 11).　As a result, there was a redistribution of PNMT in Epi neurons such that the relative amount of PNMT in the cell body rose from 2.1% in controls to 4.2% in AD (Table 12).　In addition, the fact that up to 25% of the Epi neurons were atrophic in AD suggests that the absolute concentration of PNMT in some of these neuron cell bodies was increased.　This is supported by the finding of a more dense immunohistochemical PNMT staining of the Epi neurons in an AD case with atrophic neurons (13).　When a severely affected AD case was compared to the controls, there was a twofold increase in amount of PNMT in the C-1 and C-2 neuronal cell bodies, and 15.4% of the total PNMT measured

TABLE 11. <u>PNMT activity in C-1 and C-2 neuronal cell bodies from control and Alzheimer brain</u>

Group	PNMT activity (fmole/h/neuron)		
	C-1	C-2	C-1 + C-2
Control	0.296 ± 0.035	0.496 ± 0.201	0.341 ± 0.056
Alzheimer	0.311 ± 0.073	0.424 ± 0.107	0.339 ± 0.065

PNMT in Epi neuronal cell bodies was determined by counting the number of neurons in each nucleus and measuring PNMT activity in the volume of tissue containing these nuclei according to methods described in the text. Results are the mean ± S.E. of four control and four Alzheimer cases.

TABLE 12. Distribution of PNMT between Epi cell body and projection areas in control and Alzheimer brain

Group	PNMT activity (Unit/area)		
	Cell body	Cell body + projection area	Cell body x 100 projections
Control	10.7 ± 1.9	520.9 ± 82.0	2.1 ± 0.09
Alzheimer	9.7 ± 1.2	244.8 ± 33.9[a]	4.1 ± 0.60[a]

[a]$p < 0.03$

PNMT activity was measured in neuronal cell bodies (C-1, C-2) and projection areas (locus ceruleus, hippocampus, amygdala, midfrontal cortex) in four control and five Alzheimer brains. Results are expressed as mean ± S.E.

appeared in the cell body (Table 13). In spite of this redistribution, there remained a 51% decrease in the total amount of PNMT in cell bodies plus projection areas (Table 12). A similar redistribution of PNMT was found in Epi neurons from a control case who had been treated with vindesine, a known axonal transport blocker. The vindesine-treated patient had a fourfold increase in PNMT in C-1 and C-2 neuronal cell bodies compared to control cases, and 5.6% of the total PNMT measured appeared in the cell bodies compared to 2.1% for controls (Table 14). In contrast to AD (Tables 12 and 13), there was no decrease in the total amount of PNMT in the vindesine-treated case. These results indicate that loss of the postsynaptic neuron causes an accumulation of PNMT protein in Epi neuronal cell bodies due to a decrease in axonal transport. In addition, there appears to be a decreased synthesis or increased degradation of PNMT since the total amount of PNMT is decreased in AD and not merely redistributed to the cell body.

TABLE 13. Distribution of PNMT in cell bodies and projection areas in control and an Alzheimer brain

Group	PNMT activity (fmole/h/neuron)	PNMT activity (Unit/area)			
	Cell body	Cell body	Projection area	Cell body + projections	Cell body x 100 projections
Control	0.341 ± 0.056	10.7 ± 1.9	510.2 ± 80.1	520.9 ± 82.0	2.1 ± 0.09
Alzheimer	0.660 ± 0.028	20.1 ± 0.9	130.9 ± 2.7	151.0 ± 1.8	15.4 ± 0.9

Distribution of PNMT between the Epi neuronal cell body in C-1 and C-2 regions and its axonal projections to locus ceruleus, hippocampus, midfrontal, and amygdala. Amount of PNMT protein in Epi neuronal cell bodies and projection areas was determined as outlined in the text. A severely affected Alzheimer brain is compared to four control brains. Values are the mean ± S.E.

TABLE 14. Effect of an axonal transport blocker on distribution of PNMT in a human brain

	PNMT activity (fmole/h/neuron)			PNMT activity (Unit/area)	
	C-1	C-2	C-1 + C-2	Cell body + projection area	$\dfrac{\text{Cell body}}{\text{projection area}} \times 100$
Control	0.296 ± 0.035	0.496 ± 0.201	0.341 ± 0.056	520.9 ± 82.0	2.1 ± 0.09
Vindesine	1.28 ± 0.02	1.61 ± 0.10	1.38 ± 0.02	726.5 ± 3.1	5.6 ± 0.1

PNMT activity in neuronal cell bodies and projection areas was determined as described in the text. The distribution of PNMT in brain from a patient treated with the axonal transport blocker vindesine is compared to that of four controls.

It is apparent that regulation of synthesis or degradation of neuronal proteins including PNMT is mediated by naturally occurring chemicals in these cells. In AD, due to loss of compartmentalization, these chemicals may become toxic to their neurons. We propose that Epi itself or its monoamine oxidase (MAO) metabolite, 3,4-dihydroxyphenylglycolaldehyde (DOPEGAL), may play the role of this naturally occurring autotoxin. Epi has been shown to decrease both PNMT and protein synthesis in the adrenal medulla (14,15) (Figs. 7 and 8). We have shown that compartmentalization of Epi is important in this process and that the extragranular cytoplasmic levels of Epi mediate the decrease in PNMT and protein synthesis (14,15). Histofluorescent procedures have shown an accumulation of catecholamines in C-1 and C-2 neuronal cell bodies after procedures which decrease axonal transport (7). The redistribution of PNMT in Epi neurons in AD could result in an altered compartmentalization of Epi if the storage or catabolic capacity of the neuronal cell body was unable to compensate for the increased rate of synthesis of Epi at this site in the neuron.

Another potential autotoxin is the MAO metabolite of Epi, DOPEGAL. This aldehyde may be highly reactive and potentially toxic (5). Theoretically, the aldehyde could react with amine groups on proteins and nucleic acids to form a Schiff base and, thus, interfere with intraneuronal processes (5,22,32). We have recently purified DOPEGAL and have shown it to be present in human brain (Fig. 9). It remains to be determined whether this toxic aldehyde increases in Epi neuronal cell bodies in AD.

THE DOMINO THEORY OF DEMENTIA

Anterograde vs. Retrograde Degeneration

Transsynaptic retrograde degeneration is by definition due to loss of postsynaptic neurons in contrast to anterograde degeneration which is due to loss of presynaptic inhibitory neurons (53). The LC is a major projection area of the C-1 and C-2 Epi neurons (3,13). Our correlation data (Figs. 4 and 5, Table 9) indicate that as postsynaptic neurons in LC and hippocampus die there are corresponding enzymatic and atrophic changes in Epi neurons. The LC neurons also appear to be affected by retrograde degeneration since the decrease in LC neurons correlate with the loss of postsynaptic neurons in the hippocampus (Fig. 6), whereas, there is no loss of neurons in its main afferent projection from C-1 and C-2 (3) (Table 9). To further analyze the sequence of events in this degeneration process, we examined the data from two short-duration, mildly affected AD cases (AD-1 and AD-2, Table 4). We note that the first evidence of pathology is the appearance of plaques in the hippocampus and neocortex (Table 4). While there is

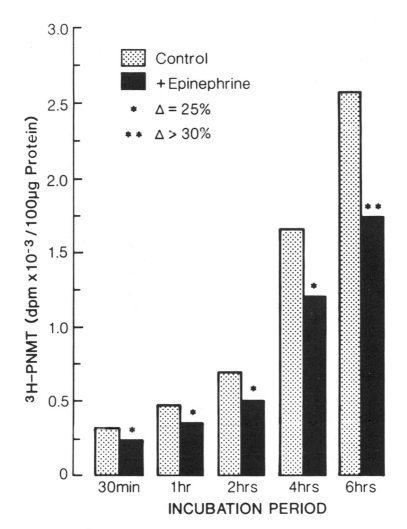

FIG. 7. [³H]Leucine incorporation into PNMT in cultured
rat adrenal medulla. Opposite halves of 30 adrenal medullae
were cultured for 20 hours at 37°C in medium 199 in the
presence or absence of 1.0 mM Epi. Tissue was changed to
fresh medium of the same composition, and 200 μCi [³H]leucine
was added to each culture dish. Three medullae were removed
from each medium at 0.5, 1, 2, 4, and 6 hours and analyzed for
[³H]leucine incorporation into PNMT (taken from Burke et al.,
Endocrinology, 113:1102, 1983).

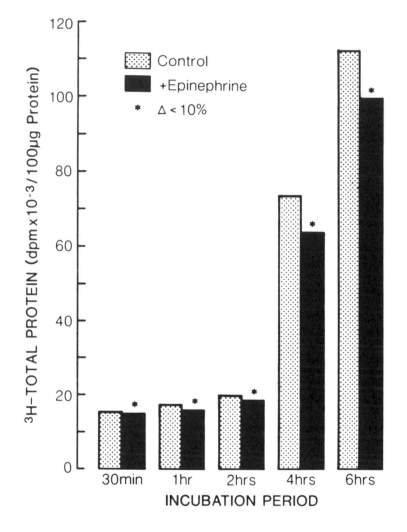

FIG. 8. [³H]Leucine incorporation into total protein in
cultured rat adrenal medulla. Opposite halves of 30 adrenal
medullae were cultured for 20 hours at 37°C in medium 199 in
the presence or absence of 1.0 mM Epi. Tissue was changed to
fresh medium of the same composition, and 200 μCi [³H]leucine
was added to each culture dish. Three medullae were removed
from each medium at 0.5, 1, 2, 4, and 6 hours and analyzed for
[³H]leucine incorporation into protein (taken from Burke
et al., Endocrinology, 113:1102, 1983).

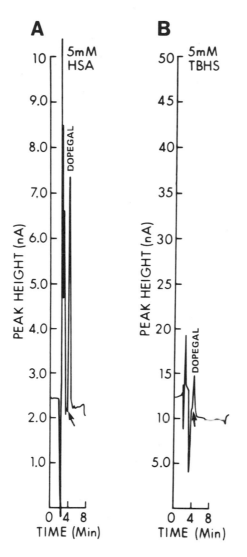

FIG. 9. Identification of DOPEGAL in human postmortem
brain. Human hippocampus, 5.5 gm (A) or 4.0 gm (B), was
homogenized in 2.75 ml (A) or 2.0 ml (B) of 0.4 N PCA. The
homogenate was centrifuged 12,000 xg for 10 min and the
supernatant adsorbed onto alumina and eluted in 500 µl 0.4 N
PCA. A 20 µl aliquot was injected into the HPLC-EC system
with either heptane sulfonic acid (HSA) (A) or tetrabutyl-
ammonium hydrogen sulfate (TBHS) (B) in the mobile phase and
analyzed for DOPEGAL.

evidence of neuronal death in cortex, the LC cell counts in
these two mildly affected AD cases were similar to those of
controls (controls: 25888 ± 1132 neurons vs. AD: 23397 ± 2730)
as was their LC PNMT (controls: 285 ± 30 units/g vs. AD:
250 ± 17). In addition, there was no atrophy of C-1 and C-2
neurons in these mildly affected cases and, in case AD-2, the
distribution of PNMT between cell body and projection areas, a
marker for a defect in transport, was 2.1%, the same as in
controls (Table 12). However, in the hippocampus where cell
loss was beginning to occur in the mildly affected cases, there
was a 19.7% decrease in PNMT (controls: 31.5 ± 3.7 units/g vs.
AD: 25.3 ± 1.6). Thus, the pathological process in AD begins
first in postsynaptic cortical neurons. In the three more
severely affected cases (AD-3 to AD-5, Table 4), there is an
increase in plaques in hippocampus indicating a greater degree
of neuronal death in cortex (Table 4). This is accompanied by
a 76% decrease in LC neurons (controls: 25888 ± 1132 neurons
vs. AD: 6166 ± 2795). The loss of LC neurons is accompanied by
a 53% decrease in PNMT (controls: 285 ± 30 units/g vs. AD:
134 ± 12). Finally, up to 25% of the C-1 and C-2 neurons are
atrophic, and the distribution of PNMT shifts to 4.9 ± 0.5% in
cell bodies of these cases compared to 2.1 ± 0.1% in controls
(Table 12). These results suggest a retrograde progression
starting with loss of cortical neurons, then LC neurons die
and, finally, C-1 and C-2 neurons are affected by a defect in
neuronal transport and atrophy.

How Transsynaptic Degeneration Could Produce Clinical Symptoms

Our findings of a correlation between the loss of hippocampal
neurons and the degree of dementia (Fig. 10) raise questions
concerning the relationship between neuronal degeneration and
loss of neurologic function. Clinical symptoms could be due to
loss of cortical neurons alone. On the other hand, clinical
symptoms may be additionally caused by the retrograde
degeneration of neurons which project onto dying hippocampal
neurons. Theoretically, this seems at least possible. For
instance, each Epi neuron may have as many as 10,000 synaptic
contacts (4). Some of these contacts may be onto neurons which
are dying. Other synapses, however, may be onto neurons which
are not only topographically separate from the dying neurons
(31) but are entirely normal. At some point in time, enough
postsynaptic neurons die to affect the function of the Epi
neurons projecting to them. At this time, we would also expect
the normal neurons onto which these Epi neurons project would
become affected by the decreased capacity of these Epi neurons
to synthesize their transmitter. Thus, at a critical level of
postsynaptic cell loss, the output of the presynaptic Epi
neuron could be reduced to all of its postsynaptic neurons,
even those unaffected directly by AD, thus, amplifying the
effect of neuronal loss to distant sites throughout the brain.

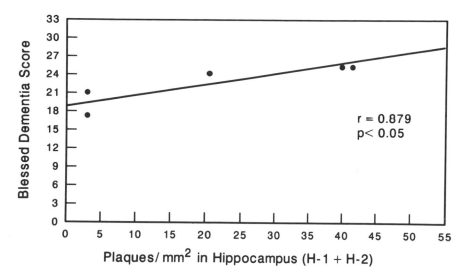

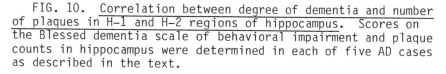

FIG. 10. Correlation between degree of dementia and number of plaques in H-1 and H-2 regions of hippocampus. Scores on the Blessed dementia scale of behavioral impairment and plaque counts in hippocampus were determined in each of five AD cases as described in the text.

There is also clinical evidence that the loss of one group of neurons may affect the function of previously normal neurons later in the disease process and give rise to new clinical symptoms. A progressive clinical decline after stroke or head trauma has been attributed to secondary anterograde transsynaptic degeneration (53). Deficits in sleep, attention, memory and behavior occurring in AD have been attributed to deficits in several transmitter systems including cholinergic, NE and Epi systems. We have presented evidence that the latter two transmitters are affected by retrograde degeneration. Pearson et al. (49) and, more recently, Burke et al. (11) have presented evidence that the cholinergic system may also be affected by secondary retrograde degeneration. Some of the symptoms due to the cholinergic deficit seem to be reversed by a drug which enhances this system (57). These results suggest that clinical symptoms may arise from loss of neurons due to secondary transsynaptic degeneration. We postulate that in AD, just as there is a progressive loss of neurons due to transsynaptic degeneration, there is a progressive increase in clinical symptomatology due to loss of functions mediated by these neurons.

FUTURE THERAPEUTIC STRATEGIES IN ALZHEIMER'S DISEASE

Our results and those of others (13,20,21,26,28,48,49,51) suggest two basic therapeutic strategies in AD. One is to devise replacement therapies for neurotransmitter deficits. The other is to devise treatments to prevent neuronal death. The first approach has been tried for the cholinergic system (48,57) and has achieved some apparent recent success. However, more than one neurotransmitter system is affected in AD (13,26). Our finding of a deficit in the Epi system in AD led us to test desipramine. This drug is known to block the synaptosomal uptake of NE and, thus, increase its availability to postsynaptic receptors. Using a rat brain synaptosomal preparation (56), we have demonstrated that desipramine also blocks the uptake of $[H^3]$ Epi into the synaptosomes (Table 15). Further studies are needed to determine the most effective drug to enhance the Epi system.

TABLE 15.   Effect of desipramine on uptake of $[H^3]$ Epi into rat hippocampal synaptosomes

Desipramine (mole/liter)	$[H^3]$ Epi uptake (cpm)
0	544.3 ± 36.9
10^{-5}	103.2 ± 16.0
10^{-6}	109.7 ± 19.6
10^{-8}	334.3 ± 8.9
10^{-9}	575.1 ± 77.5

Desipramine was added at concentrations noted to 1.0 ml of buffered reaction mixture containing 50 ul of rat hippocampal synaptosomes and 0.5 µCi of 4 µM $[H^3]$ Epi. After incubation at 37°C for 5 min, the uptake was stopped and aliquots analyzed as outlined in the text. Blanks for each concentration were run at 0°C. Each value is the mean ± S.E. of duplicate determinations.

While the primary cause of neuronal death in cortical neurons is unknown, our data indicates that there is secondary and tertiary neuronal loss and atrophy due to retrograde transsynaptic degeneration. Some of the progressive mental decline could be due to this secondary neuronal loss. If agents could be found which would prevent early retrograde changes, it is conceivable that the progression of cell loss and clinical manifestations of this neuronal loss in AD could be halted. One explanation of our results is that the postsynaptic neuron produces substances necessary for maintenance of the presynaptic neuron. There are a number of growth factors which may fit this role including nerve growth factor and brain derived growth factor (2,27,29,33,39). In this regard, intraventricular injection of nerve growth factor has been shown to halt degeneration of rat forebrain cholinergic neurons after transsection of their axonal processes (28,29).

Another strategy to prevent neuronal death would be to determine the specific intraneuronal processes which lead to retrograde cell death and attempt to reverse these processes. For instance, it is conceivable that in the CA neurons some of the damage could be due to the MAO-A metabolite DOPEGAL which is potentially toxic (5). This would be analogous to the recent finding in Parkinson's disease that the toxic effects of 1-methyl-4-phenyl-1,2,4,6-tetrahydropyridine are produced by its MAO-B metabolite, the pyridinium form (MPP^+) (54). Further studies are needed to determine which naturally occurring brain chemicals are potentially toxic and how their toxicity can be prevented.

REFERENCES

1. Alexander, M.P., and Geschwind, N. (1984): In: Clinical Neurology of Aging, edited by M.L. Albert, pp. 254-276. Oxford University Press, New York.
2. Appel, S.H. (1981): Ann. Neurol., 10:499-505.
3. Aston-Jones, G., Ennis, M., Pieribone, V.A., Nickell, W.T., and Shipley, M.T. (1986): Science, 234:734-737.
4. Black, I.B., Adlers, J.E., Dreyfus, C.F., Jonakait, G.M., Katz, D.M., LaGamma, E.F., and Markey, K.M. (1984): Science, 225:1266-1270.
5. Blaschko, H. (1952): Pharmacol. Rev., 4:415-453.
6. Blessed, G., Tomlinson, B.E., and Roth, M. (1968): Br. J. Psychiatry, 114:797-811.
7. Blessing, W.W., Goodchild, A.K., Dampney, R.A.L., and Chalmers, J.P. (1981): Brain Res., 221:35-55.
8. Bondareff, W., Mountjoy, C.O., and Roth, M. (1982): Neurology, 32:164-168.
9. Bowen, D.M., Smith, C.B., White, P., and Davison, A.N. (1976): Brain, 99:459-496.
10. Bowen, D.M., Smith, C.B., White, P., Goodhardt, M.J., Spillane, J.A., Flack, R.H.A., and Davison, A.N. (1977): Brain, 100:397-426.
11. Burke, W.J., Chung, H.D., Joh, T.H., Mattammal, M.B., Luque, F.A., Cruz-Rodriguez, R., Nakra, B.R.S., Grossberg, G.T., Richardson, A., Haring, J.H., Huang, J.S., and Strong, R. (1987): In: Proceedings of the Sixth International Catecholamine Symposium, edited by M. Sandler, (in press). Alan R. Liss, Inc., New York.
12. Burke, W.J., Chung, H.D., Nakra, B.R.S., Grossberg, G.T., and Joh, T.H. (1987): Ann. Neurol. (in press).
13. Burke, W.J., Chung, H.D., Strong, R., Marshall, G.L., Davis, J.W., and Joh, T.H. (1987): In: Geriatric Clinical Pharmacology, edited by W.G. Wood and R. Strong, pp. 47-69. Raven Press, New York.

14. Burke, W.J., Davis, J.W., and Joh, T.H. (1983): Endocrinology, 113:1102-1110.
15. Burke, W.J., Davis, J.W., Joh, T.H., Reis, D.J., Horenstein, S., and Bhagat, B. (1978): Endocrinology, 103:358-367.
16. Burke, W.J., Hanson, D.M., and Chung, H.D. (1986): Proc. Soc. Exp. Biol. Med., 181:66-70.
17. Cowan, W.M. (1970): In: The Contemporary Research Methods in Neuroanatomy, edited by J.J.H. Nauta and S.D.E. Effeson, pp. 217-251. Springer-Verlag, New York.
18. Coyle, J.T., and Snyder, S.H. (1981): In: Basic Neurochemistry, edited by G.J. Siegel, R.W. Albers, B.W. Agranoff, and R. Katzman, pp. 205-218. Little, Brown, and Co., Boston, Massachusetts.
19. Curcio, C.A., and Kemper, T. (1984): J. Neuropathol. Exp. Neurol., 43:359-367.
20. Davies, P., Katzman, R., and Terry, R.D. (1980): Nature, 228:279-280.
21. Davies, P., and Maloney, A.J.F. (1976): Lancet, 2:1403.
22. Erwin, V.G. (1973): In: Frontiers in Catecholamine Research, edited by E. Usdin and S.H. Synder, pp. 161-166. Pergamon Press, New York.
23. Fuller, R.W. (1982): Annu. Rev. Pharmacol. Toxicol., 22:31-55.
24. Gajdusek, D.C. (1985): N. Engl. J. Med., 312:714-719.
25. Goldstein, M., Pearson, J., Sauter, K., Veta, K., Asano, T., Engel, J., Passeltiner, P., Hokfelt, T., and Fuxe, K. (1980): In: Central Adrenaline Neurons, edited by K. Fuxe, M. Goldstein, and T. Hokfelt, pp. 49-55. Pergamon Press, Oxford.
26. Hardy, J., Adolfsson, R., Alafuzoff, I., Bucht, G., Marcusson, J., Nyberg, P., Perdahl, E., Wester, P., and Windblad, B. (1985): Neurochem. Int., 7:545-563.
27. Hefti, F. (1983): Ann. Neurol., 13:109-110.
28. Hefti, F. (1986): Ann. Neurol., 20:275-281.
29. Hefti, F. (1987): In: Proceedings of the International Meeting on Alzheimer's Disease and Related Neuro-degenerative Disorders, edited by A. Fisher, (in press). Raven Press, New York.
30. Hirano, A., and Inoue, K. (1980): Neurol. Med. (Tokyo), 13:148-160.
31. Hokfelt, T., Johansson, O., and Goldstein, M. (1984): Science, 225:1326-1334.
32. Holtz, P., Stock, K., and Westerman, E. (1964): Nature, 203:656-658.
33. Huang, S.S., Tsai, C.C., Adams, S.P., and Huang, J.S. (1987): Biochem. Biophys. Res. Commun. (in press).
34. Inoue, K., and Hirano, A. (1979): Neurol. Med. (Tokyo), 11:448-455.

35. Joh, T.H., and Ross, M.E. (1983): In: Immunohisto-
    chemistry, IBRO Handbook Series, Vol. 3, edited by
    A.C. Cuello, pp. 131–138. John Wiley and Sons,
    Chichester.
36. Kemper, T. (1984): In: Clinical Neurology of Aging,
    edited by M.L. Albert, pp. 9–52. Oxford University
    Press, New York.
37. Khachaturian, Z.S. (1985): Arch. Neurol., 42:1097–1105.
38. Kuhar, M.J., and Atwen, S.F. (1978): In: Reviews of
    Neuroscience, Vol. 3, edited by S. Ehrenpreis and
    I.J. Kopin, pp. 35–76. Raven Press, New York.
39. Levi-Montalcini, R. (1982): Annu. Rev. Neurosci.,
    5:341–362.
40. Marcyniuk, B., Mann, D.M.A., and Yates, P.O. (1986):
    J. Neurol. Sci., 76:335–345.
41. Marcyniuk, B., Mann, D.M.A., and Yates, P.O. (1986):
    Neurosci. Lett., 64:247–252.
42. McGaugh, J.L. (1983): Am. Psychol., 38:161–174.
43. McGeer, E., and McGeer, P.L. (1976): In: Neurobiology of
    Aging, Vol. 3, edited by R.D. Terry and S. Gershom,
    pp. 389–403. Raven Press, New York.
44. McGeer, E., McGeer, P.L., and Wada, J.A. (1971):
    J. Neurochem., 18:1647–1658.
45. McGeer, P.L., and McGeer, E.G. (1976): J. Neurochem.,
    26:65–76.
46. McGeer, P.L., and McGeer, E.G. (1981): In: The Molecular
    Basis of Neuropathology, edited by R.H.S. Thompson and
    A.N. Davison, pp. 631–648. Edward Arnold, London.
47. McKhann, G., Drachman, D., Folstein, M., Katzman, R.,
    Price, D., and Stadlan, E.M. (1984): Neurology,
    34:939–944.
48. Mohs, R.C., Davis, B.M., Johns, C.A., Mathe, A.A.,
    Greenwald, B.S., Horvath, T.B., and Davis, K.L. (1985):
    Am. J. Psychiatry, 142:28–33.
49. Pearson, R.C.A., Sofroniew, M.V., Cuello, A.C., Powell,
    T.P.S., Eckenstein, E., Esiri, M.M., and Wilcock, G.K.
    (1983): Brain Res., 289:375–379.
50. Perry, E.K., Gibson, P.H., Blessed, G., Perry, R.H., and
    Tomlinson, B.E. (1977): J. Neurol. Sci., 34:247–265.
51. Perry, E.K., Tomlinson, B.E., Blessed, G., Perry, R.H.,
    Cross, A.J., and Crow, T.J. (1981): J. Neurol. Sci.,
    51:279–287.
52. Ross, R.A., Joh, T.H., and Reis, D.J. (1975): Brain Res.,
    92:57–72.
53. Saji, M., and Reis, D.J. (1987): Science, 235:66–69.
54. Snyder, S.H., and D'Amato, R.J. (1986): Neurology,
    36:250–258.
55. Squire, L.R. (1986): Science, 232:1612–1619.
56. Strong, R., Samorajski, T., and Gottesfeld, Z. (1984):
    J. Neurochem., 43:1766–1768.

57. Summers, W.K., Majouski, L.V., Marsh, G.M., Tachiki, K., and Kling, A. (1986): N. Engl. J. Med., 315:1241–1245.
58. Terry, R.D. (1985): In: Textbook of Neuropathology, edited by R.L. Davis and D.M. Robertson, pp. 824–841. Williams and Wilkins, Baltimore.
59. Turner, B.B., Katz, R.J., and Carroll, B.J. (1979): Brain Res., 166:426–430.
60. Vijayashankar, N., and Brody, H. (1979): J. Neuropathol. Exp. Neurol., 38:490–497.
61. Warsh, J.J., Godse, D.D., Li, P.P., and Cheung, S.W. (1981): J. Neurochem., 36:902–907.
62. Whitehouse, P.J., Price, D.L., Clark, A.W., Coyle, J.T., and Delong, M.R. (1981): Ann. Neurol., 10:122–126.
63. Wolozin, B.L., Pruchnick, A., Dickson, D.W., and Davies, P. (1986): Science, 232:648–650.
64. Wurtman, R.J., and Axelrod, J. (1966): J. Biol. Chem., 241:2301–2305.
65. Yamamoto, T., and Hirano, A. (1985): Ann. Neurol., 17:573–577.
66. Zemcov, A., Barclay, L.L., Brush, D., and Blass, J.P. (1984): J. Am. Geriatr. Soc., 32:801–842.

*Central Nervous System Disorders of Aging:
Clinical Intervention and Research*, edited by
Randy Strong et al. Raven Press, New York
© 1988.

EFFECT OF ORAL PHYSOSTIGMINE IN SENILE DEMENTIA PATIENTS:

UTILITY OF BLOOD CHOLINESTERASE INHIBITION AND NEUROENDOCRINE

RESPONSES TO DEFINE PHARMACOKINETICS AND PHARMACODYNAMICS

Kathleen A. Sherman,* Vinod Kumar,[+] J. Wesson Ashford,[+]
John W. Murphy,[+] Rodger J. Elble,[§] and Ezio Giacobini*

Departments of *Pharmacology, [+]Psychiatry,
[+]Laboratory Medicine, and [§]Internal Medicine,
Southern Illinois University School of Medicine,
Springfield, Illinois 62708

Recent demonstrations of marked impairment of brain
cholinergic mechanisms in patients with Alzheimer's disease
have led to a resurgence of interest in pharmacotherapies which
potentiate central cholinergic neurotransmission. Alzheimer's
disease is a major cause of dementia and severe behavioral
debilitation in the elderly, but thus far a therapeutic approach
has yet to be devised which reproducibly results in more than,
at best, modest improvement of performance on neuropsychological
tests.
     Cholinergic deficits in Alzheimer's disease have now been
well-documented. Choline acetyltransferase (ChAT), the synthetic
enzyme for acetylcholine (ACh), is consistently reduced by 50 to
95% in cortex and hippocampus of Alzheimer patients compared
to age-matched controls (8,17,63,67). Reductions are also
observed in high affinity choline uptake (HACU) (73,77), in vitro
synthesis of ACh during depolarization (7,61), presynaptic
muscarinic receptor binding (53), and the ACh content of cortex
(68) and cerebrospinal fluid (CSF) (46). The reduction of these
presynaptic cholinergic markers is associated with a marked loss
of cells in the nucleus basalis of Meynert which project to
cortex (89). By contrast, postsynaptic muscarinic receptor
mechanisms appear to be relatively spared in Alzheimer patients
(17,52,67). The reductions of cortical and CSF cholinergic
markers are closely correlated with the extent of neuropathology
(e.g., senile plaques) and with the severity of cognitive
impairment (8,30,33,46,61,63).

These severe cholinergic losses in Alzheimer's disease are superimposed on functional deficits in both pre- and postsynaptic cholinergic mechanisms which occur in brain during "normal" aging. In animal studies, we and others have shown presynaptic dysfunction with age including reductions in brain ACh turnover (34), HACU (31,76) and ACh release (62). Cholinergic muscarinic receptor binding (31,51,80) and electrophysiological response to cholinergic stimulation (51,75) are also impaired with age in certain brain regions. These cholinergic deficits may underlie the less marked deterioration of cognitive function which occurs during normal aging and also contribute to the age-related predisposition to Alzheimer's disease (31).

Experimental evidence provides further support for the hypothesis that disruption of cholinergic transmission plays a major role in the deterioration of cognitive function in Alzheimer's disease (3,15,27). Administration of muscarinic receptor antagonists, such as scopolamine, to young normal subjects leads to memory impairments which are qualitatively similar to those which occur in the early stages of Alzheimer's disease (24-27,78). In experimental animals, lesions of the cholinergic pathways affected in Alzheimer's disease result in impaired memory-related performance (31,42,59,60); and these retention impairments are reversed by administration of the cholinesterase (ChE) inhibitor, physostigmine (PHYSO) (42,59,60). At certain doses PHYSO also improves cognitive performance in young normal subjects (22) and in patients with amnesic syndrome (12,65).

Several studies found consistent, albeit quite modest, improvement in the neuropsychological test performance of Alzheimer patients after i.v. infusion of PHYSO (6,13,19,46) or tacrine (THA) (82). However, in dose-response studies, the maximum improvement varied considerably across patients, and only about 20 to 25% of patients showed pronounced and reproducible improvement at their optimum doses of PHYSO (13,46) or THA (82). Other studies and case reports have confirmed a beneficial effect of i.v. administration of these reversible ChE inhibitors in some, but not all, patients with dementia of the Alzheimer type (58,70,81). Discrepant results after a single fixed dose (0.5 mg) of PHYSO (1) may reflect a relatively narrow therapeutic window for the drug with i.v. administration (13,46). Mixed results were also obtained after i.m. or s.c. PHYSO, but a number of patients did improve when the drug was given alone (49) or with a low dose of lecithin (66). Case studies (58,79) found no change in recall, but reductions in frequency of intrusions and constructional praxis were found in Alzheimer patients after parental PHYSO. However, no significant effect was found in two other studies with 6 to 7 patients each after 1 mg PHYSO i.m. (23) or 10 and 20 µg/kg PHYSO s.c. with lecithin pretreatment (88).

Encouraging results have been reported when PHYSO or THA were administered orally to Alzheimer patients (4,20,21,49,56,57,64,

66,83-87). In these studies the ChE inhibitors were given in combination with lecithin (49,64,66,83-87) and/or given repeatedly up to seven times a day for several days prior to neuropsychological testing. Peters and Levin (66) reported sustained improvement for up to three to ten months in patients treated with oral PHYSO/lecithin combination. However, other studies which tested only after one or more months of repeated oral PHYSO alone (11,48) or with lecithin (88) were negative. The diminishing efficacy of PHYSO (66,87) or THA (83) after prolonged administration in "responders" may be due to the breakthrough of the progressive degenerative losses of the disease. Alternatively, this may indicate that tolerance to the therapeutic effect of ChE inhibitors occurs with prolonged administration analogous to that reported in schizophrenics during oral PHYSO treatment (72) and in animals during treatment with irreversible ChE inhibitors.

The efficacy of a single oral administration of PHYSO remains unknown. Therefore, we have begun a preliminary examination of neuropsychological test performance and mood after acute oral ingestion of PHYSO as a prelude to comparing efficacy with repeated oral or other routes of PHYSO administration. Moreover, in these studies we sought to determine whether inhibition of plasma and red blood cell (RBC) ChE activity could be used to define the kinetics of oral PHYSO and to assess interpatient variability. A recent study of pharmacokinetic parameters in surgical patients receiving PHYSO by bolus i.v., i.m. or s.c. routes using high performance liquid chromatographic (HPLC) determinations of plasma drug levels revealed marked variation (43). Such interindividual pharmacokinetic differences may contribute to the variability in the effect of the drug on neuropsychological test performance which has been notable in virtually all positive studies of PHYSO in Alzheimer patients. Inhibition of plasma and RBC ChE activity is readily quantified after administration of irreversible ChE inhibitors and RBC enzyme inhibition correlated with behavioral manifestations (9,36). Our laboratory recently reported that in dogs plasma ChE activity was inhibited 50% after 25 μg/kg PHYSO i.v. bolus (54), the lowest dose tested. Plasma prolactin, cortisol and adrenocorticotrophic hormone (ACTH) levels were also examined in the Alzheimer patients after oral PHYSO as putative markers of central cholinergic stimulation. Elevation of these neuro-endocrines has been reported after PHYSO in relatively high i.v. doses (18,50,69), and the magnitude of the response was highly correlated with the effect of drug on mood (45). Our previous results (32) indicate that peripheral markers of drug efficacy can be very useful in identifying subgroups of Alzheimer patients who respond to treatments such as piracetam/lecithin combination. Development of analogous markers for the efficacy of PHYSO may help to establish the optimal regimen for consistent cognitive improvement in Alzheimer dementia.

MEASUREMENT OF RESPONSES TO ORAL PHYSOSTIGMINE

Subjects

The ten patients participating in this study were diagnosed as having dementia of the Alzheimer type using the NINCDS-ADRDA criteria (55) after examination by a neurologist, an internist, a geriatric psychiatrist, and a neuropsychologist. All patients and their next of kin signed an informed consent form. Each patient was screened to exclude other possible causes of dementia with a laboratory test battery which included a computerized tomographic (CT) head scan or magnetic resonance imaging (MRI) scan, chest x-ray, blood chemistry, Westergren erythrocyte sedimentation rate, serum protein electrophoresis, and syphilis serology. All patients were evaluated with Mini Mental State (MMS) exam (29), Blessed Dementia Scale (7), Hachinski Ischemic Score (38) and Hamilton Depression Scale (40). Subjects with a Hachinski score greater than 3 or a Hamilton score greater than 16 were excluded. Regardless of the Hachinski score, subjects with a history of stroke, abrupt onset, fluctuating course, or focal neurological signs or symptoms were excluded (71). In addition, patients who met DSM III criteria for depressive illness were excluded. Six of the ten patients were female; patient age ranged from 51 to 80 with mean of 71.6 ± 2.9 years (S.E.), weight ranged from 52.5 to 96 kg with mean of 75.4 ± 4.3 kg, and severity of dementia ranged from mild to moderate (44).

Drug Administration

PHYSO salicylate (Antilirium) (60 µg/kg) was diluted in 50 cc of carbonated beverage (pH ≤ 3.5) within 15 minutes of consumption by the subject. Neostigmine bromide (Prostigmine) (7.5 mg) was administered as a peripherally active placebo control. The neuropsychologist, the research nurse and the patient were blind to the randomized cross-over condition for the two sessions which occurred at least one week apart. Baseline testing began promptly at 8:30 a.m. after 30 minutes acclimatization.

Blood Cholinesterase and Neuroendocrine Determinations

Venous blood (10 ml) was drawn into green top Vacutainer[R] tubes containing 143 U heparin at 30-minute intervals before drug or placebo administration (two samples) and up to 3 hours after administration. The blood was immediately placed on ice and within 5 minutes RBC and plasma were separated by centrifugation at 1500 rpm for 10 minutes. Any residual cells (platelets and leukocytes) were removed by centrifugation at 15,600 g (Brinkman Model 5414) for 2 minutes. Aliquots of plasma and RBC were diluted in Triton-X buffer (0.5% in 10 mM EDTA, pH 7.4): 10 volumes for plasma and 100 volumes for RBC.

Samples were stored at -90°C until assay by the radiometric method of Johnson and Russell (47). ChE activity was measured during 15 minutes at 37°C using 2.5 mM ^{3}H-ACh iodide (New England Nuclear) as substrate. RBC activity was expressed per mg hemoglobin (Hb) for each sample as determined spectrophotometrically at 540 nm. To determine the effect of tissue dilution, the time of incubation was varied to stay within the linear range of ChE activity. Separate aliquots of microfuged plasma were prepared and stored at -90°C for the determination of prolactin (Abbott), cortisol (Diagnostic Products Corporation) and ACTH (Immuno Nuclear Corporation) by radioimmunoassay.

Neuropsychological Performance

Cognitive function was assessed in one-hour blocks using a 30-minute neuropsychological test battery split into 15-minute sessions alternated with 15-minute rest periods. Eight counter balanced forms of the test were used; each form included assessment of short-term verbal memory (Rey word list learning, noun recognition), long-term memory (Boston naming, category fluency), short-term visual memory (postcard recognition, design recognition), attention (digit span, Smith symbol digit), motor coordination (tapping) and perceptual speed (7's cancellation test).

Subjective ratings related to mood items and side effects including nausea/loss of appetite were obtained at hourly intervals. The patients were asked to rate on a scale from 0 (not present) to 9 (present in severe form) their feelings regarding depression, helplessness, hopelessness, worthlessness, tearfulness, loss of energy, drowsiness, loss of appetite, and nausea; ratings were recorded by the tester.

CHOLINESTERASE INHIBITION AND NEUROENDOCRINE RESPONSES

Cholinesterase Inhibition

Inhibition of plasma ChE increased to a maximum at 60 minutes after oral administration of 60 µg/kg PHYSO (Fig. 1). Plasma ChE activity was inhibited compared to predrug baseline in all patients, but varied quantitatively from 12% (patient 10) to 33% (patient 1) maximum inhibition (Table 1). The low level of inhibition in patient 10 was replicated in a trial several months later. In most patients, maximum inhibition was at 60 minutes and then declined; but in one (patient 7) the peak inhibition was broader with a maximum at 120 minutes, and in two the maximum inhibition was at 90 minutes postdrug (Table 1). Mean inhibition at 60 minutes was 23.9 ± 2.2%, and mean peak inhibition was 25.1 ± 2.0% (n = 10). Inhibition of plasma ChE activity then declined from 60 to 120 minutes, but plateaued at 15 to 17% inhibition from 120 to 180 minutes. Thus, 60% of the

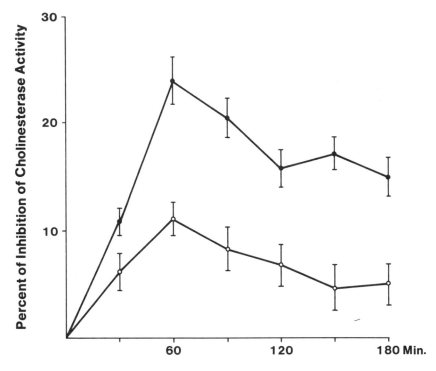

FIG. 1. Inhibition of plasma and RBC ChE activity after a
single oral dose (60 μg/kg) of PHYSO. Inhibition of ChE in
plasma (●) and RBC (o) is expressed as a percent of the mean of
the two predrug values as baseline. Results are mean + S.E. as
percent for ten patients. ChE activity was determined in
triplicate for all plasma samples and for RBC baseline and
60-minute points. RBC activity was expressed per mg hemoglobin
in each sample.

maximal effect on plasma ChE persisted for up to 3 hours after
oral PHYSO.
    RBC ChE activity is specific for ACh as substrate, which
contrasts with plasma ChE which has little specificity. RBC ChE
activity was also inhibited maximally at 60 minutes. However,
the magnitude of inhibition of RBC activity was less than in
plasma (Fig. 1) ($\overline{X}$ 11.1 + 1.5% at 60 minutes), and both the
magnitude and timing of peak inhibition were more variable (4 to
21%, 60 to 150 minutes).

TABLE 1. Summary of biological correlates of oral physostigmine administration by individual patient

Patient	Maximum ChE inhibition		Neuroendocrine response			
	Plasma (%)	RBC (%)	Prolactin (ng/ml)	Cortisol (μg/dl)		ACTH (pg/ml)
1	33.4	10.5	54.2[a]	21.8[b]	23.4[c]	51.7[b]
2	29.7	11.0	5.2	17.8	20.9	24.7
3	29.2	20.6	18.4	20.5	22.3	91.6
4	28.7	4.0	34.2	12.7	15.0	75.1
5	27.5	17.7	-2.4	21.2	27.1	70.4
6	25.1	10.4	-2.1	-3.4	-2.3	13.1
7	25.3	10.5	+0.9	+3.3	7.7	12.4
8	23.1	14.6	-1.5	8.0	6.4	39.1
9	17.1	15.3	-7.5	-1.9	5.3	7.7
10	12.1	10.1	+1.7	-9.2	-5.4	11.6

[a]Difference from baseline at 90 minutes after drug administration.
[b]Maximum difference compared to mean baseline value.
[c]Maximum difference compared to placebo day.

The degree of ChE inhibition by PHYSO in vitro is dependent on a number of factors including substrate concentration and enzyme dilution. The dilution of tissue necessitated for convenient assay of ChE activity within the linear range might, therefore, lead to an underestimation of the magnitude of inhibition in vivo (5). To test this possibility, baseline and maximally inhibited plasma and RBC samples were assayed across a broad range of tissue dilutions, varying time of incubation in order to stay within the linear range of the enzyme assay. Percent inhibition in plasma was constant over the range of 2.5- to 110-fold final tissue dilution, and RBC enzyme inhibition was constant from 66- to 100-fold final dilution. Thus, the effect of tissue dilution on inhibition by in vitro addition of reversible ChE inhibition does not appear to influence inhibition by in vivo administration. These results are consistent with inhibition due to the temporary accumulation of carbamylated enzyme (37).

Neuroendocrine Response

The neuroendocrine responses investigated, including prolactin, cortisol and ACTH, each showed more interindividual variation and a different temporal pattern than ChE inhibition. Prolactin was markedly increased in only three of the ten patients (Table 1). In all three patients, plasma prolactin levels were unchanged for the first 60 minutes after drug administration and then rose sharply to a peak at 90 minutes. Prolactin was increased 220%, 514% and 600% of baseline levels in these patients. Prolactin then declined in all three patients and returned to baseline by 150 minutes. It is noteworthy that all patients who showed the prolactin response after PHYSO had close to 30% inhibition of plasma ChE activity at 60 minutes (Table 1).

Marked elevation of plasma cortisol content also occurred only in a subset of the patients. Again, the five patients who showed a clear-cut increase were those who had the greatest inhibition of plasma ChE activity (> 27%). In these patients, plasma cortisol declined slightly in the first 60 minutes after drug ingestion and then increased sharply by 90 minutes, reaching a peak from 120 to 150 minutes after drug administration. The elevation of cortisol was much more sustained than for prolactin, and cortisol had not returned to baseline in any of the five patients by 180 minutes. In the remaining five patients, both elevation and reduction of cortisol levels were observed after PHYSO; and the magnitude of the effect depended somewhat on whether the value was expressed relative to baseline or relative to the neostigmine placebo control (Table 1).

Elevation of plasma ACTH occurred in all five of the patients with greater than 27% inhibition of plasma ChE, but was also elevated in one patient who showed only a moderate increase of cortisol (Table 1). The ACTH response was again delayed until 90 minutes, reaching a maximum from 90 to 120 minutes. The elevation of ACTH was more transient than the cortisol response, and ACTH levels returned toward baseline by 3 hours after PHYSO ingestion.

CLINICAL EFFECTS

Side Effects

Patient 1 experienced an extreme drug reaction, consisting of shaking, confusion and slight nausea followed by somnolence. She was, therefore, untestable. Patient 4 was nauseous and patient 2 vomited. As shown in Table 2, these reactions occurred in the patients with greatest plasma ChE inhibition, but were not strictly correlated with the prolactin, ACTH or cortisol responses.

Mood Ratings

Only patient 4 showed a marked increase in subjective ratings related to depression (hopelessness, worthlessness and helplessness). Several patients reported anxiety/tension, and the frequency and severity of these effects were greater with increasing plasma ChE inhibition. The only mood item significantly different for the group as a whole after PHYSO

TABLE 2. Summary of biological and psychological changes after 60 µg/kg physostigmine by patient

Patient	Plasma ChE	Prolactin	Cortisol	ACTH	Side effects	Depressed mood	Anxiety/ tension	Anergia	Cognitive tests
1	33.4	++++	+++	++	+++	ND[a]	ND	ND	ND
2	29.7	+	+++	+	++		++	0	0
3	29.2	+++	+++	++++			+	+	+
4	28.7	++++	++	+++	++	++++	+++	+	+
5	27.5	(+)	+++	+++			0	++	++
6	25.1	(-)	(-)	(+)		-	++	++	-
7	25.3	(+)	±	(+)			0	0	-
8	23.1	(-)	+	+		+	+	++	-
9	17.1	-	0	(+)			+	+++	++
10	12.1	(+)	-	(+)		±	0	++	(-)

[a]ND = not determined

compared to placebo was "loss of energy" ($p < .05$). Since
fatigue and anergia could antagonize any beneficial effect of
PHYSO on neurophysiological test performance, we examined the
relationship of ratings for anergia with plasma ChE inhibition.
However, ratings for this item were inversely related to total
plasma ChE inhibition across the 3-hour test period ($r = .71$,
$n = 9$, $p < .05$).

Neuropsychological Test Performance

Analysis of variance of the neuropsychological test scores
showed no significant difference between performance after PHYSO
and neostigmine as active placebo. In both drug conditions,
performance tended to deteriorate by 3 hours. Many of the
patients showed considerable variability in baseline performance
on particular tests across the two test days, and this makes it
difficult to assess whether individual patients were improved
on particular cognitive tests. The sum of the test scores and
the sum of closely related tests were relatively stable at
baseline across days, and these sum scores were used to provide
a preliminary assessment of whether the individual patient
improved relative to baseline and neostigmine (Table 2). It
must be emphasized that the degree of improvement was, at best,
quite small and that patient 9 showing the greatest improvement
was also the most erratic in terms of baseline performance.
Patient 2 continued neuropsychological testing despite the
emesis produced by PHYSO; performance was not affected after
PHYSO, but it is also notable that patient 2 was the least
impaired of all patients.

PHARMACOKINETICS, PHARMACODYNAMICS AND CLINICAL RESPONSE

A trend toward improvement of cognitive function has been
observed in many trials of reversible ChE inhibitors for senile
dementia of the Alzheimer type, but the variability in efficacy
has been considerable. Our results suggest that measurement of
ChE inhibition and neuroendocrine levels in blood may provide a
relatively simple and cost effective means to monitor pharmacokinetic differences between individuals and to compare the net
"dosage" achieved after administration of these drugs across
patients and different routes of administration in order to
standardize across studies. However, a single oral dose of
PHYSO produced no significant change in overall neuropsychological test performance, and the change in any individual
patient was small. Although a relatively high dose of oral
PHYSO was used; maximum inhibition of plasma ChE activity was
only 25%, and RBC AChE activity was reduced only 11%. The peak
inhibition was very transient. Thus, treatment failure may
simply be due to the failure to inhibit ChE sufficiently to
alter cholinergic activity after acute administration of PHYSO.
Moreover, the plasma neuroendocrine levels measured as putative

markers of central cholinergic stimulation were only significantly affected in half of the patients; these patients all had greater than 27% plasma ChE inhibition. The frequency of adverse side effects was also high in this subgroup of patients, which is consistent with the observations of other investigators that the therapeutic window for PHYSO is very narrow after acute administration. Although peak inhibition was transient after acute oral administration of PHYSO, our results show that submaximal inhibition persists from 2 to 3 hours postdrug. This suggests the possibility of cumulative inhibition to much higher levels when PHYSO is given every 2 hours, 7 times daily for several days, as in previous positive studies of oral PHYSO (56,57,84-87). The half-life of biological efficacy also appears to be longer than previously believed (see 87). This may explain the reported successes in several studies which used this multiple dose regimen of oral PHYSO administration.

Despite a strong rationale for the use of cholinomimetics such as PHYSO for Alzheimer's dementia, thus far, experience has shown the response to this drug to be quite variable and relatively circumscribed (21,57,87). Several factors have been raised as possible explanations of the limited and variable response (10,14,16,86).

Brinkman and Gershon (10) reviewed the literature with respect to the neuropsychological tasks used in studies of cholinergic manipulations and concluded that the selective reminding task used in many of the positive PHYSO trials is most sensitive to cholinergic and anticholinergic drugs. We have included a broad battery of neuropsychological tests in order to better identify the cognitive domains affected by PHYSO. However, we found that day-to-day variation in baseline performance is problematic when individual tests are examined. Relatively unstable baseline performance in Alzheimer patients is also apparent by comparison of placebo days in the dose-finding and replication phases of the studies by Davis and coworkers (19,56) and Schwartz and Kohlstaedt (74). In our study, the sum scores for the entire battery and for closely related clusters of tests provided a baseline which was more stable across days; and these sum scores were used as a preliminary assessment of whether an individual patient was improved. Even among those who improved compared to baseline and placebo, the particular neuropsychological test affected after PHYSO was not consistent. This is in agreement with previous findings (81). In addition, the dose-response curve for PHYSO may be task-dependent (70).

These findings raise questions about the generality of cognitive improvement after PHYSO and, in particular, whether any impact would occur on the performance of Alzheimer patients outside the experimental setting. For example, Thal et al. (87) observed improvement of verbal memory in the selective reminding paradigm, but no effect on constructional ability or performance of activities of daily living during prolonged oral administration of PHYSO to Alzheimer patients responsive to short-term treatment. On the other hand, Mohs and coworkers (56) found just the opposite: scores on the Alzheimer Dementia Rating Scale related to memory were not affected by PHYSO, but scores for praxis and activities of daily living improved 19% and 39%, respectively.

The dose of PHYSO used is also considered a critical factor (13,19,56,74,85), but the optimum dose for improvement remains ill defined. In rats, the dose-response curve for improvement of retention performance after ChE inhibitors and receptor agonists is clearly an inverted U-shaped function, with no improvement or a decrement occurring at supra-optimal doses (e.g., 28,42). However, in lesioned rats the dose-effect curve was altered (42).

In patients, adverse side effects may limit tolerance to PHYSO before the optimum dose for cognitive improvement can be attained. In Alzheimer patients on multiple daily doses of oral PHYSO, gastrointestinal intolerance occurred at doses above 2.5 mg every 2 hours (87). Several dose-titration studies have indicated that the optimum dose varies from patient to patient (10,19,56,74,85), but as yet there has been no attempt to test the reproducibility of apparent differences in the dose-response curves. Moreover, the majority of patients respond optimally to the highest dose tested unless that dose reliably induces nausea and vomiting (4,13,56). In our study, gastrointestinal symptoms occurred in three of the five patients who showed greater than 27% inhibition of plasma ChE, the degree of inhibition associated with neuroendocrine responses indicative of central cholinergic stimulation. Anergia and subjective feelings of fatigue might also be expected to limit improvement of cognitive performance, but we found that the degree of anergia was inversely related to plasma ChE inhibition. Marked depression of mood only occurred in one patient who had 29% plasma ChE inhibition. Thus, GI discomfort rather than anergia or mood changes appears to be the most important side effect limiting the therapeutic index for stimulation of central cholinergic activity. The degree to which tolerance may develop to the GI symptoms induced by ChE inhibitors and the extent to which the therapeutic index may broaden during repeated administration of these compounds remains to be determined. Rapid tolerance to GI distress has been reported during i.c.v. bethanechol administration (41). Close to half of the patients treated with oral THA experienced gastrointestinal symptoms which were ameliorated by a peripheral anticholinergic or dose reduction (83). Thus, GI distress appears to be a significant liability of all cholinomimetic therapies, and further investigation of methods to reduce or avoid these side effects are warranted.

The role of differences in the pharmacokinetics of PHYSO as a factor underlying variability in degree of cognitive improvement or the "best-dose" also has not been systematically investigated. Our results show marked differences in the maximum reduction of plasma ChE activity ranging from 12 to 33%. These differences were reproduced in repeated trials of some patients. Moreover, the neuroendocrine measures of biological efficacy showed marked differences between patients, but were closely related to the degree of plasma ChE inhibition. Marked elevations of plasma cortisol and prolactin only occurred in those with greater than 27% inhibition, and all of these subjects had elevated ACTH levels. These findings indicate that differences in systemic absorption and metabolism play a dominant role in interpatient variability. Hartvig et al. (43) observed 3- to 7-fold differences in various pharmacokinetic parameters for PHYSO in anesthetized patients after bolus i.v. administration which were not correlated with age or body weight. Thus, the variability in pharmacokinetics does not appear to be restricted to the elderly Alzheimer population or to the oral route of administration. In two of the positive repeated oral PHYSO studies, the degree of cognitive improvement was found to be highly correlated with measures of biological efficacy (56,87). Thal et al. (87) found that both the improvement on retrieval tests and reduction of intrusions were positively correlated with the inhibition of ChE activity in c.s.f. It is noteworthy that reduction of intrusions did not show any tendency towards an inverted U-shaped "dose"-effect curve; retrieval scores improved incrementally to 50% ChE inhibition, but were less improved in one patient with 70% ChE inhibition (87). The degree of improvement after repeated oral doses of PHYSO was also related to the elevation of nocturnal cortisol levels in plasma (56). These findings support the need for readily accessible measures with which to titrate dosage of ChE inhibitors for Alzheimer studies.

The ability of PHYSO to augment cholinergic transmission in a disease in which cholinergic neurons degenerate has also been questioned. In rat studies, it has been shown that PHYSO is effective in increasing ACh content after lesion (52) and in reversing memory deficits produced by nucleus basalis lesion (42,59,60). Indeed, it is notable that the doses which reverse deficits in the lesioned animal are doses which impair performance in intact controls (42,59,60). This phenomenon may contribute to variability in the "best-dose" for improvement of cognitive function in Alzheimer patients and account for the poor response to ChE inhibitors observed in mildly impaired or misdiagnosed patients (46,83). On the other hand, PHYSO may not be able to reverse the effect of more extensive degeneration; and this, coupled with the development of multiple neurotransmitter deficits, may account for treatment failure in Alzheimer patients with severe stages of illness (16,82,83). The finding that both very mild and very severe stages of illness are less responsive to ChE inhibitors (82,83) may resolve discrepancies regarding the relationship of cognitive improvement after PHYSO to severity of illness (49,74,82,83,88).

Especially in view of the evidence from animal models that higher doses of PHYSO are required to reverse lesion-induced deficits than to improve control performance, it is reasonable to question whether the degree of inhibition of blood ChE observed in our studies reflects sufficient change in brain acetylcholinesterase (AChE) to augment central cholinergic neurotransmission. Plasma ChE inhibition after the relatively high dose of oral PHYSO (3.2 to 5.8 mg) we tested was 33% or less. This is considerably less than the degree of inhibition induced by irreversible ChE inhibitors with CNS action (e.g., 36) and is considerably less than the plasma inhibition resulting from the lowest parental doses of PHYSO tested in dogs and rats (25 and 100 µg/kg, respectively) (39,54). Inhibition of RBC AChE activity was even less marked in the Alzheimer patients after oral PHYSO, averaging only 11%. Surprisingly, the degree of RBC inhibition did not appear to be correlated with plasma inhibition, neuroendocrine response or psychological factors. By contrast, overt CNS symptoms after irreversible ChE inhibitors were correlated with RBC AChE inhibition, occurring after 30 to 60% reduction of activity (9,36). The inhibition of plasma and RBC ChE after i.v. infusion of 1 mg PHYSO is comparable in magnitude (Sherman and coworkers, unpublished results) indicating that the low level of inhibition after oral PHYSO is not a peculiarity of this route of administration. The consideration of how accurately ChE inhibition assayed in vitro reflects the magnitude of enzyme inhibition in vivo has been raised (5), because factors such as dilution of tissue and substrate concentration influence the inhibition produced by in vitro addition of drugs (5). However, we found a constant level of inhibition across a broad range of plasma or RBC dilutions, in agreement with a previous study indicating that tissue dilution has minimal effect on the apparent magnitude of inhibition after in vivo administration of carbamate inhibitors (2). These results further suggest that the inhibition measured is due to the presence of carbamylated enzyme (37) rather than competitive inhibition by any free PHYSO present (which would decrease proportionate to tissue dilution).

Evidence from animal models further suggests that blood ChE inhibition provides an accurate assessment of the effects in brain. Studies in our laboratory indicate that in rats, brain AChE inhibition and PHYSO concentration are highly correlated with both plasma and RBC enzyme inhibition (39). The neuro-chemical changes associated with the lower degree of inhibition relevant to clinically tolerated doses have not yet been examined in animal models.

The neuroendocrine results suggest that stimulation of central cholinergic activity may occur when greater than 27% inhibition of plasma ChE is achieved. The significance of neuroendocrine responses to PHYSO has been questioned by investigators who found an association of the response with nausea and emesis (18,50). Although these adverse side effects were more prevalent in patients with greater than 27% ChE inhibition, the neuroendocrine responses did not specifically correlate with occurrence or timing of adverse reactions in our study or in the study by Risch et al. (69).

The blood measures of ChE inhibition and neuroendocrine response may also help define the time course of PHYSO's action. The peak inhibition of plasma and RBC ChE activity occurred 60 minutes after PHYSO ingestion, in agreement with blood levels of PHYSO determined by HPLC after oral PHYSO (35). However, neuroendocrine responses occurred with a delay beginning at 90 minutes. ACTH peaked from 90 to 120 minutes and the rise in prolactin levels peaked sharply at 90 minutes; both returned to near baseline by 3 hours. The increase of cortisol also peaked from 90 to 150 minutes but was more sustained. The time course of neuroendocrine responses we observed after oral PHYSO was similar to that after i.v. infusion (50,69), but the delay was approximately 30 minutes longer. It is noteworthy that after parental administration of PHYSO in rats the elevation of brain ACh content occurred with a delay of about 30 minutes after the peak of drug concentration and AChE inhibition in brain (39). Behavioral effects occur with a similar latency. These findings suggest a delay in the consequences of PHYSO's action on cholinergic neurotransmission which may be an important consideration in the timing of neuropsychological tests.

Inhibition of plasma and RBC activity persisted at submaximal levels until 3 hours after ingestion, which indicates a longer duration of biological efficacy than measurement of drug levels would suggest (35). Cumulative inhibition of enzyme when PHYSO is given orally every 2 to 3 hours may account for the more marked cognitive improvement observed when Alzheimer patients are treated with the multiple dose regimen. Consistent with this possibility, Thal and coworkers (86,87) observed that improvement was not marked until the second day of treatment and that improvement lasted 17 hours after withdrawal from multiple oral doses. Elevation of nocturnal cortisol secretion in patients on this regimen (57) may also suggest a more prolonged duration of effect.

CONCLUSION

In conclusion, among the many difficulties involved in devising a successful treatment strategy for Alzheimer's dementia, inability to demonstrate that the drug has the intended biological efficacy in a given patient is among the foremost. In the case of PHYSO, considerable variation in the pharmacokinetics of absorption and metabolism, as well as the low efficacy of the doses which can be tolerated by most patients, may account for the modest and inconsistent clinical action of the drug after acute administration. However, our studies suggest that blood measures of ChE inhibition and neuro-endocrine response may be useful for monitoring the biological efficacy of other inhibitors such as THA or other regimens including the multiple-dose daily administration of PHYSO which appear to have a higher therapeutic index than acute PHYSO.

ACKNOWLEDGEMENTS

This work was supported in part by funds from the Alzheimer's Disease and Related Disorders Association, the National Institute on Aging Grant AG 05416-01A1, the Southern Illinois University Alzheimer Research Project, and the E.F. Pearson Foundation. We thank Linnea Larson, Andrew Kurtner, Constance Higgins, Sandra Best, and Pamela Ray for their assistance in data collection, and Salie Fluckiger for manuscript preparation.

REFERENCES

1. Ashford, J.W., Soldinger, S., Schaeffer, J., Cochran, L., and Jarvik, L.F. (1981): Am. J. Psychiatry, 138:829-830.
2. Barrow, M.E.H., and Johnson, J.K. (1966): Br. J. Anaesth., 38:420-431.
3. Bartus, R.T., Dean, R.L., III, Beer, B., and Lippa, A.S. (1982): Science, 217:408-417.
4. Beller, S.A., Overall, J.E., and Swann, A.C. (1985): Psychopharmacology, 87:147-151.
5. Benveniste, D., Hemmingsen, L., and Juul, P. (1967): Acta Anaesthesiol. Scand., 11:297.
6. Blackwood, D.H.R., and Christie, J.E. (1986): Biol. Psychiatry, 21:557-560.
7. Blessed, G., Tomlinson, B.E., and Roth, M. (1968): Br. J. Psychiatry, 114:797-811.
8. Bowen, D.A., Smith, C.B., White, P., and Davison, A.M. (1976): Brain, 99:459.
9. Bowers, M.B., Goodman, E., and Sim, V.M. (1964): J. Nerv. Ment. Dis., 138:383-389.
10. Brinkman, S.D., and Gershon, S. (1983): Neurobiol. Aging, 4:139-145.
11. Caltagirone, C., Gainotti, G., and Musullo, C. (1982): Int. J. Neurosci., 16:247-249.
12. Catsman-Berrevoets, C.F., Van Harkamp, F., and Appelhof, A. (1986): J. Neurol. Neurosurg. Psychiatry, 49:1088-1089.
13. Christie, J.E., Shering, A., Ferguson, J., and Glen, A.I.M. (1981): Br. J. Psychiatry, 138:46-50.
14. Corkin, S. (1981): Trends Neurosci., 3:287-290.
15. Coyle, J.T., Price, D.L., and DeLong, M.R. (1983): Science, 219:1184-1190.
16. Davidson, M., Mohs, R.C., Hollander, E., Davis, B.M., Ryan, T., Horvath, T.B., and Davis, K.L. (1986): Psychopharmacol. Bull., 22:101-105.
17. Davies, P. (1979): Brain Res., 171:319-327.
18. Davis, B.M., Brown, G.M., Miller, M., Friesen, H.G., Kastin, A.J., and Davis, K.L. (1982): Psychoneuro-endocrinology, 7:347-354.

19. Davis, K.L., and Mohs, R.C. (1982): Am. J. Psychiatry, 139:1421-1424.
20. Davis, K.L., Mohs, R.C., Davis, B.M., Horvath, T.B., Greenwald, B.S., Rosen, W.G., Levy, M.I., and Johns, C.A. (1983): Psychopharmacol. Bull., 19:451-453.
21. Davis, K.L., Mohs, R.C., Rosen, W.G., Greenwald, B.S., Levy, M.I., and Horvath, T.B. (1983): N. Engl. J. Med., 308:721.
22. Davis, K.L., Mohs, R.C., Tinklenberg, J.R., Pfefferbaum, A., Hollister, L.E., and Kopell, B.S. (1978): Science, 201:272-274.
23. Delwaide, P.J., Devoitille, J.M., and Ylieff, M. (1980): Acta Psychiatr. Belg., 80:748-754.
24. Drachman, D.A., Glosser, G., Fleming, P., and Longenecker, G. (1982): Neurology, 32:944-950.
25. Drachman, D.A., and Leavitt, J. (1974): Arch. Neurol., 30:113-121.
26. Drachman, D.A., Noffsinger, D., Sahakian, B.J., Kurdziel, S., and Fleming, P. (1980): Neurobiol. Aging, 1:39-43.
27. Drachman, D.A., and Sahakian, B.J. (1980): In: The Psychobiology of Aging, edited by D.G. Stein, pp. 347-368. Elsevier, New York.
28. Flood, J.F., Smith, G.E., and Cherkin, A. (1985): Psychopharmacology, 86:61-67.
29. Folstein, M.F., Folstein, S.E., and McHugh, P.R. (1975): J. Psychiatr. Res., 12:189-198.
30. Francis, P.T., Palmer, A.M., Sims, N.R., Bowen, D.M., Davison, A.N., Esiri, N.M., Neary, D., Snowden, J.S., and Wilcock, G.K. (1985): N. Engl. J. Med., 313:7-11.
31. Friedman, E., Brennan, M.J., Lerer, B.E., Sherman, K.A., Schweitzer, J.W., and Kuster, J. (1986): In: Alzheimer's and Parkinson's Diseases: Strategies in Research and Development, Vol. 29, edited by A. Fisher, I. Hanin, and C. Lachman, pp. 393-405. Plenum Press, New York.
32. Friedman, E., Sherman, K.A., Ferris, S.H., Reisberg, B., Bartus, R.T., and Schneck, M.K. (1981): N. Engl. J. Med., 304:1490-1491.
33. Fuld, P.A., Katzman, R., and Davies, P. (1982): Ann. Neurol., 11:155-159.
34. Gibson, G.E., Peterson, C., and Sansone, J. (1981): Neurobiol. Aging, 2:165-172.
35. Gibson, M., Moore, T., Smith, C.M., and Whelpton, R. (1985): Lancet, i:695-696.
36. Grob, D., Harvey, A.M., Langworthy, O.R., and Lilienthal, J.L., Jr. (1947): Johns Hopkins Hosp. Bull., 81:257-266.
37. Groff, W.A., Ellin, R., and Skalsky, R.L. (1977): J. Pharm. Sci., 66:389-391.

38. Hachinski, V.C., Iliff, L.D., Zilhka, E., Du Boulay, G.H., McAllister, V.L., Marshall, J., Russell, R.W.R., and Symon, L. (1975): Arch. Neurol., 32:632-637.
39. Hallak, M., and Giacobini, E. (1986): Neurochem. Res., 11:1037-1048.
40. Hamilton, M. (1960): J. Neurol. Neurosurg. Psychiatry, 23:56-62.
41. Harbaugh, R.E., Roberts, D.W., Coombs, D.W., Saunders, R.C., and Reeder, T.M. (1984): Neurosurgery, 15:514-518.
42. Haroutunian, V., Kanof, P., and Davis, K.L. (1985): Life Sci., 37:945-952.
43. Hartvig, P., Wiklung, L., and Lindstrom, B. (1986): Acta Anaesthesiol. Scand., 301:177-182.
44. Hughes, C.P., Berg, L., Danziger, W.L., Coben, L.A., and Martin, R.L. (1982): Br. J. Psychiatry, 140:566-572.
45. Janowsky, D.S., Risch, C., Parker, D., Huey, L., and Judd, L. (1980): Psychopharmacol. Bull., 16:29-33.
46. Johns, C.A., Levy, M.I., Greenwald, B.S., Rosen, W.G., Horvath, T.B., Davis, B.M., Mohs, R.C., and Davis, K.L. (1983): In: Biological Aspects of Alzheimer's Disease, Banbury Report 15, edited by R. Katzman, pp. 435-449. Cold Spring Harbor Laboratory.
47. Johnson, C.D., and Russell, R.L. (1975): Anal. Biochem., 64:229-238.
48. Jotkowitz, S. (1983): Ann. Neurol., 14:690-691.
49. Kaye, W.H., Sitaram, N., Weingartner, H., Ebert, M.H., Smallberg, S., and Gillin, J.C. (1982): Biol. Psychiatry, 17:275-280.
50. Lewis, D.A., Sherman, B.M., and Kathol, R.G. (1984): J. Clin. Endocrinol. Metab., 58:570-573.
51. Lippa, A.S., Pelham, R.W., Beer, B., Critchett, D.J., Dean, R.L., and Bartus, R.T. (1980): Neurobiol. Aging, 1:13-19.
52. London, E., and Coyle, J.T. (1978): Biochem. Pharmacol., 27:2962-2965.
53. Mash, D.C., Flynn, D.D., and Potter, L.T. (1985): Science, 228:1115-1117.
54. Mattio, T., McIlhany, M., Giacobini, E., and Hallak, M. (1986): Neuropharmacology, 25:1167-1177.
55. McKhann, G., Drachman, D., Folstein, M., Katzman, R., Price, D., and Stadlan, E.M. (1984): Neurology, 34:939-944.
56. Mohs, R.C., Davis, B.M., Johns, C.A., Mathe, A.A., Greenwald, B.S., Horvath, T.B., and Davis, K.L. (1985): Am. J. Psychiatry, 142:28-33.
57. Mohs, R.C., Davis, B.M., Greenwald, B.S., Mathe, A.A., Johns, C.A., Horvath, T.B., and Davis, K.L. (1985): J. Am. Geriatr. Soc., 33:749-757.
58. Muramoto, O., Sugishita, M., and Anda, K. (1984): J. Neurol. Neurosurg. Psychiatry, 47:485.

59. Murray, C.L., and Fibiger, H.C. (1985): Neuroscience, 14:1025-1032.
60. Murray, C.L., and Fibiger, H.C. (1986): Behav. Neurosci., 100:23-32.
61. Neary, D., Snowden, J.S., Mann, D.M.A., Bowen, D.M., Sims, N.R., Northern, B., Yates, P.O., and Davison, A.N. (1986): J. Neurol. Neurosurg. Psychiatry, 49:229-237.
62. Pedata, F., Slavikova, J., Kotas, A., and Pepeu, G. (1983): Neurobiol. Aging, 4:31-35.
63. Perry, E.K., Tomlinson, B.E., Blessed, G., Bergmann, K., Gibson, P.H., and Perry, R.H. (1978): Br. J. Med., 42:1457-1459.
64. Peters, B.H., and Levin, H.S. (1979): Ann. Neurol., 6:219-221.
65. Peters, B.H., and Levin, H.S. (1977): Arch. Neurol., 34:215-219.
66. Peters, B.H., and Levin, H.S. (1982): In: Alzheimer's Disease: A Report of Progress, Vol. 19, edited by S. Corkin, K.L. Davis, J.H. Growdon, E. Usdin, and R.J. Wurtman, pp. 421-426. Raven Press, New York.
67. Reisine, T., Yamamura, H.I., Bird, E.D., Spokes, E., and Enna, S.J. (1978): Brain Res., 159:477-481.
68. Richter, J.A., Perry, E.K., and Tomlinson, B.E. (1980): Life Sci., 26:1683-1689.
69. Risch, S.C., Cohen, R.M., Janowsky, D.S., Kalin, D.H., and Murphy, D.L. (1980): Science, 209:1545-1546.
70. Rose, R.P., and Moulthrop, M.A. (1986): Biol. Psychiatry, 21:538-542.
71. Rosen, W.G., Terry, R.D., Fuld, P.A., Katzman, R., and Peck, A. (1980): Ann. Neurol., 7:486-488.
72. Rosenthal, R., and Bigelow, L.B. (1973): Compr. Psychiatry, 14:489-494.
73. Rylett, R.J., Ball, M.J., and Colhoun, E.H. (1983): Brain Res., 289:169-175.
74. Schwartz, A.S., and Kohlstaedt, E.V. (1986): Life Sci., 38:1021-1028.
75. Segal, M. (1982): Neurobiol. Aging, 3:121-124.
76. Sherman, K.A., Kuster, J.E., Dean, R.L., III, Bartus, R.T., and Friedman, E. (1981): Neurobiol. Aging, 2:99-104.
77. Sims, N.R., Bowen, D.M., Allen, S.J., Smith, C.C.T., Neary, D., Thomas, D.J., and Davison, A.N. (1983): J. Neurochem., 40:503-509.
78. Sitaram, N., Weingartner, H., and Gillin, J.C. (1978): Science, 201:274-276.
79. Smith, C.M., and Swash, M. (1979): Lancet, i:42.
80. Strong, R., Hicks, P., Hsu, L., Bartus, R.T., and Enna, S.J. (1980): Neurobiol. Aging, 1:59-63.

81. Sullivan, E.V., Shedlock, K.J., Corkin, S., and
     Growdon, J.H. (1982): In: Alzheimer's Disease: A Report
     of Progress, Vol. 19, edited by S. Corkin, K.L. Davis,
     J.H. Growdon, E. Usdin, and R.J. Wurtman, pp. 361-367.
     Raven Press, New York.
82. Summers, W.K., Viesselman, J.O., Marsh, G.M., and
     Candelora, K. (1981): Biol. Psychiatry, 16:145-153.
83. Summers, W.K., Majorski, L.V., Marsh, G.M., Tachiki, K.,
     and Kling, A. (1986): N. Engl. J. Med., 315:1241-1245.
84. Thal, L.J., and Fuld, P.A. (1983): N. Engl. J. Med.,
     308:720.
85. Thal, L.J., Fuld, P.A., Masur, D.M., and Sharpless, N.S.
     (1983): Ann. Neurol., 13:491-496.
86. Thal, L.J., Masur, D.M., Fuld, P.A., Sharpless, N.S., and
     Davies, P. (1983): In: Biological Aspects of Alzheimer's
     Disease, Banbury Report 15, edited by R. Katzman,
     pp. 461-469. Cold Spring Harbor Laboratory.
87. Thal, L.J., Masur, D.M., Sharpless, N.S., Fuld, P.A., and
     Davies, P. (1986): Prog. Neuropsychopharmacol. Biol.
     Psychiatry, 10:627-636.
88. Wettstein, A. (1983): Ann. Neurol., 13:210-212.
89. Whitehouse, P.J., Price, D.L., and Stuble, R.G. (1982):
     Science, 215:1238-1239.

Central Nervous System Disorders of Aging:
Clinical Intervention and Research, edited by
Randy Strong et al. Raven Press, New York
© 1988.

EVALUATION OF NEURODEGENERATIVE DISORDERS

WITH DIAGNOSTIC IMAGING MODALITIES

James W. Fletcher

Nuclear Medicine Service, Veterans Administration Medical
Center; and Department of Internal Medicine,
St. Louis University School of Medicine,
St. Louis, Missouri 63106

The development of powerful new imaging techniques such as positron emission tomography (PET), nuclear magnetic resonance imaging (NMRI), and single photon emission computed tomography (SPECT) has provided exciting new probes for evaluating metabolic functions in the brains of intact humans. The fundamental concept, which has led to the development of PET and which still represents the major cornerstone of this modality, is that a certain number of radionuclides, which happen to decay by the emission of positrons, exhibit chemical properties which make them particularly useful as biologic probes and tracers. The most important of these very short-lived "physiologic tracers" are carbon-11, oxygen-15, nitrogen-13, and fluorine-18. Significant advances have already been made in a variety of neurodegenerative disorders using PET to study 2-deoxyglucose uptake and to image neurotransmitter receptors such as dopamine, opiate, and benzodiazepine receptors. Presently, the major limitation of PET is technological. PET isotopes have very short half-lives and the production of the isotopes and synthesis of labeled ligands must be carried out at the site of the scanning. SPECT may be the logical and economic developmental outgrowth of PET that would allow the study of these metabolic functions using equipment that is already available in most academic centers. Significant development in radiopharmaceuticals suitable for SPECT imaging must occur before SPECT can match the current potential of PET. Presently, 123-iodine and 99m-technetium labeled ligands are being evaluated for use with SPECT in neurodegenerative disorders. NMRI has, thus far, been restricted to studies of protons permitting the visualization of anatomic structures, but not studies of metabolism. In the near future it may be possible to study phosphorus metabolism

using high-field NMRI. This paper will describe the present
application of these three diagnostic imaging modalities in the
evaluation of neurodegenerative disorders. The emphasis will
be on senile dementia of the Alzheimer's type (DAT)
(Alzheimer's disease) as the majority of work has been
performed on patients with this diagnosis. Applications of
these modalities in other neurodegenerative diseases such as
Huntington's disease (HD) and Parkinson's disease (PD) will
also be described.

COMPARISON OF DIAGNOSTIC IMAGING TECHNIQUES

Positron Emission Tomography

   PET is a technique that measures the distribution of
systemically administered substances labeled with a radioactive
isotope that decays through the emission of positrons. The
fundamental concept, which has led to the development of PET
and which still represents the major cornerstone of this
modality, is that a certain number of radionuclides, which
happen to decay by the emission of positrons, exhibit chemical
properties which make them particularly useful as biologic
probes and tracers. The principle of PET is based on the
release of a positron from these unstable radionuclides that
have an excess number of protons compared to neutrons. When
the nucleus attempts to achieve stability by converting a
proton to a neutron, a positron is released. The positron
moves away from the nucleus a few millimeters and encounters an
electron. The interaction of the positron and electron results
in the annihilation of the combined mass of these two parti-
cles. This annihilation of matter is accompanied by the
release of energy in the form of two high-energy photons that
fly away from each other in opposite directions. The ability
to simultaneously detect these two photons signals the decay of
a positron along a line connecting the two points of detection. This basic localization mechanism is one of the main
attractions of positron imaging compared to SPECT.
Characteristics of the commonly used "physiologic tracers" are
presented in Table 1. It is clear from the inspection of the
data in Table 1 that the short half-lives for these tracers
will require that they be produced at or very near the site of
intended use.
   Thus, for most institutions, there is the requirement not
only for the PET scanning device, but also for a local source
of positron emitting radionuclides, a cyclotron. While this
technology is very elegant and capable of measurements of brain
metabolism, blood flow, receptor site mapping/binding studies
and functional imaging, its complexity has limited its
widespread acceptability and diffusion. It is often stated
that PET is too complicated because it involves physicists,
chemists, biochemists, and a broad variety of other
professional constituents, but the main reason leveled by

TABLE 1. Radionuclides for PET

Radionuclide	Half-life (min)	Positron Decay Events (%)
Carbon-11	20.42	99.9
Nitrogen-13	9.96	100
Oxygen-15	2.07	99.9
Fluorine-18	109.70	96.9
Gallium-68	68.10	90
Bromine-75	76.00	76

critics is that PET is too expensive (33). Recent cost
comparisons based on annualized expenditures would indicate
procedure charges which are similar to those of NMRI (12,35).
Considering the implications of PET for clinical decision-
making and the other cost factors resulting from a diagnosis,
many feel that PET is not too costly.

Single Photon Emission Computed Tomography

Although PET and SPECT have the same image reconstruction
process in common, it would be a mistake to consider these two
modalities as only variations on a theme, as there are
considerable fundamental conceptual and technological differences which affect their clinical application and utility.
SPECT was developed as an imaging technique to provide tomographic information from radionuclides that are readily available
and used conventionally for planar imaging in nuclear medicine.
Developments in this technology have been very slow since its
introduction in the early 1960s. It is likely that much of the
early lack of enthusiasm and slow development derived from the
limited success of attempts to adapt the conventional Anger
gamma camera for SPECT application. Within the past five to
ten years, there has been renewed interest in the potential of
SPECT, particularly when SPECT can be combined with certain
newly developed radiopharmaceuticals (11,34). A considerable
amount of work is being directed toward structuring radiopharmaceuticals for SPECT that can compete with those utilized
with PET. It is probable that a portion of the biochemical
information acquired by PET can be transferred to SPECT through
the development of appropriate radiopharmaceuticals. This
would be highly desirable as the present cost of SPECT instrumentation for imaging is considerably lower than PET instrumentation, and the requirement for a cyclotron, an on-site
source of positron emitters, is not necessary for SPECT. It
appears, at this time, that the broader dissemination of SPECT
in nuclear medicine will depend on the rate of development of
newer clinically-useful radiopharmaceuticals and also the

availability of instrumentation optimized specifically for
SPECT (38).

Nuclear Magnetic Resonance Imaging

The phenomenon of NMRI was identified in the mid 1940s by
Bloch and Purcell who received the Nobel Prize for their
discovery. Until the early 1970s, NMRI was not applied to
diagnostic imaging but was developed as a highly useful
analytical probe in chemistry, providing chemists with unique
information about the molecular form and structure of molecules
with nuclides capable of providing NMRI signals. In the early
1970s, the ability to detect NMRI signals from biologic tissues
was applied to the development of a new diagnostic imaging
procedure for evaluating biologic structures in vivo.
Paul Lauterbur described this technique as "Zeugmatography"
(27), although it has come to be more generally known as
nuclear magnetic resonance imaging (NMRI or MRI). Certain
professional groups have recommended MRI as the preferred
terminology claiming it to be less alarming to the public,
although certainly ignoring the fact that the origin of the
useful and necessary signal derives from the nucleus. The
historical experience with NMRI as a powerful analytical tool
in chemistry suggested that NMRI would be an extremely powerful
technique for characterizing the biochemical or physicochemical state of living tissue, in vivo, in a manner similar
to that of SPECT and PET. Unfortunately, this promise has yet
to be fulfilled; and at the present time, the major application
of NMRI is in obtaining images providing primarily morphologic
information similar to computed tomography (CT). A partial
explanation for the lack of NMRI to provide useful tissue
"characterizing" information can be seen in examining Table 2.

TABLE 2.   Concentrations of nuclides capable of providing
NMR signals in soft tissue

Nuclide	Typical concentration in tissue (atoms/g $\times 10^{20}$)	Isotopic abundance (%)	NMRI sensitivity relative to ^1H at constant field	Imaging index relative to ^1H
^1H	460	100	1	46,000
^{31}P	0.60	100	0.07	10^{-4}
^{23}Na	0.42	100	0.09	10^{-4}
^{13}C	24	1	0.016	10^{-4}
^{19}F	–	100	0.83	–

Adapted from P.L. McGeer in National Conference on
Biological Imaging, National Academy of Sciences, 1983

The extremely low concentration in normal tissues of "NMRI nuclides", other than protons, the relatively low sensitivity of other nuclides compared to the proton, and the relatively low signal-to-noise ratio produced when the NMRI signal is used to create images are all factors which have limited NMRI to its inherently low specificity and current primary role as a technique for providing exquisitely detailed structural information on biologic organ systems.

Areas of potential development which are now receiving considerable attention by the research and development groups of major universities and NMRI instrument manufacturers include: (1) "flow imaging" for evaluation of circulatory hemodynamics, spectroscopic fat/H_2O imaging which can distinguish between water and hydrogen (aliphatic) bound protons through the natural chemical frequency shifts between "fat" protons and "water" protons; (2) the use of NMRI "contrast" agents which act by modifying or shortening the intrinsic relaxation rate of tissue protons; (3) the development of images based on distribution of phosphorus-31 and sodium-23; and (4) the use of the same NMRI instrumentation for imaging as well as measurement of biochemical events through NMRI spectroscopy for hydrogen and phosphorus. While it is unlikely that NMRI will ever compete successfully with SPECT or PET in the realm of tracer methodology, since NMRI studies of this nature require administration of large quantities of tracer material, it is important to remember that NMRI has the capability of measuring the physicochemical state of the image-forming nuclide and in certain applications is unchallenged by nuclear medicine imaging techniques. One example in this regard is the ability of NMRI to distinguish between intracellular and extracellular sodium. The relative sensitivity and resolution of NMRI and PET are presented in Table 3.

TABLE 3.   Sensitivity and resolution of NMRI and PET

Technique	Approximate sensitivity limits units/g tissue x 10^{20}	Resolution	
		Present	Estimated achievable
NMR	4	$(3~mm)^3$	$(1~mm)^3$
PET	10^{-12}	$(8~mm)^3$	$(3~mm)^3$

Adapted from P.L. McGeer in National Conference on Biological Imaging, National Academy of Sciences, 1983.

At the present time, the resolution of NMRI for protons and the estimated achievable resolution far exceeds that of PET, however, the sensitivity of PET is 10^{12} times greater than NMRI. It is, therefore, unlikely that NMRI will ever be able to compete with PET in providing images of such parameters as regional glucose metabolism, regional blood flow, or neurore-ceptor distribution.

EXPERIENCE WITH PET IN THE STUDY OF NEURODEGENERATIVE DISORDERS

Glucose Metabolism in Dementia of the Alzheimer's Type

A fairly large number of studies have been published evaluating regional cerebral metabolism of glucose in DAT. Almost all of these studies have used a technique developed by Sokoloff (37), using a tracer amount of ^{18}F-fluorodeoxyglucose (FDG) which is injected systemically. PET is then used to determine regional cerebral metabolic rate for glucose (rCMRgl) in various brain regions. Several studies have confirmed that the rCMRgl is reduced in DAT compared with age-matched controls, but information on the effects of aging itself are in conflict. Kuhl et al. (25) studied 17 men and 23 women between 18 and 78 years and found a small but significant decrement in cortical metabolism with age. Duara et al. (9) reported on a similar study in 40 healthy men aged 21 to 83 years. The rCMRgl of 4.6 to 4.7 mg/kg min^{-1} did not change significantly with age although there was a mild trend towards lower values in older people. Other investigators (1,7) have failed to find a significant difference in rCMRgl between young and elderly normals. Chase et al. (5) evaluated rCMRgl in 17 patients with DAT and 5 healthy age-matched controls. Results of rCMRgl were correlated with performance on tests of global intellectual function. The rCMRgl as determined by PET was 30% lower in the DAT group. There was also a significant correlation between degree of overall dementia and amount of metabolic reduction. Chase also described a close relationship between the predom-inant cognitive deficit and the foci of cortical hypometab-olism. Thus, patients with disproportionate language failure all manifested conspicuous involvement of the left parasylvian region; those with major visual-spatial dysfunction consistently had a right posterior parietal hypometabolic focus. Patients with relatively severe dyscalculia and other aspects of the Gerstmann syndrome had left angular gyrus hypometabolism, while those with prominent attentional deficits and personality changes appeared to have relatively severe frontal lobe involvement. Other studies by Foster et al. (15), Farkas et al. (13), and Friedland et al. (19) have confirmed these findings. In each of these studies, some areas of cortex were more heavily involved than others, but there was no consistent pattern. Asymmetric patterns of diminished metabolism in the frontal, parietal or temporal regions in DAT were emphasized by Foster et al. (15); whereas, Duara et al. (10) recently reported metabolic asymmetries to a small degree in patients with mild DAT, but more prominently in the moderate cases of DAT. There was no predilection for the right or left side, but the changes were most prominent in the parietal regions.

Significant decreases in rCMRgl were noted only in the severely demented patients. Duara et al. concluded that right/left metabolic asymmetry for rCMRgl occurs early in the course of DAT when there may only be mild memory loss and becomes more prominent as the disease progresses. All of these findings suggest that PET studies of rCMRgl may be useful in establishing the diagnosis of DAT in the early course of the disease. Limitations for these studies include the facts that: 1) in most patients, the diagnosis of DAT is presumptive and not definitive as cortical biopsy is infrequently indicated or performed for pathologic confirmation of the disease; and 2) the effect of aging is uncertain, and pathologic changes brought on by DAT are imposed on a constantly shifting normal baseline (31).

Glucose Metabolism in Huntington's and Parkinson's Diseases

HD, which is a genetic neurodegenerative disorder, causes progressive dementia and chorea and pathologically demonstrates widespread neuronal cell loss, particularly in the caudate, putamen and cerebral cortex. Kuhl et al. (26) examined 13 patients with HD between 17 and 71 and 15 subjects 12 to 53 years old who were "at risk" for the disease. In contrast to CT where the caudate is intact in the early stages of HD and atrophies only in the late stages, glucose metabolism in the caudate was dramatically reduced compared to age-matched controls in the early stages of the disease. Metabolic defects appear to precede the structural changes as determined by the discrepancy between CT anatomic findings and PET rCMRgl measurements. In Kuhl's study, approximately 50% of the subjects "at risk" for HD demonstrated caudate hypometabolism. A more recent report by Phelps et al. (34) has confirmed these findings and shown that the metabolic lesions begin in the caudate and spread to the putamen as the disease progresses. Glucose utilization is typically normal in the rest of the brain in HD. Mazziotta et al. (30) have recently described measurement of rCMRgl by PET in a larger series of patients "at risk" for HD. In their study, PET demonstrated graded, bilateral reductions in metabolism of the caudates despite normal appearing CT studies. The ratio of rCMRgl between the caudate and hemisphere (Cd/Hem) was reduced by more than 2.5 standard deviations from normal in 13/44 subjects "at risk" for HD. Individual risk estimates were averaged for the "at risk" population and resulted in the prediction that the average probability of having the clinically unexpressed HD gene was 30%. This was consistent with the 30% (13/44) probability actually found using PET studies. Only a small number of patients with PD have been studied for rCMRgl by PET. Compared with age-matched controls, patients with PD had rCMRgl moderately (18%) and uniformly reduced (24). With development

of dementia and increased severity of bradykinesia, global
hypometabolism was seen to develop.

PET Measurements of Flow and Oxygen Metabolism

PET has been used in aging studies and in the evaluation of
neurodegenerative disorders to measure cerebral blood flow and
cerebral metabolic rate for oxygen ($CMRO_2$) using ^{15}O-labeled
H_2O and ^{15}O-oxyhemoglobin, or ^{15}O-O_2 by inhalation.   In
general, regional cerebral blood flow (rCBF) and $rCMRO_2$ have
correlated, although focal flow metabolism mismatches have been
found in certain disorders, particularly stroke.   Several
investigators (16,28) using continuous inhalation of ^{15}O-
labeled CO_2 and O_2 showed a decrease with age in rCBF and
$rCMRO_2$ in grey matter but not in white matter.   Frackowiak et
al. (17) used the ^{15}O-O_2 steady-state technique to study cerebral flow and metabolism in 22 patients with DAT and multi-
infarct dementia (MID) and matched normal controls.   Their
results indicated that the DAT group had diminished rCBF and
$rCMRO_2$ compared to normals that were proportional to the severity of the disease.   Thus far, these techniques have not been
applied to large numbers of subjects with DAT or other
neurodegenerative disorders.   In general, one would expect the
results to be comparable to those observed with the use of FDG
or of earlier studies (4,42) ^{133}Xe clearance technique for CBF.

Neuroreceptor Mapping and Binding

Until the advent of neuroreceptor imaging in vivo by PET,
the quantitative analysis of human neuroreceptors was
restricted to studies on homogenates of human brain or receptor
autoradiography (ARG).   This area represents a relatively new
application for PET imaging, and it is still quite dependent on
the information which has been previously obtained by
homogenate and ARG studies for development and direction.   In
this area, PET has the unique capability not only to generate
information noninvasively, that is presently accessible only
with in vitro methods, but also to elucidate the properties of
receptors that may be recognizable only through in vivo binding
studies.   PET scans will, therefore, make it possible to assess
the state of neurotransmitter receptors, such as the dopamine,
serotonin, muscarinic cholinergic, opiate, and benzodiazepine
receptors, in anatomically distinct regions in normal persons
and in patients with neurodegenerative and neuropsychiatric
diseases.   Certain properties of neurotransmitter receptors are
important in determining their role in disease.   Since only
certain neurons possess certain receptors, dysfunction in
specific neural systems should lead to changes in specific
receptors.   Also, the presence of receptors on membranes and
the affinity of receptors for neurotransmitters may be
disrupted prior to actual death of the neuron and serve as an
early sign of pathologic events.   Finally, as many neuroactive

drugs act through stimulating or blocking receptors, a better
understanding of receptor changes in disease may lead to
improvements in therapy. Selected examples of neuroreceptor
alterations Table 4 (44).

TABLE 4. <u>Receptor alterations in neurodegenerative disorders</u>

Disease	Region	Receptor
Amyotrophic lat- eral sclerosis	Ventral horn	Muscarinic cholinergic (M2 receptor)
Huntington's Disease	Caudate	Muscarinic cholinergic (M1, M2 receptor) dopamine, benzodiazepine
Alzheimer's Disease	Amygdala	Muscarinic cholinergic (M2 receptor)

The changes which have been observed by study of tissue
homogenates and ARG are quite significant. For example, the
muscarinic cholinergic receptors in amyotrophic lateral
sclerosis are decreased 74% compared to average control
receptor concentration. The M2 muscarinic cholinergic
receptors in Alzheimer's disease are decreased 72% in the
basolateral portion of the amygdala and basal ganglia regions
which receive dense innervation from the basal forebrain
cholinergic system. These findings, reported by Whitehouse et
al. (45) using ARC, have been confirmed through tissue
homogenate studies (29).   At the present time, the majority of
PET studies for quantitative imaging of neuroreceptors have
been performed using a variety of ^{11}C-labeled radiotracers. An
example of the types of substances which are available are
presented in Table 5.

TABLE 5. ^{11}C-Labeled radiotracers for receptor studies

Receptor	Ligand
Dopamine D-2	3-N-Methylspiperone
Dopamine D-1	SCH-23390
Opiate "mu"	Carfentanil
	Diprenorphine
Muscarinic	Dexetimide/levetimide
Serotonin S-2	N-Methylketanserin
	N-Methyl-bromo-LSD
Benzodiazepine	Suriclone

For a radioactive drug to be identified as binding specifically to a neuroreceptor, certain criteria must be fulfilled: 1) the binding must be saturable at low concentrations of drug because of the small number of receptor sites; 2) the binding must be blocked by high concentrations of the drug; and 3) the distribution within the brain should correspond to known sites of the receptors (40). While the majority of work in this area is still very preliminary and requires confirmation by others, some of the early findings are very exciting and promising. Wagner et al. (41) have reported on the imaging of dopamine receptors in the human brain with PET. These investigators have compared the amount of radioactivity in the caudate, an area rich in D2 dopamine receptors, with that of the cerebellum, an area which has no such receptors. The ratio of radioactivity in caudate and cerebellum was noted to rise as a linear function of time in normal volunteers and in patients with neuropsychiatric disorders. With regard to aging, a marked decline with increasing age was observed in the caudate-cerebellar ratio in 44 normal volunteers (49). These same investigators have recently reported on a method for not only visualizing these dopamine receptors, but also for quantification of the rate of binding and measurement of the receptor density and affinity (47,48).

EXPERIENCE WITH SPECT IN THE STUDY
OF NEURODEGENERATIVE DISORDERS

Measurement of Cerebral Blood Flow in Alzheimer's Disease

As contrasted with PET, the overall experience with SPECT is much more limited. The majority of work accomplished with SPECT has been in relation to the study of cerebral blood flow using radioactive inert gasses or newer radiopharmaceuticals labeled with ^{99m}Technetium or radioiodine, usually ^{123}I. The experience with inert gasses such as ^{133}Xe for measuring rCBF dates back to the early and mid 1960s (20). The inert gasses can be given intravenously or by inhalation. The procedure is noninvasive and relatively inexpensive and has been applied extensively in the study of stroke and neuropsychiatric disorders. It is subject to potential errors, has not been used to study neurodegenerative disorders, requires special instrumentation beyond a modified Anger-type gamma camera, and does not provide the same degree of anatomic localizing information that is available through SPECT with other tracers and PET. The most promising work with SPECT for the measurement of rCBF has been obtained using radiotracers that behave like microspheres and which can be labeled with radionuclides that have suitable characteristics for use with standard imaging instrumentation. The agent which has had the widest application is N-isopropyl-p-[^{123}I]-iodoam-phetamine (^{123}I-IMP). This material was introduced in 1980 by

Winchell (46), and the regional distribution of IMP correlates
well with blood flow (22). Sharp et al. (36) have recently
reported on their experience with IMP in the study of 47
patients with dementia. In those patients diagnosed as having
DAT, a bilateral reduction in IMP uptake in the temporo-
parietal-occipital region was seen in all subjects with DAT
including those with mild disease. It is of interest to note
that in 64% of these subjects, NMRI was entirely normal; and a
much closer correlation was observed between SPECT and NMRI in
patients with multi-infarct dementia. Derouesne et al. (8)
using IMP in DAT suggested that the temporo-parietal-occipital
flow deficits are not seen in all patients with DAT, but only
those most severely affected. A more limited study by Cohen et
al. (6) studying DAT with IMP reported the ability to correctly
identify subjects with DAT compared to those with MID. In most
of these studies, patients with DAT had marked decreases in the
parietal area, suggesting that this might represent a signature
of the disease. This premise was further evaluated by Johnson
et al. (23) who compared IMP activities in the parietal,
frontal, temporal and striate cortex with activity in the
cerebellum. The study population consisted only of patients
with DAT and normals. The cortical cerebellar ratios were
significantly lower for most regions of the cortex in patients
with DAT, but the posterior parietal cortex was the most
sensitive marker of DAT. Uptake in this area was decreased in
13 of 15 patients with DAT. These results with IMP are similar
to those discussed above for PET although it should be
emphasized that values of absolute rCBF are not readily
obtainable with IMP. Another agent developed by Troutner et
al. (39) based on a complex of [99m]Technetium and propyleneamine
oxine (PnAO), is very promising for the study of rCBF in human
subjects. There is very little experience with this agent in
the neurodegenerative disorders, although it should be a very
powerful tool when combined with SPECT as the [99m]Technetium
label is generally better suited for imaging than radioiodine
labeled agents.

Receptor Studies with SPECT

The only legitimate SPECT receptor imaging agent is [123]I-
labeled (R)-3-quinuclidinyl-4-iodobenzilate (^{123}I-QNB). This
compound was developed by Eckelman et al. (11), for visualization of cerebral muscarinic-acetylcholine receptors. Holman
et al. (21) have recently reported on the use of SPECT in
combination with ^{123}I-QNB in a patient with DAT. These
investigators used the ratio of radioactivity between the
caudate and cerebellum as an index of the specificity of the
tracer for muscarinic binding sites. They reported a 15-fold
greater concentration of tracer in the caudate than the
cerebellum which is consistent with previously measured
concentrations of muscarinic acetylcholine receptor sites in
these two areas of the brain (43). Their conclusion was that

muscarinic acetylcholine receptor concentrations may be
relatively preserved in patients with DAT despite profound
decreases in blood flow to the temporo-parietal cortex. They
did note, however, that the QNB activity ratio between temporo-
parietal cortex and caudate was lower than the corresponding
ratio in the age-matched normal subject. While Holman's study
is rather preliminary, it does demonstrate the potential of
SPECT when combined with an appropriate pharmaceutical. Future
directions include efforts to develop tracers for evaluation of
somatostatin receptors or binding sites for corticotropin-
releasing factor as both of these have been described as
abnormal in DAT by tissue homogenate and ARG studies (2,3).
The immediate future for SPECT is likely to be in the
evaluation of CBF and in assisting with the differential
diagnosis of the dementias as the perfusion patterns appear to
be sensitive and discriminating.

EXPERIENCE WITH NMRI IN THE NEURODEGENERATIVE DISEASES

NMRI has proven to be superior to most other imaging
modalities in the evaluation of the central nervous system in
providing improved sensitivity for the detection of disease,
improved structural detail, and ability to view abnormalities
in multiple projections. Despite this fact, very little
information is available on the value of NMRI in neurodegenerative disorders as only a few publications have
addressed this topic. As expected, NMRI has demonstrated
limitations similar to CT in applying a structural approach to
the evaluation of neurodegenerative diseases. An example of
this limitation is reported by McGeer et al. (32) who examined
13 patients with DAT using CT, NMRI and PET with [18]FDG. These
investigators reported PET findings for DAT similar to others
and showed that the deficits in neuropsychologic testing
generally correlated with those predicted from loss of regional
cortical metabolism. In contrast, the degree of atrophy
identified by CT and NMRI did not correlate with the
neuropsychologic deficit, and significant atrophy was reported
in some of the controls. Fazekas et al. (14) also reported
preliminary findings in 10 patients with dementia examined with
NMRI. Eight were determined to have DAT, two had MID. In 8 of
these 10, periventricular bands of signal hyperintensity were
noted on T2 scans. Two DAT patients who did not have this
finding had mild disease. Discreet areas of cortical
hyperintensity were also seen in 4 DAT and 2 MID patients.
These authors concluded that on T2 weighted NMRI scans
confluent periventricular white matter abnormalities and
discrete cortical hyperintense lesions are features of both
vascular and degenerative dementia, distinguishing these
patients from healthy elderly controls. In general, findings
on NMRI are also similar to findings on CT: 1) The brain
decreases in size with aging. This phenomenon known as brain
atrophy is manifested by decreased tissue volume, enlarged

ventricles, and widened sulci. 2) Ventricular enlargement and sulcal widening are greater in senile dementia that in normals of comparable age; and 3) Some senile dementia cases have no detectable atrophy while some normals show considerable atrophy. Sharp et al. (36) in evaluating 47 patients with dementia by SPECT also performed NMRI examinations in these patients and reported that NMRI findings were normal in 64% of the sites where iodoamphetamine (IMP) activity was clearly decreased. Because of the more significant structural changes associated with brain infarction, a much closer agreement was found between NMRI and IMP findings in patients with MID. These authors concluded that when the NMRI and IMP findings were concordant and symmetric, MID was more likely to be the cause of the dementia than DAT. Thus, while CT and NMRI provide accurate information about cortical atrophy and periventricular white matter changes, neither of these modalities appears to offer as much sensitivity or discriminatory information in the neurodegenerative disorders as SPECT or PET. Future work with NMRI that involves chemical shift imaging, flow imaging or use of nuclides other than the proton will be likely to contribute additional useful information for evaluating the neurodegenerative disorders.

REFERENCES

1. Alavi, A., Reivich, M., and Ferris, S. (1982): Exp. Brain Res. (Suppl.), 5:187-195.
2. Beal, M.F., Muzurek, M.F., and Tran, V.T. (1985): Science, 229:289-291.
3. Bissette, G., Reynolds, G.P., and Kilts, C.D. (1985): JAMA, 254:3067-3069.
4. Butler, R.W., Dickinson, W.A., Katholi, C., and Halsey, J.H., (1983): Ann. Neurol., 13:155-159.
5. Chase, T.N., Foster, N.L., Fedio, P., Brooks, R., Mansi, L., and De Chiro, G. (1984): Ann. Neurol. (Suppl.), 15:170-174.
6. Cohen, M.B., Graham, L.S., and Lake, R. (1986): J. Nucl. Med., 27:769-774.
7. De Leon, M.J., George, A.E., and Ferris, S.J. (1984): J. Comput. Assist. Tomogr., 8:88-94.
8. Deroucsne, C., Rancurel, G., and Le Poncin Lafitte, M., (1985): Lancet, i:1282 (Abstract).
9. Duara, R., Grady, C., and Haxby, J. (1984): Ann. Neurol., 16:702-713.
10. Duara, R., Grady, C., Haxby, J., Sundaram, M., Cutler, N.R., Heston, L., Moore, A., Schlageter, N., Larson, S., and Rapoport, S.I. (1986): Neurology, 36:879-887.
11. Eckleman, W.C., Reba, R.C., and Rzeszotarski, R. (1984): Science, 223:291-292.
12. Evens, R.G., Siegel, B.A., and Welch, M.J. (1983): Am. J. Roentgenol., 131:1073-1076.

13. Farkas, T., Ferris, S.H., and Wolf, A.P. (1982): <u>Am. J. Psychiatry</u>, 139:352-353.
14. Fazekas, F., Alavi, A., McCarthy, K., Chawluk, J., and Zimmerman, R.A. (1986): <u>J. Nucl. Med.</u>, 27:969 (Abstract).
15. Foster, N.L., Chase, T.N., Fedio, P., Patronas, N.J., Brooks, R., and DiChiro, G. (1983): <u>Neurology</u>, 33:961-965.
16. Frackowiak, R.S., Lenzi, G-L., Jones, T., and Heather, J.D. (1980): <u>J. Comput. Assist. Tomogr.</u>, 4:727-736.
17. Frackowiak, R.S., Pozzilli, C., and Legg, N.J., (1981): <u>Brain</u>, 104:753-778.
18. Friedland, R.P., Budinger, T.F., and Ganz, E. (1983): <u>J. Comput. Assist. Tomogr.</u>, 7:590-598.
19. Friedland, R.P., Budinger, T.F., Koss, E., and Ober, B.A. (1985): <u>Neurosci. Lett.</u>, 53:235-240.
20. Hoedt-Rasmussen, L., Sveinsdottir, E., and Lassen, N.A. (1966): <u>Circ. Res.</u>, 18:237-247.
21. Holman, B.L., Gibson, R.E., Hill, T.C., Eckelman, W.C., Albert, M., and Reba, R.C. (1985): <u>JAMA</u>, 254:3063-3066.
22. Holman, B.L., Lee, R.G.L., and Hill, T.C. (1984): <u>J. Nucl. Med.</u>, 25:25-30.
23. Johnson, K.H., Mueller, S.T., and Walshe, T.M. (1985): <u>Neurology</u> (Suppl 1.), 35:235 (Abstract).
24. Kuhl, D.E., Metter, E.J., and Riege, W.H. (1984): <u>Ann. Neurol.</u>, 15:419-424.
25. Kuhl, D.E., Metter, E.J., Riege, W.H., and Phelps, M.E. (1982): <u>J. Cereb. Blood Flow Metab.</u>, 2:163-171.
26. Kuhl, D.E., Phelps, M.E., Markham, C.H., Metter, E.J., Riege, W., and Winter, J. (1982): <u>Ann. Neurol.</u>, 12:425-432.
27. Lauterbur, P.C. (1973): <u>Nature</u>, 242:190-191.
28. Lebrun-Grandie, P., Baron, J.C., Soussaline, F., Loch'h, C., Sastre, J., and Bousser, M.G. (1983): <u>Arch. Neurol.</u>, 40:230-236.
29. Mash, D.S., and Potter, L.T. (1983): <u>Soc. Neurosci.</u> (Abstract), 9:582.
30. Mazziotta, J.C., Phelps, M.E., Pahl, J., Huang, S.C., Wapenski, J., Baxter, L.R., Riege, W., Kuhl, D.E., Selin, C., Sumida, R., and Markham, C. (1986): <u>J. Nucl. Med.</u>, 27:920 (Abstract).
31 McGeer, P.L. (1986): <u>Br. Med. Bull.</u>, 42:24-28.
32. McGeer, P.L., Kamo, H., Harrop, R., and Li, D.K. (1986): <u>Can. Med. Assoc. J.</u>, 134:597-607.
33. Phelps, M.E., Mazziotta, J.C., Schelbert, H.R., Hawkings, R.A., and Engle, J., Jr. (1986): <u>J. Nucl. Med.</u>, 26:1353-1358.
34. Phelps, M.E., Mazziotta, J.C., Wapenski, J., Riege, W., and Baxter, L.R. (1985): <u>J. Nucl. Med.</u>, 26:47 (Abstract).

35. Phelps, M.E., Schelbert, H.R., and Mazziotta, J.C. (1984):
    Continuing Education Lecture Series, CEL 34, Society of
    Nuclear Medicine, New York (Audiovisual).
36. Sharp, P., Gemmell, H., Cherryman, G., Besson, J.,
    Crawford, J., and Smith, F. (1986): J. Nucl. Med.,
    27:761-768.
37. Sokoloff, L., Reivich, M., and Kennedy, C. (1977): J.
    Neurochem., 28:897-916.
38. Ter-Pogossian, M.M. (1986): J. Nucl. Med., 26:1387-1398
    (Abstract).
39. Troutner, D.E., Volkert, W.A., and Hoffman, T.J. (1984):
    J. Nucl. Med., 24:10 (Abstract).
40. Wagner, H.N. (1986): Semin. Nucl. Med., XVI:51-62.
41. Wagner, H.N., Burns, H.D., Dannals, R.F., Wong, D.F.,
    Langstrom, B., Duelfer, T., Frost, J.J., Ravert, H.T.,
    Links, J.M., Rosenbloom, S., Lukas, S.E., Kramer, A.V.,
    and Kuhar, M.J. (1983): Science, 221:1264-1266.
42. Wang, H.S., Obrist, W.D., and Busse, E.W. (1970): J.
    Psychiatry, 126:1205-12.
43. Wastek, G.J., and Yamamura, H.I. (1978): Med. Pharmacol.,
    13:768-780.
44. Whitehouse, P.J. (1985): Trends Neurosci., 8:434-437
    (Abstract).
45. Whitehouse, P.J., Rajagopalan, R., Kitt, C.A, Jones, B.E.,
    Niehoff, D.L., Kuhar, M.J., Price, D.L. (1984):
    Neurology (Suppl. 1), 34:121.
46. Winchell, H.S., Baldwin, R.M., and Lin, T.H. (1980): J.
    Nucl. Med., 21:940-946.
47. Wong, D.F., Gjedde, A., and Wagner, H.N. (1986): J. Cereb.
    Blood Flow Metab., 6:137-136.
48. Wong, D.F., Gjedde, A., Wagner, H.N., Dannals, R.F.,
    Douglass, K.H., Links, J.M., and Kuhar, M. (1986): J.
    Cereb. Blood Flow Metab., 6:147-153.
49. Wong, D.F., Wagner, H.N., and Dannals, R.F. (1984):
    Science, 226:1393-1396.

Central Nervous System Disorders of Aging:
Clinical Intervention and Research, edited by
Randy Strong et al. Raven Press, New York
© 1988.

THE DIAGNOSTIC DILEMMA OF DEPRESSIVE PSEUDODEMENTIA

George T. Grossberg and Raj Nakra

Division of Geriatric Psychiatry,
Department of Psychiatry and Human Behavior,
St. Louis University Medical Center,
St. Louis, Missouri 63104

Dementia and depression are the two most common mental disorders of later life (19). It is estimated that 5 to 15% of people over age 65 are moderately demented, with approximately 2 million people currently affected (12). Estimates of the prevalence of depression vary from 5 to 44% (2). One study found symptoms of major depressive illness in 3.7% of the elderly and dysphoric symptoms in 14.7% (2). Particularly alarming is the rise in suicides in the elderly, with the suicide rate in men over 65 years of age being 3 times that of the general population (8).

In this chapter, when speaking of dementia, we will be referring to DAT, which accounts for nearly 70% of the progressive dementias (25). Evidence is mounting that many patients diagnosed as having dementia of the Alzheimer's type (DAT) are being misdiagnosed (5). The notion of depression mimicking a dementing illness such as DAT has been termed depressive pseudodementia. Obviously, the need to be able to differentiate depression from dementia is crucial, as depression in the elderly is reversible in most cases.

In this chapter, the authors will review current diagnostic criteria for dementia as well as depression and highlight the controversy over the term depressive pseudodementia. We will explore how and why the signs and symptoms of depression in the elderly may resemble those of DAT and offer the reader some help in differential diagnosis (20).

DEMENTIA AND DEPRESSION

Definitions

Table 1 contains the diagnostic criteria for dementia as adapted from the Diagnostic and Statistical Manual (DSM) III of the American Psychiatric Association. DSM III divides the dementias into three major groups: (1) primary degenerative dementia, which includes DAT and Pick's disease. Additional criteria for DAT would be an "insidious onset with a uniformly progressive course" and "exclusion of other specific causes of dementia" (6); (2) multi-infarct dementia; and (3) dementias arising from other etiologies. The major feature of primary degenerative dementia is a broad decline in intellectual functioning which interferes with the individual's social and/or occupational functioning. In order to fulfill the diagnostic criteria for dementia, the patient must show memory impairment as well as at least one of a variety of other symptoms or signs. Importantly, the state of consciousness should not be clouded, i.e., the patient should be fully alert.

TABLE 1. Dementia

Diagnostic criteria

A. Loss of intellectual abilities of sufficient severity to interfere with social or occupational functioning.
B. Memory impairment.
C. At least one of the following:
   1. Impaired abstract thinking
   2. Impaired judgment
   3. Other disturbances of higher cortical functioning, e.g., aphasia, apraxia, agnosia, constructional difficulty
   4. Personality change, i.e., alteration of accentuation of premorbid traits
D. State of consciousness not clouded.
E. Either 1 or 2:
   1. Evidence from a physical examination, lab tests, or history of specific organic factor judged to be etiologically related
   2. In the absence of such evidence (see 1 above), must rule out conditions other than organic mental disorders; and the behavioral change must represent cognitive impairment in a variety of areas

---

The backbone for diagnosing major depression in younger, as well as older, patients is highlighted in Table 2.

TABLE 2. Diagnostic criteria for major depressive episode[a]

A. Dysphoric mood or loss of interest or pleasure in almost all usual activities and pastimes. Mood should be prominent, relatively persistent, and characterized by the patient's feeling depressed, sad, blue, hopeless, low, down in the dumps, or irritable.
B. At least four of the following symptoms occur nearly every day for at least two weeks:
   1. Poor appetite or significant weight loss
   2. Insomnia or hypersomnia
   3. Psychomotor agitation or retardation (objective)
   4. Loss of interest or pleasure in usual activities, or decrease in sexual drive
   5. Loss of energy, fatigue
   6. Feelings of worthlessness, self reproach, or excessive or inappropriate guilt
   7. Complaint or evidence of decreased concentration or ability to think
   8. Recurrent thoughts of death, suicidal ideation or suicide attempt
C. Clinical picture not dominated solely by either:
   1. Delusion or hallucination, or
   2. Bizarre behavior
D. Not superimposed on schizophrenia, schizophreniform, or paranoid disorder
E. Not due to organic mental disorder or uncomplicated bereavement

[a]Adapted from DSM III

   To diagnose a patient's major or endogenous depression which would require chemical, i.e., antidepressant, intervention, one first needs a prominent and persistent lowering of mood. Additionally, there should be at least four key symptoms (Table 2) on a day-to-day basis for at least two weeks. This criteria was established to exclude milder, less severe depressive reactions such as grief and situational depressions where some of these symptoms may be found, but not daily for two weeks.

Pseudodementia Terminology Controversy

   Though some investigators (15,18) have advocated either abandoning or changing the term depressive pseudodementia, there is little disagreement that the features of major depression in the elderly can resemble those seen with dementia. Kiloh (14) was the first to systematically study the syndrome of depressive pseudodementia. He defined depressive pseudodementia as a condition in which the picture of dementia may be very closely mimicked at the outset, but the subsequent course of the illness is such that it is incompatible with a diagnosis of dementia. In the patients he described, depressive pseudodementia was not only associated with endogenous depression, but also with hysteria and other psychiatric syndromes. Kiloh also found that a past psychiatric history, a short course of illness with abrupt onset, and the results of a therapeutic trial of antidepressants were the most sensitive diagnostic tools in differentiating depression from dementia.

Wells (24), in his study of ten patients, noted that depressive pseudodementia could be associated with a variety of primary psychiatric illnesses including personality disorders and depression. He also outlined several clinical features which together can help differentiate depressive pseudodementia from dementia. Table 3 lists clinical features which we have found particularly helpful in differentiating between depressive pseudodementia and dementia.

TABLE 3. Differences between depressive pseudodementia
and dementia[a]

Depressive Pseudodementia	Dementia
Clinical course and history	
Family aware of dysfunction and its severity	Family often unaware
Onset can be dated fairly precisely	Vague, insidious onset
Prior history of psychiatric illness	No psychiatric history
Rapid progression of symptoms after onset	Show progression throughout
Complaints and clinical behavior	
Patients frequently complain of cognitive loss	Patients rarely complain
Patients communicate strong sense of distress	Patients often appear unconcerned
Clinical features related to memory, cognitive and intellectual dysfunction	
"Don't know" answers typical (patients unwilling to hazard guesses)	Near-miss answers typical (patients will guess if encouraged)
Recent and remote memory loss equally severe	Memory loss for recent events more severe
Variability in performance on tasks of similar difficulty	Consistently poor performance on tasks of similar difficulty

[a]Adapted from Wells (24).

More recently, investigators (15,23) have pointed out that though a variety of functional psychiatric syndromes can resemble dementia, it is the "dementia syndrome of depression" (9), a reversible syndrome of dementia often found in older adults with major depression, which poses the greatest challenge in differential diagnosis. The "dementia syndrome of depression" arises from the fact that elderly patients with major depression may present with memory and concentration problems. How does one make the differential diagnosis?

DIFFERENTIAL DIAGNOSIS

Differentiating major depression from dementia in the elderly may be difficult. Poor appetite, sleep disturbance, agitation, loss of interest, concentration and thinking problems (see Table 2) are commonly found in varying degrees in dementia as well as major depression in the elderly. Cummings and Benson's (5) DAT inventory may be helpful in identifying patients with dementia. The inventory includes aphasia, amnesia, abnormal cognition and visuospatial skills, inappropriate lack of concern, and normal motor functions. However, it is least useful in early stages of disease when such features as aphasia are not fully developed and in late dementia when motor functions become impaired. Straker (22) has proposed that trained clinicians can "empathically" differentiate between the "disorganized confusion" seen in demented patients versus the "despairing helplessness" of depressives. Rabins et al. (17) have proposed the following criteria for diagnosing reversible dementia caused by depression: a past history of affective disorder, subacute onset, persistently depressed or dysphoric mood, poor appetite and weight loss, and delusions of self blame, hopelessness, or physical ill health. These suggest a treatable cause of dementia.

In our experience, the most difficult cases to properly diagnose are:

(1) older adults with atypical presentations of depression, i.e., those whose presenting complaint is not one of depression, but who upon further exploration may be found to have major depression (see Masked Depression section);

(2) individuals with coexisting early dementia and depression (16). Some investigators have found that nearly 25% of patients with dementia also are depressed and that depression is most common early in the course of dementia (17,19). This relationship between dementia and major depression is intriguing, especially from a neurochemical standpoint. As far back as 1970, Schildkraut (21) implicated noradrenaline as the neurotransmitter most likely to be disturbed in depression. Elsewhere in this volume, Burke et al. document extensive impairment in noradrenergic neurotransmission in dementia, possibly indicating a neurochemical basis for the overlap of depression and dementia.

(3) the so-called "pseudodepressive patients" (7) referred for depression who are found to have a primary dementing illness.

Perhaps the key is to become familiar with the diagnostic hallmarks of major depression in the elderly, keeping in mind that geriatric patients may not present with the full panoply of DSM III signs and symptoms, but instead may present with the following features, some of which are only rarely found in younger depressives (11).

Decreased Activity Level

One of the first signs of impending major depression, discovered through talking with the patient or his family, may be a lack of interest in usual clubs or activities. The 85-year-old patient in the nursing home who used to enjoy bingo but no longer participates is a common example.

Masked Depression

The patient presents with a multiplicity of vague, nonspecific, somatic complaints such as headaches, low back pain, and gastrointestinal problems. Typically, no organic cause is found, and the patient is given medication for symptomatic relief. These patients often "shop around" from physician to physician, and their symptoms do not respond to somatic treatments. What the physician often fails to do is to sit down with the patient and the patient's family and inquire about what is going on in that person's life. Have there been recent stresses or losses? Is it possible that a major depression is presenting in atypical fashion?

Persistent Complaints of Lack of Energy

Geriatric patients often complain of a profound lack of energy. They may say, "I don't know what's wrong with me. If only I had more pep." This symptom may be the hallmark of a major depression in the geriatric patient.

Role Reversal

The formerly active geriatric patient who becomes increasingly dependent on others in the environment may be suffering from major depression. This phenomenon, also called "regression," is not uncommon in institutional settings or postoperatively (10). Regression can lead to increased morbidity/mortality and should always be aggressively treated, particularly in the postoperative geriatric patient (10).

Preoccupation with the Past

Life review, or reminiscence, may be the most important psychological task in the final phase of life (3). Older patients have a need to review their past; and by coming to accept the past as they lived it, they help prepare themselves for eventual death. However, some patients become so overly preoccupied with the past, perhaps even with a trivial wrong, that they can no longer focus on the here and now. These patients are at risk for major depression of perhaps psychotic proportions.

Malnutrition

Elderly patients are more likely than younger persons to suffer a very serious depression in which they may become almost mute, refuse to eat and drink, and take to bed. These depressions are life-threatening because most older people cannot tolerate dehydration and malnutrition (11). Such patients often have delusions, particularly somatic delusions about cancer or other intractable illnesses. These patients most often live alone and are more vulnerable to the development of hypothermia, delirium, and other medical complications if appropriate therapy is delayed. Such patients should be promptly hospitalized for assessment of nutritional status and treatment of depression.

Suicidal Ideation

The elderly depressive patient should always be questioned about suicidal ideation and intent (11). The suicide rate for elderly white men is three to four times the national average. Successful suicides in elderly depressive patients occur most often early (within six months of onset) (4). Predictors of suicide risk include increased age, male sex, widowed or divorced status, isolation, alcohol or drug abuse, and the presence of debilitating diseases (1). The suicide rate peaks for men between the ages of 80 and 90, and for women between the ages of 50 and 65 (1). A psychotically depressed patient is at great risk for suicide, especially if he hears voices commanding him to hurt himself or if his delusions center around the idea that his family would be better off without him.

Memory and Concentration Problems

Elderly patients with major depression may present with deteriorating memory and ability to concentrate. They may fear that they have Alzheimer's disease. In 1982, Jarvik (13) noted that as many as one third of patients diagnosed as demented may suffer from depression that may closely mimic the cognitive loss experienced in dementia. Depressed patients complain of being forgetful, may neglect their hygiene, and may even show severe apathy. Noteworthy is rapid progression of symptoms in cognitive loss, patchy loss of memory, impaired concentration, and frequent responses of "I don't know," "I can't remember," or "ask my son or daughter". Memory loss is frequently a complaint of the patients themselves, as opposed to family complaints, in cases of dementia. Mental status examination and observation of the patient are helpful in the diagnosis. The depressed patient may show evidence of rapid progression of memory loss and psychomotor retardation. They also frequently manifest anxiety, agitation, multiple somatic complaints, lack of appetite, loss of weight, loss of sleep, loss of interest in hobbies, and other symptoms typical of depression. Patients with dementia generally show gradual decline in memory and intellectual functions without loss of appetite.

Thorough physical, neurological, mental status and cognitive evaluations; a review of the patient's prescribed and over-the-counter medications to rule out drugs that may precipitate depression in the elderly; a basic hematologic workup including electrolytes, chemistry panel, complete blood count with differential, T_3, T_4, TSH levels, and serum B_{12} and folic acid levels may uncover depressive reactions secondary to underlying illnesses. In some instances, neuropsychological testing may help to further elucidate the diagnosis. If depression is suspected, a vigorous treatment trial is warranted (7).

SUMMARY

Major depression may mimic dementia (DAT) in the elderly. Careful review of signs and symptoms of depression in the elderly and awareness of atypical presentations can help differentiate between depression, a largely remediable problem, and dementia, a progressive brain disease.

REFERENCES

1. Avant, R. (1983): Fam. Pract. Recertification, 5(Suppl. 1): 41-48.
2. Blazer, D., and Williams, C.D. (1980): Am. J. Psychiatry, 137:439-444.
3. Butler, R.W. (1963): Psychiatry, 26:65.
4. Charatan, F.B. (1985): Psychiatr. Ann., 15:313-316.
5. Cummings, J.L., and Benson, F. (1986): J. Am. Ger. Soc., 34:12-19.
6. Diagnostic and Statistical Manual, Ed. 3, American Psychiatric Association, 1980.
7. Feinberg, T., and Goodman, B. (1984): J. Clin. Psychiatry, 45:99-103.
8. Finlayson, R.E., and Martin, L.E. (1982): Mayo Clin. Proc., 57:115-120.

9. Folstein, M.F., and McHugh, P.R. (1978): In: Alzheimer's Disease: Senile Dementia and Related Disorders (Aging, Vol. 7), edited by R. Katzman, R.D. Terry, and K.L. Bick. Raven Press, New York.
10. Grossberg, G.T. (1984): In: Anesthesia and the Geriatric Patient, edited by S.W. Krechel, pp. 63-72. Grune & Stratton, New York.
11. Grossberg, G.T., and Nakra, B. (1986): Comprehensive Therapy, 12:16-22.
12. Hamill, R.W., and Buell, S.J. (1982): J. Am. Ger. Soc., 30:781-787.
13. Jarvik, L.F. (1982): Consultant, 22:141-146.
14. Kiloh, L.G. (1961): Acta Psychiatr. Scand., 37:336-351.
15. McAllister, T. (1983): Am. J. Psychiatry, 140:528-533.
16. McAllister, T., and Price, T. (1982): Am. J. Psychiatry, 139:626-629.
17. Rabins, P.V., Merchant, A., and Nestedt, G. (1984): British Journal of Psychiatry, 144:488-492.
18. Reifler, B. (1982): J. Am. Ger. Soc., 30:665-668.
19. Reifler, B. (1986): J. Clin. Psychiatry, 47:354-356.
20. Reifler, B., Larson, E., Teri, L., and Poulsen, M. (1986): J. Am. Ger. Soc., 34:855-859.
21. Schildkraut, J.J. (1970): Neuropsychopharmacology and the Affective Disorders. Little, Brown and Co., Boston.
22. Straker, M. (1984): Psychiatr. Ann., 14:2:96-99.
23. Thase, M., and Reynolds, C. (1984): Psychosomatics, 25:256-260.
24. Wells, C. (1979): Am. J. Psychiatry, 136:7:895-900.
25. Winokur, G., and Clayton, P. (1986): The Medical Basis of Psychiatry, pp. 10-20. W.B. Saunders Co., Philadelphia.

Central Nervous System Disorders of Aging:
Clinical Intervention and Research, edited by
Randy Strong et al. Raven Press, New York
© 1988.

PRESENT STATUS OF TARDIVE DYSKINESIA

Edward F. Domino

Department of Pharmacology
University of Michigan
Ann Arbor, Michigan 48109-0010

Tardive dyskinesia (TD) is one of the major problems in the treatment of schizophrenic patients (1,5,13). The seriousness of TD cannot be overemphasized. In a patient taking chronic antipsychotic (neuroleptic) medication (especially if he or she is older, or she is edentulous and postmenopausal), the risk of developing TD is as high as 75%. TD is a major problem that seriously limits the usefulness of current neuroleptic medication. Many day care and outpatient facilities for schizophrenic patients only exist because of the concurrent use of neuroleptics. There is an incredible lack of support for basic and clinical research on the best medication to use chronically, as well as whether drug-free holidays promote or reduce the risk of developing TD. It is still not clear at present whether the risk of TD is less with the chronic use of a neuroleptic like thioridazine, which has significant atropine-like properties, versus the use of haloperidol, which does not. Does the concurrent use of atropine-like antiparkinsonian drugs with neuroleptics like haloperidol enhance or reduce the development of TD?

The prevalence of TD dramatically increases as patients age. Geriatric patients in their seventies may show a sixfold greater prevalence of TD than young adults under 40 years of age. Jeste and Wyatt (6) have summarized much of the literature which emphasizes the importance of aging in the manifestations of TD. Fig. 1 is reproduced from their review, which illustrates this fact.

Elderly patients, particularly those in nursing home settings, are often prescribed neuroleptic drugs for psychoses that are not due to schizophrenia. For example, neuroleptics

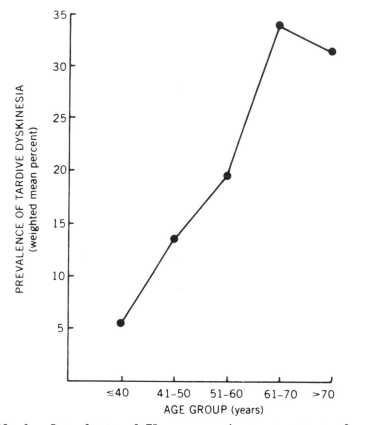

FIG. 1. 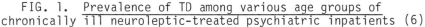 Prevalence of TD among various age groups of
chronically ill neuroleptic-treated psychiatric inpatients (6)

may be prescribed to manage patients with dementia who are
agitated and difficult to control. Ideally, such patients
should be given neuroleptics that have minimal extrapyramidal
side effects in very small dosages. However, the
anticholinergic properties of neuroleptics which have less
acute extrapyramidal effects tend to detract from their
utility. Thus, their enhanced susceptibility to TD makes
management of demented and psychotic geriatric patients very
difficult. Furthermore, geriatric patients tend to have senile
dyskinesia even if never given neuroleptics. Such senile
dyskinesia is similar in its signs and symptoms to TD, but a
history of neuroleptic use is lacking. This makes
identification of TD in geriatric patients more difficult.

A simple way of preventing TD is to not prescribe
neuroleptics to patients who are nonresponders. Of course,
neuroleptic drug therapy should only be given to patients when
such therapy is indicated and when benefits outweigh the risks
of side effects and the economic costs of chronic medication.

This issue is especially pertinent in the current medical-legal climate in the United States where a physician can be sued for either not medicating or overmedicating a patient, and especially for not informing all concerned persons of the risks and benefits of neuroleptic therapy.

SIDE EFFECTS OF NEUROLEPTIC AGENTS

There are many different antipsychotic or neuroleptic drugs. All of the agents listed in Table 1 have some pharmacological actions in common with the prototype drug, chlorpromazine. However, many of the current agents do have significant pharmacological differences that result in a variety of side effects and differ qualitatively and quantitatively from chlorpromazine.

TABLE 1. Various neuroleptics currently available

Class and generic name	Trade name
Phenothiazines	
Aliphatic	
Chlorpromazine	Thorazine
Triflupromazine	Vesprin
Piperidine	
Thioridazine	Mellaril
Mesoridazine	Serentil
Piperazine	
Trifluoperazine	Stelazine
Fluphenazine	Prolixin, Permitil
Acetophenazine	Tindal
Perphenazine	Trilafon
Thioxanthenes	
Chlorprothixene	Taractan
Thiothixene	Navane
Butyrophenones	
Haloperidol	Haldol
Dibenzoxazepines	
Loxapine	Loxitane
Dihydroindolones	
Molindone	Moban

We probably do not need so many different agents, although it is important that some drug options be available to treat specific patients. The oral dose range and mg potency of the various neuroleptic drugs vary widely, yet they all show equal efficacy. That is, each drug is equally effective in treating about two of three schizophrenic patients. Although some patients do not respond to one class of medication but do respond to another, the total percentage of patients responding

is the same--about 66% on the average. It is possible to list
the equivalent dosages of various agents as shown in Table 2.

TABLE 2. Equivalent dosage of various neuroleptics

Neuroleptic	Approximate dosage (mg/day)	Potency (mg equivalents)
Chlorpromazine	400-1000	100
Thioridazine	400-800	100
Loxapine	40-120	10
Molindone	40-120	10
Trifluoperazine	20-60	5
Thiothixene	20-60	5
Fluphenazine	10-40	2
Haloperidol	10-40	2

The neuroleptics produce many different adverse or unwanted
side effects. These are summarized in Table 3. Some of the
most devastating side effects from a social and occupational
standpoint are the extrapyramidal motor side effects of
neuroleptics. These are summarized in Table 4. There is a
close relationship between abnormal movements induced by
neuroleptics and age and disease (Table 5). In addition, some
symptoms are exacerbated by drug overdose and others by drug
withdrawal. The response to anticholinergic therapy together
with a history may be helpful in determining the etiology of
the motor side effects.

TABLE 3. Adverse effects produced by neuroleptics

Autonomic
  Dry mouth
  Constipation, ileus
  Blurred near vision
  Urinary retention
  Delayed ejaculation
Behavioral
  Sedation
  Tardive psychosis (?)
  Seizures
Cardiovascular
  Orthostatic hypotension
  EKG changes
Endocrine and metabolic
  Amenorrhea
  Galactorrhea
  Gynecomastia
  Weight gain

Extrapyramidal
  Pseudoparkinsonism
  Dystonic reactions
  Akathisia
  Tardive dyskinesia
  Tardive dystonia
Pigmentation
  Corneal, lenticular
  Retinopathy
  Skin
Toxic and allergic
  Skin
  Hematologic
Neuroleptic
malignant syndrome

TABLE 4. Extrapyramidal side effects of neuroleptics

PSEUDOPARKINSONISM
Akinesia:
Rigidity and immobility
Stiffness and slowness of
    voluntary movement
Mask-like facial expression
Drooling (sialorrhea)
Stooped posture
Shuffling, festinating gait
Slow, monotonous speech
Tremor:
Regular rhythmic oscillations
    of extremities, especially
    hands and fingers, pill-
    rolling movement of fingers

AKATHISIA
Inability to sit still,
constant pacing; continuous
agitation and restless
movements; rocking or
shifting of weight while
standing; shifting of
leg, tapping of feet while
sitting

TARDIVE DYSKINESIA
Mouth: Rhythmical involuntary
    movements of tongue, lips or
    jaw; protrusion of tongue,
    puckering of mouth, chewing
    movements (buccal-lingual-
    masticatory triad)
Choreiform: Irregular purpose-
    less involuntary quick
    movements of the extremities;
    flailing movements
Athetoid: Continuous arrhythmic
    worm-like slow movements
    of the extremities
Axial hyperkinesis: To and fro
    clonic movements of spine

DYSTONIC REACTIONS
Oculogyric crisis: Fixed
    upward gaze
Torticollis: Neck twisting
Opisthotonos: Arching of back
Trismus: Clenched or lockjaw
Others: Spasm of muscles
    resulting in facial
    grimaces, exaggerated
    posturing of head or
    jaw, and difficulty
    in speech and swallowing

TABLE 5. Motor side effects of neuroleptics

Syndrome	Neuroleptic Related		Age and Disease Related
	Overdose	Withdrawal	
Dystonia	Acute or Prolonged Anticholinergic Sensitive	Tardive Dystonia Anticholinergic Resistant	Senile Dystonia Anticholinergic Resistant
Parkinsonism	Acute or Prolonged Rabbit (Meigs') Syndrome	?	Advancing age Influenza Self-administration of N-methyl phenyl-tetra-hydropiperidine
	Anticholinergic Sensitive		Anticholinergic Sensitive
Hyperkinesia	Initial Akathisia Stereotypes Anticholinergic Sensitive Sensitive	Tardive Akathisia Tardive Dyskinesia Anticholinergic Resistant	Senile akathisia Schizophrenic Akathisia Senile Dyskinesia Schizophrenic Stereotypes Anticholinergic Resistant

It is important to recognize that the neuroleptic drugs differ widely in their profile of side effects. This is summarized in Table 6. The extrapyramidal side effects are inversely related to the degree of anticholinergic activity. However, with increasing anticholinergic activity, there is an increase in two other unwanted side effects, sedation and hypotension.

TABLE 6. Degree of side effects of various neuroleptics

Drug	Sedation	Extrapyramidal	Anticholinergic	Hypotension
Haloperidol	1	4	1	1
Fluphenazine	1	4	2	1
Thiothixene	2	3	2	1
Trifluoperazine	2	3	2	2
Loxapine	2	3	2	2
Molindone	2	3	2	2
Chlorpromazine	4	2	3	4
Thioridazine	4	1	4	4

1=least; 4=greatest

DIAGNOSIS AND EVALUATION OF TARDIVE DYSKINESIA

The differential diagnosis of TD requires exclusion of a variety of neurologic diseases including Huntington's, Meigs' and Wilson's. In addition, there are idiopathic dyskinesias associated with psychoses and old age that are non-neuroleptic related. A very small number of patients with hyperthyroidism, hypoparathyroidism, chorea, lupus erythematosus, and a dyskinetic postencephalitic syndrome may occasionally be confused with true TD.

Obtaining an adequate drug history is important in diagnosing TD. It is not generally realized that a large variety of drugs can induce hyperkinesia. Although neuroleptics are by far the most likely offenders, under rare circumstances anticholinergics, antihistaminics, anticonvulsants, antimalarials (chloroquine-like), amphetamines, estrogens, and lithium salts can induce increased motor activity that may be confused with TD if an adequate drug history is not obtained.

Two TD rating scales that have been used extensively since the 1970s are the Abnormal Involuntary Movements Scale and the Dyskinesia Rating Scale. Both have advantages and disadvantages. Our own experience with Abnormal Involuntary Movements Scale has been satisfactory (4). Patients on chronic neuroleptics should be periodically evaluated and an objective assessment of their involuntary movements using a rating scale should be included as part of their permanent medical records. The major clinical features of TD include akathisia, a darting tongue (fly-catching), body rocking, repetitive movements, marching-in-place, and oral-lingual-buccal dyskinesia.

Crow (3) in England has pointed out that there are two major types of schizophrenic patients: type I, those that respond well to antipsychotic drugs; and type II, those who do not. Patients with paranoid schizophrenia or patients with "good prognosis" schizophrenia, as well as schizophreniform disorder, and reactive schizophrenia represent type I schizophrenia. Type II patients are process schizophrenics with a "defect state." Schizophrenic patients can go from type I to type II, but it is unlikely that they will progress from type II to type I. Type I patients may develop type II disease. Type I patients have more positive symptoms, delusions, hallucinations, and significant paranoid thoughts, as opposed to type II patients who have negative symptoms, flattened affect, reduced speech, and loss of drive. Type I patients are more acutely psychotic. Type II patients have the more chronic forms of schizophrenia. Especially important from a therapeutic point of view, type I patients respond well to neuroleptic drugs, whereas, type II patients respond poorly. In type I patients, intellectual impairment is generally absent, whereas, in type II patients there may be some intellectual impairment. Type I schizophrenia is associated with disturbed dopaminergic neurotransmission. Some drug-free, type I schizophrenic patients have about a 30% increase in the number of dopamine receptors in their brain. In contrast, type II schizophrenic patients have a normal level of dopamine receptors but a relatively mild, unknown type of neuronal cell loss that produces mild or "soft" structural changes in the brain such as dilated ventricles. Inasmuch as type II schizophrenic patients do not respond well to neuroleptic medication, it may very well be that the risks of drug therapy far outweigh the benefits. Hence, neuroleptic medication is not indicated chronically, but only during acute exacerbations of their illness.

NEURAL MECHANISMS AND TREATMENT OF TD

Our knowledge of the neural mechanisms of TD is very limited (2,7-10). The dopamine receptor hypersensitivity hypothesis is only partially applicable to some TD patients. After chronic neuroleptic medication, it is postulated that pharmacological denervation supersensitivity occurs with up-regulation of dopamine receptors. Hence, neuroleptic withdrawal unmasks an excess of dopamine receptors and leads to the signs and symptoms of TD. If this were the only mechanism for producing TD, one would expect that symptoms of TD would resolve in a matter of months pending down-regulation of dopamine receptors. Only some patients show reversal of their TD symptoms in a matter of months; many do not. The dopamine receptor hypersensitivity theory has led to the novel use of levodopa desensitization therapy in the treatment of TD. Since too much dopamine and too little gamma-aminobutyric acid and possibly acetylcholine may also involve the neural mechanisms of TD, there has been a great deal of interest in giving acetylcholine precursors or gamma-aminobutyric acid potentiators like the benzodiazepines to enhance the activity of those neurotransmitters. Catecholamine synthesis inhibitors like alpha-methyl-para-tyrosine or catecholamine depletors like reserpine or tetrabenazine reduce dopamine. Only very modest therapeutic success has resulted from such therapies. Hence, the current treatment of TD is very unsatisfactory (7,11). Once a diagnosis of TD is made, the issue of whether neuroleptic medication should be stopped must be addressed immediately. If the psychotic state is not manageable without medication or if the psychosis returns or is markedly exaggerated, then appropriate medical consultations with informed written consent involving the patient, the legal guardian, and key family members must be undertaken. Subsequently, one may resume neuroleptic medication using the lowest dose possible of a "broad spectrum" agent. If no psychosis emerges upon withdrawal of neuroleptic medication and the symptoms of TD are mild, no further drug treatments are indicated, except perhaps the use of a benzodiazepine if the patient is agitated. On the other hand, if the resultant psychosis is severe, then use of reserpine or levodopa desensitization, alpha-methyl-para-tyrosine, and benzodiazepines are indicated. Our experience with lecithin has been disappointing (4), although it certainly may be tried as the side effects are minimal.

CONCLUSIONS

As illustrated in Fig. 2, there are many factors influencing the incidence of TD, of which the duration and the total dose of neuroleptic treatment are most important. Increasing age, female sex, prolonged drug-free holidays, lack of teeth or ill-fitting teeth, biological predisposition including presence or absence of significant psychiatric or neurologic diseases, and other unknown factors are clearly involved. The reasons why the elderly are especially prone to TD are unknown. Further research is needed to clarify each of these variables before significant progress in the prevention and treatment of TD can occur. Recently, it has been reported (12) that moderate to severe facial dyskinesia is associated with a shortened life expectancy in psychiatric patients with schizophrenia or manic-depressive psychosis. Data of this type underscore the importance of constant monitoring and the use of minimal effective amounts of the neuroleptics. TD probably results from a combination of factors including the primary mental disease and long-term neuroleptic medication. The role of polypharmacy in the elderly and the problem of drug-drug interactions further complicate the problems of those who are also mentally ill.

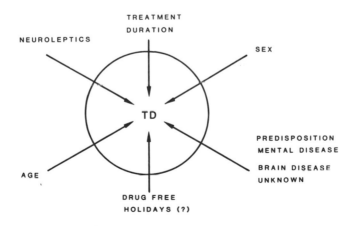

FIG. 2. Factors determining tardive dyskinesia

REFERENCES

1. Baldessarini, R.J., Cole, J.O., Davis, J.M., Gardos, G.,
   Simpson, G., and Tarsy, D. (1980): Tardive Dyskinesia,
   Task Force Report No. 18, American Psychiatric
   Association, Washington, D.C.
2. Baldessarini, R.J., and Tarsy, D. (1979): Int. Rev.
   Neurobiol., 21:1-45.
3. Crow, T.J. (1980): Br. J. Psychiatry, 137:383-386.
4. Domino, E.F., May, W.W., Demetriou, S., Mathews, B.,
   Tait, S., and Kovacic, B. (1985): Biol. Psychiatry,
   20:1189-1196.
5. Fann, W.E., Smith, R.C., Davis, J., and Domino, E.F.,
   editors (1985): Tardive Dyskinesia: Research and
   Treatment. Spectrum Publications, New York.
6. Jeste, D.V., and Wyatt, R.J. (1981): Am. J. Psychiatry,
   138:297-309. Reprinted by permission of APA.
7. Jeste, D.V., and Wyatt, R.J. (1982): Understanding and
   Treating Tardive Dyskinesia. Guilford Press, New York.
8. Jeste, D.V., and Wyatt, R.J. (1982): Arch. Gen. Psychiatry,
   39:803-816.
9. Johns, C.A., Greenwald, B.S., Mohs, R.C., and Davis, K.L.
   (1983): Psychopharmacol. Bull., 19:185-197.
10. Klawans, H.L. (1973): Am. J. Psychiatry, 130:82-86.
11. Kobayashi, R.M. (1977): N. Engl. J. Med., 296:257-260.
12. McClelland, A., Kerr, T.A., Dutta, D.K., and Metcalfe, A.
    (1986): Br. J. Psychiatry, 148:310-316.
13. Simpson, G.M., Varga, E., Lee, J.H., and Zoubok, B. (1978):
    Psychopharmacology, 58:117-124.

Central Nervous System Disorders of Aging:
Clinical Intervention and Research, edited by
Randy Strong et al. Raven Press, New York
© 1988.

AGING AND SLEEP APNEA

John W. Shepard, Jr.

Geriatric Research, Education, and Clinical Center,
Veterans Administration Medical Center; and
Department of Internal Medicine,
St. Louis University School of Medicine,
St. Louis, Missouri 63125

Death marks the cessation of the aging process. Its time
of occurrence has been shown to follow a circadian pattern
with peak death rates occurring between 0400 and 0700 (66).
Sleep-related breathing disorders leading to nocturnal
hypoxemia and potentially lethal cardiac arrhythmias have been
suggested as one pathophysiological mechanism contributing to
this nocturnal peak in human mortality. Snoring, obesity and
hypertension, which increase as a function of age, have all
been identified as risk factors for sleep apnea. When the
snoring pattern becomes periodic during sleep, sleep apnea
usually is present. The fluctuations in blood pressure and
heart rate which coincide with the disordered breathing events
may contribute to premature aging of the cardiovascular
system. Although ventricular ectopy usually decreases during
sleep in healthy individuals, nocturnal hypoxemia has been
associated with life-threatening ventricular tachyarrhythmias
as well as serious bradyarrhythmias. Progress in the field of
sleep medicine has allowed us to diagnose and effectively
treat the majority of individuals with sleep disordered
breathing.

NORMATIVE CHANGES IN SLEEP WITH AGE

Sleep is divided into two major states: rapid eye movement
(REM) sleep in which dreaming predominates and non-rapid eye
movement (NREM) sleep. NREM sleep is further subdivided into
four stages with stages 1 and 2 being considered light sleep
and stages 3 and 4 deep or slow wave sleep. The percentage of
time spent in NREM stages 3 and 4 has been consistently
reported to decrease with age (Fig. 1) (15,47). Sleep

efficiency, defined as total sleep time divided by time in bed, also decreases with age. This occurs primarily because the elderly demonstrate an increased number of awakenings which increase wake time after sleep onset. Although total sleep time tends to decrease with age in overnight studies, the inclusion of daytime naps might actually increase total daily sleep. While a shift toward the lighter stages of NREM sleep may be intrinsic to aging, many investigators now feel that the underlying reason for this shift is the high incidence of sleep pathologies (nocturnal myoclonus and sleep apnea) in the elderly. Once established, daytime napping habits may further contribute to poor consolidation of sleep during the nocturnal hours. Percent time spent in REM sleep remains constant over the adult life span until decreasing in the very old.

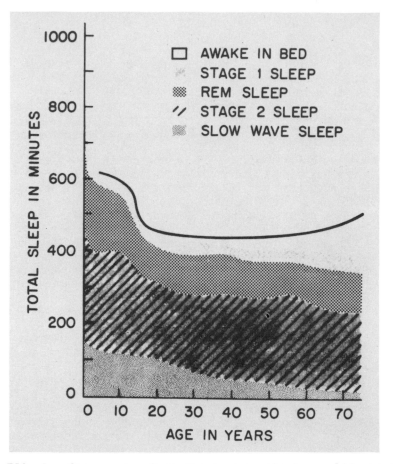

FIG. 1. Changes in sleep stages over the human life span. (From reference 15 with permission.)

SNORING

Snoring was generally considered to be a social nuisance prior to the publication of research linking snoring to more serious medical conditions. In a large scale epidemiological study of snoring, Lugaresi et al. (45) reported that 53% of adult males and 38% of the adult females snored while 31% of the men and 19% of the women were habitual snorers. Six percent of the habitual snorers reported sudden awakenings with the sensation of suffocation. The prevalence of snoring increased with age in both men and women up to 70 years of age, after which it declined. Snoring was associated with obesity as 70% of the obese subjects reported snoring. Only 7% of nonsnorers were obese while 21% of the snorers were obese. Snoring was also linked to hypertension as 14% of habitual snorers were hypertensive while only 7% of the nonsnorers had elevated blood pressures. Pulmonary and systemic pressures were greater in the snorers than nonsnorers, and snorers with overt sleep apnea were even more hypertensive (Fig. 2).

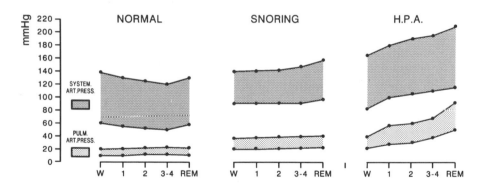

FIG. 2. Systemic and pulmonary blood pressures in normals, heavy snorers, and patients with hypersomnia and periodic apneas (HPA) during sleep and wakefulness. (From reference 45 with permission.)

In a study of 7,511 subjects from Finland, 30% of men and 15% of women aged 40 to 69 were reported as "often" or "habitual" snorers (30). There was a small increase in habitual snoring with age in men and a larger increase in women. Snoring was again found to be significantly associated with obesity and hypertension. The association between snoring and hypertension was significant even after correcting for body mass index. In addition, habitual snoring was significantly associated with angina pectoris in men. This association persisted even after statistically adjusting for hypertension and body mass index. In women, no association with angina pectoris was detected.

In addition to these studies linking snoring to hypertension, angina and obesity, periodic or cyclical snoring is a well-established finding in patients with sleep apnea. Although early published reports stressed the loudness of the snoring, it is the repetitive fluctuations in snoring intensity which strongly suggest coexistent sleep disordered breathing. The cyclical cessation of snoring corresponds with the periods of apnea, and usually last between 10 and 45 seconds (Fig. 3). In the absence of turbulent airflow, tissue vibration in the upper airway and snoring cease. In contrast, regularity of snoring intensity and vibratory frequency suggest greater stability of the breathing pattern. Nighttime recordings of snoring patterns have been used to detect sleep disordered breathing (35,50).

oximeter

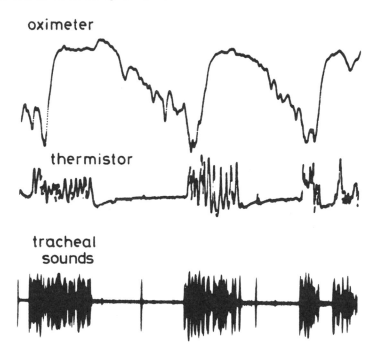

thermistor

tracheal sounds

FIG. 3. Example of an obstructive apnea indicated by the absence of thermistor deflections, tracheal breath sounds and oxyhemoglobin desaturation. (From reference 50 with permission.)

SLEEP APNEA

Definitions

Apnea is defined as the cessation of ventilation for greater than 10 seconds. Hypopnea is generally defined as a reduction in ventilation of sufficient magnitude to result in arterial oxyhemoglobin desaturation. Apneas are subdivided into central, obstructive, and mixed depending on whether respiratory effort is absent, present or begins after a period of initial absence as illustrated in Fig. 4. When the number of apneas exceeds 30 during an overnight sleep study or the apnea index (number of apneas per hour sleep) exceeds 5, a diagnosis of sleep apnea syndrome is usually made. Individuals are classified as having central, obstructive or mixed sleep apnea according to the predominant type of apnea present. While central apneas are commonly observed with noninvasive monitoring, the majority of apneas in adults are either obstructive or mixed. Because patients with pure central sleep apnea are less common, this diagnosis should raise one's suspicion that respiratory effort may have evaded detection by the noninvasive methodologies used in most sleep labs. Esophageal pressure recordings may be required to detect low levels of respiratory effort.

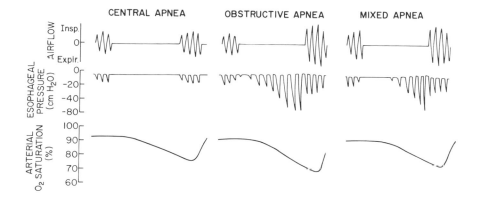

FIG. 4. Patterns of airflow, respiratory effort (esophageal pressure) and arterial oxyhemoglobin saturation in central, obstructive, and mixed apneas. (From Shepard, J.W., Jr., Pathophysiology and medical therapy of sleep apnea. Ear Nose Throat J., 63:198-213, 1984.)

Hypopneas may be due to reductions in ventilatory effort, in which case they are classified as central. When they occur secondary to increased upper airway resistance, they are

appropriately designated obstructive hypopneas. Hypopneas are
usually terminated by arousals and, therefore, contribute to
sleep fragmentation as do apneas. As a result, many
investigators include hypopneas in their calculation of apnea
index or report them as a combined apnea plus hypopnea index.
Individuals with a combined index of less than 20 per hour
would be considered to have mild disease in terms of
frequency, whereas, patients with greater than 60 events per
hour are severely affected. An equally important variable in
assessing apnea severity is the degree of arterial
oxyhemoglobin desaturation. Desaturations below 65% are
considered to be severe and have been associated with
significant cardiac arrhythmias (61).

Prevalence

Lavie et al. (37) have estimated that approximately 3% of
the middle-aged male population has sleep apnea. In elderly
adults, the prevalence of sleep apnea syndrome has been
reported to range from 0 to 62% of the population (2,3,6-9,11,
14,46,55,57,65). The prevalence depends substantially on the
sex and the methods employed to recruit the subjects (Table 1).
Sleep apnea has consistently been found to be more prevalent
in the male population. When elderly subjects were highly
selected for good health and the absence of sleep complaints,
low prevalences of sleep apnea were observed (6,57). In
contrast, 25 to 30% of elderly subjects are found to have
sleep apnea when randomly recruited (2).
    Although sleep apnea is present in a substantial proportion
of the elderly when defined as an apnea index greater than 5,
the frequency of apneic events in these studies has generally
been in the mild to moderate range. In subjects with
diagnosed sleep apnea syndrome, the mean frequency of
disordered breathing events ranged between 10 and 20 per hour
in 5 studies and between 20 and 30 per hour in the 2 other
studies reporting these data.

Pathophysiology

Considerable discussion has centered around distinguishing
between central and obstructive apneic events. While this
distinction is often therapeutically relevant, it is important
to remember that cyclical fluctuations in respiratory center
output occur in both types of apnea. Whether the upper airway
collapses producing the obstructive apneic pattern may largely
depend on co-existing anatomical variables as well as the
relative neural outputs to the upper airway muscles versus the
thoracic musculature (54). Mixed apneas clearly illustrate
the overlap between central and obstructive events.

TABLE 1. Prevalence of sleep apnea syndrome in the elderly

Study	No. of Subjects		Prevalence		
	Men	Women	Men	Women	Both
REYNOLDS: J. Am. Geriatr. Soc. 28:164, 1980	18	9	28%	0%	
BLOCK: Am. J. Med. 69:75, 1980	--	20	--	5%	
COLEMAN: J. Am. Geriatr. Soc. 29:289, 1981	60	23	--	--	40%
CARSKADON: J. Gerontol. 36:420, 1981	18	22	44%	32%	
ANCOLI-ISRAEL: Sleep 4:349, 1981	11	13	55%	23%	
McGINTY: Neurobiol. Aging 3:337, 1982	26	--	62%	--	
BLIWISE: Exp. Aging Res. 9:77, 1983	26	40	--	--	33%
SMALLWOOD: Sleep 6:16, 1983	24	6	46%	0%	
CATTERALL: Am. Rev. Respir. Dis. 132:86, 1985	9	11	44%	27%	
ANCOLI-ISRAEL: J. Gerontol. 40:419, 1985	73	72	--	--	28%
BIXLER: J. Appl. Physiol. 58:1597, 1985	25	35	0%	3%	
REYNOLDS: Sleep 8:20, 1985	19	21	11%	10%	

Periodic breathing is commonly observed at the time of sleep onset. Fluctuations in the state of wakefulness as one drifts off to sleep are accompanied by fluctuations in respiratory center output. These cyclical changes in central output are believed to be responsible for the periodic changes in tidal volume which occur (52). When an individual becomes hypoxic during the hypoventilatory phase (as occurs at high altitudes), the increase in hypoxic ventilatory drive accentuates the ensuing ventilatory phase which, in turn,

reduces carbon dioxide tension below the apneic threshold
while simultaneously increasing oxygen tension (16). As a
result, both hypoxic and hypercapnic ventilatory drives are
suppressed, leading to subsequent hypoventilation or apnea.
Once established, this oscillatory pattern in the chemical
drives to breathe accentuates the periodicity in tidal
volume. When apneas intervene, the pattern is commonly
referred to as Cheyne-Stokes breathing. Cheyne-Stokes
breathing implies central reductions in ventilatory effort.

TABLE 2. Determinants of upper airway occlusion

INITIATION	TERMINATION
	Arousal response to:
1. Airway anatomy	
2. Intraluminal pressure	1. Hypercapnic-acidosis
3. EMG activity of upper airway muscles	2. Hypoxia
	3. Mechanical loading

     In obstructive apneas, the interaction of three major
variables determine whether or not the upper airway will
collapse: 1) anatomical narrowing and compliance of the
airway; 2) intraluminal pressure; and 3) the electromyographic
(EMG) activity of the upper airway muscles (Table 2). The
negative airway pressures developed during inspiration which
act to collapse the upper airway are opposed by the EMG
activity of the dilatory muscles. Collapse occurs when
negative airway pressures exceed the counteracting force
generated by the dilatory muscles. Obstructive apneas do not
occur during wakefulness when there is sufficient EMG activity
in the upper airway musculature. In contrast, upper airway
collapse is more likely to occur during REM sleep because of
the severe reductions in EMG activity which occur during REM
sleep. Upper airway narrowing predisposes to airway collapse
by increasing the negativity of the inspiratory pressures
needed to maintain tidal ventilation plus the Venturi effect.
Gravitational forces acting to prolapse the soft palate and
tongue against the posterior pharyngeal wall are believed
responsible for the increased frequency of airway collapse in
the supine position (Fig. 5) (10).
     Because disordered breathing events are generally
terminated by arousals, body movements and myoclonic jerks are
frequently observed. Arousals are considered to result from
the multiple stimuli associated with apneas and hypopneas.
These include hypercapnia, acidosis, hypoxemia and, in the
case of upper airway obstruction, mechanical loading of the
respiratory system. During REM sleep, when the arousal

thresholds to these stimuli are increased, prolongation of the disordered breathing events occurs. This results in more severe oxyhemoglobin desaturation (Fig. 6).

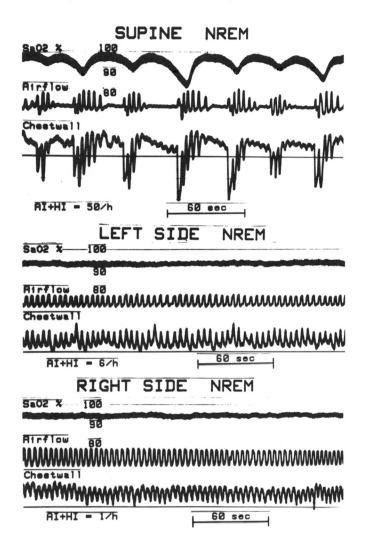

FIG. 5. Effect of sleep position on disordered breathing. Top panel shows repetitive obstructive apneas in the supine position. The middle and lower panels were representative of sleep in the left and right lateral decubitus positions, respectively. (From Shepard, J.W., Jr., Cardiopulmonary problems during sleep in the elderly. Geriatrics, 42:51-60, 1987, with permission.)

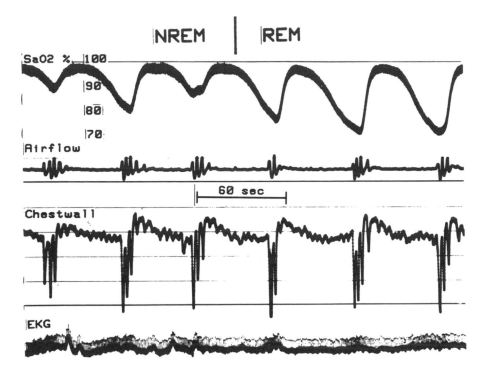

FIG. 6. Transition from NREM to REM sleep showing
increasing apnea duration and severity of oxyhemoglobin
desaturation. (From Shepard, J.W. Jr., Cardiopulmonary
problems during sleep in the elderly. Geriatrics, 42:51-60,
1987, with permission.)

Cardiopulmonary Consequences

Several recent reviews are available which detail the
effects of apneic and hypopneic events on gas exchange and
hemodynamics (58,61,62). The rapidity and extent to which
arterial oxyhemoglobin saturation falls is a complex function
of event duration, oxygen stores within the body, cardiac
output and the distribution of blood flow within the lung
(20,61). Lung volume and apnea duration are the major
variables determining the severity of the arterial hypoxemia.
Obesity contributes to more severe oxyhemoglobin desaturation
by lowering lung volume and the contained stores of oxygen.
The decreases in lung volume result from increased abdominal
pressures which push the diaphragm cephalad.

Apneas are acutely associated with a decrease in heart rate
(apneic-bradycardia). The bradycardia frequently begins at
the onset of the apnea indicating a neurally mediated

process. Progressive reductions in heart rate occur over the apneic interval in direct relationship to the severity of oxyhemoglobin desaturation (75). Increased vagal efferent (parasympathetic) activity is responsible for the bradycardia as atropine has been documented to prevent the bradycardiac response (36,60).

Despite the reductions in heart rate, systemic and pulmonary arterial pressures increase (60-62). The magnitude of the pressure elevations are significantly related to the severity of the hypoxemia. Although hypoxia is a widely recognized stimulus for pulmonary vasoconstriction (21), its effects on the systemic circulation are more complex. The direct effect of hypoxia is to produce vasodilation of systemic vascular beds. However, under apneic conditions, hypoxia initiates cardiovascular reflexes which selectively vasoconstrict the systemic circulation in order to maintain perfusion of the heart and central nervous system (19). Cardiac output has been recently shown to decrease during major apneic events (26).

With the resumption of ventilation, heart rate and cardiac output abruptly increase, contributing to maximal elevations in systemic pressures and myocardial oxygen demands (62). Because poorly oxygenated blood continues to perfuse the coronary circulation for a limited period of time, high levels of myocardial blood flow may be required to maintain myocardial oxygen balance (Fig. 7). This effect, along with a shift from parasympathetic to sympathetic dominant neural tone, is considered to increase the susceptibility of the myocardium to ventricular tachyarrhythmias (Fig. 8) (63,64). Significant bradyarrhythmias have been reported in association with severe oxyhemoglobin desaturation in 10% of patients with sleep apnea (Fig. 9) (25,48,61). At the present time, the frequency and pathophysiological sequence(s) leading to nocturnal deaths in sleep apnea are not known.

Clinical Consequences

Aside from the immediate cardiopulmonary consequences, apneas result in sleep fragmentation as they are terminated by arousals. As disordered breathing begins, individuals may have little trouble falling asleep but will complain of increasingly frequent nocturnal awakenings. This problem, referred to as sleep maintenance insomnia, may be more common in the elderly. Because of increased difficulty in falling back to sleep, the elderly are more likely to experience prolonged awakenings and greater sleep disruption. Nocturnal awakenings following apneas usually occur without accompanying clinical symptoms. However, a substantial percent of patients will report hearing themselves snore while awakening. Because a decrease in the arousal threshold to auditory stimuli has been reported with aging, the sound generated by the snoring

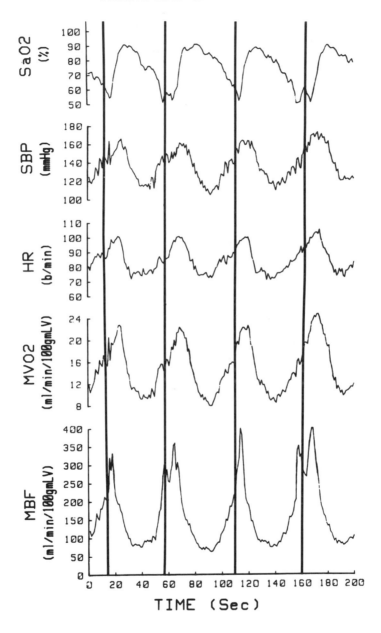

FIG. 7. Sequential changes in arterial oxyhemoglobin saturation (SaO2), systolic blood pressure (SBP), heart rate (HR), calculated myocardial oxygen consumption (MVO2) and myocardial blood flow (MBF) with repetitive obstructive apneas in one subject. Apnea termination is indicated by the vertical lines. (From reference 62 with permission.)

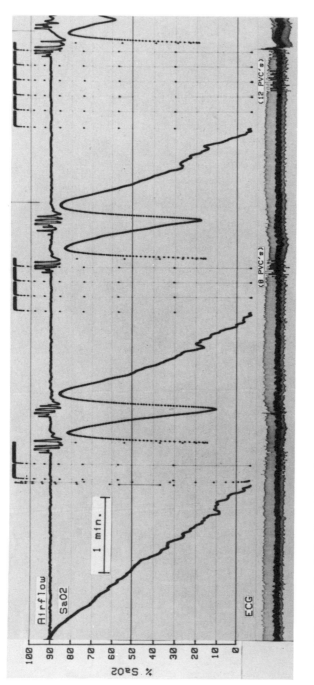

FIG. 8. Ventricular bigeminy occurring near the nadir of severe episodes of oxyhemoglobin desaturation secondary to obstructive apneas of 2 minutes duration. (From reference 63 with permission.)

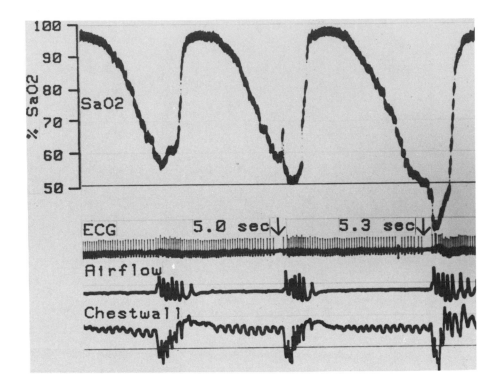

FIG. 9. Prolonged sinus pauses occurring immediately prior to the termination of obstructive apneas during REM sleep.

may actually contribute to arousals (73,74). Less frequently, sleep apneics will complain of dyspnea. When patients awaken with the sensation of dyspnea related to an apneic event, it should spontaneously resolve within less than a minute. Since the sensation of dyspnea likely results from the persisting chemical stimuli of hypercapnia, acidosis and hypoxemia, one should suspect that relatively severe apneas have preceded these awakenings. More prolonged episodes of dyspnea upon awakening suggest alternative diagnoses such as chronic obstructive pulmonary disease, asthma, or congestive heart failure.

As the frequency of apneic events disrupting sleep increases, excessive daytime sleepiness and fatigue develop along with irritability, difficulty in maintaining concentration and other neuropsychiatric symptoms. The extent of personality change and hypersomnolence is often underestimated by the patient as the symptoms have developed insidiously over time. Questioning of the spouse, friends or relatives usually provides more accurate information on the degree of impairment. Individuals with greater than 30 arousals per hour are usually clinically symptomatic.

While some experts argue that sleep fragmentation is the major variable leading to clinical impairment, others feel that the degree of nocturnal hypoxemia is the major determinant (49). It seems logical that both variables are important but perhaps in different ways. For example, ventricular ectopy linked to severe oxyhemoglobin desaturations could potentially result in sudden death during sleep. Alternatively, patients with an apnea index of 100 per hour, who never desaturate below 90%, may be hypersomnolent to the point of falling asleep while driving. Clearly, sleep fragmentation and oxyhemoglobin desaturation are important variables which should be assessed in every individual suspected of having sleep disordered breathing.

In addition to the neuropsychiatric consequences, systemic hypertension has been reported in 50 to 95% of subjects with sleep apnea. Conversely, sleep apnea is present in approximately 30% of hypertensives (23,29). Increased sympathetic neural activity resulting from recurrent hypoxemia and sleep fragmentation may be responsible for this association as urinary catecholamines have been reported to be elevated in sleep apnea (12,24). Diurnal hypertension combined with cyclical elevations during sleep may importantly contribute to deterioration of the cardiovascular system with age.

Mechanisms Linking Aging and Apnea

At the present time, there is no holistic theory which can account for the greater prevalence of sleep apnea in the older population. However, evidence does exist suggesting that the problem is multifactorial with variables influencing both central ventilatory control as well as the anatomic structure of the upper airway.

The ventilatory responses to both hypoxia and hypercapnia have been reported to decrease with age (34,51). While the ventilatory responses to these chemical stimuli are decreased during sleep (4,5,16,18), it is not known whether aging further modifies the sleep-related decrement in ventilatory drives. The importance of the ventilatory responses to these chemical stimuli in the pathophysiology of sleep apnea is not entirely clear. Initially, it was felt that low ventilatory drives contributed to the development of sleep apnea. However, women, who have less sleep apnea, have lower ventilatory drives than men (71). More recently, convincing evidence has been presented suggesting that a brisk ventilatory response to hypoxia actually contributes to oscillatory instability of the respiratory center (16). While there is disagreement regarding the exact role(s) played by these chemical drives, there is agreement that insufficient neural drive to the dilators of the upper airway contributes to obstruction and collapse of the upper airway (54). The possibility exists that neural output to upper airway muscles may selectively decrease with age.

Because arousal represents the final respiratory defense mechanism preventing asphyxia during sleep, changes in arousal threshold with age may be important and need further investigation. Sleep deprivation has been shown to worsen sleep apnea in a small group of elderly patients (27) as well as to decrease the ventilatory responses to hypercapnia and hypoxia (59,72). Although a more recent study failed to confirm an effect on the ventilatory response to hypercapnia, a decrease in genioglossal EMG activity was noted with carbon dioxide rebreathing in the older male subjects (41). This effect would favor narrowing and collapse of the upper airway in older men. Furthermore, by blunting the arousal response to hypoxia, hypercapnia and resistive loading, sleep fragmentation would further worsen sleep apnea by increasing apnea duration and oxyhemoglobin desaturation. Sleep deprivation has been shown to decrease the perception of resistive ventilatory loads by the elderly during wakefulness (1).

The widespread use of sedative-hypnotics and alcohol are additional factors which would act to increase the incidence and severity of sleep apnea in the elderly. These drugs have been shown to increase sleep disordered breathing as well as to decrease the EMG activity of the dilating muscles of the upper airway (17,27,28,33,42,68). Kripke et al. (31,32) have postulated that sleep apnea may be a contributing factor in the increased death rates associated with the use of sleeping pills.

The development of neurological disorders affecting the respiratory centers in the brainstem with age could certainly produce ventilatory dysfunction. However, studies of the prevalence of sleep apnea in the elderly have excluded subjects with overt neurological disease. While sleep studies conducted in patients with dementia have revealed severe fragmentation of the normal sleep-waking pattern, they have not revealed sleep apnea of substantial severity (53,56).

In contrast to variables affecting ventilation centrally, anatomic changes in the upper airway may occur with age which predispose to disordered breathing. Probably the most important variable is the age-associated increase in body weight which probably leads to narrowing of the upper airway in selected individuals. Palatomegaly, resulting from vibrational tissue trauma associated with snoring may further contribute to upper airway narrowing (13). Dimensional changes in upper airway anatomy and compliance with age are currently under investigation in nonobese subjects without clinically evident upper airway pathology.

Disorders leading to nasal obstruction increase sleep fragmentation and contribute to the development of sleep apnea (39,43). Furthermore, experimental nasal obstruction has been shown to lead to the development of sleep apnea in normal subjects (38,40,67,69,76). Consequently, the prevalence of nasal obstruction in the elderly population can be expected to influence the prevalence of sleep apnea.

Treatment

Successful treatment is importantly predicated on correct diagnosis. In the mid 1970's, there were an insufficient number of laboratories specializing in the diagnosis and treatment of sleep disorders. Fortunately, the magnitude and implications of sleep disordered breathing have been recognized and a large number of sleep laboratories recently established. Table 3 offers a brief schematic outline of the major therapeutic interventions judged appropriate for varying degrees of sleep apnea severity. Because the rate of progress in this field has been rapid, it is important to remember that therapeutic management may change in the near future and that alternative forms of therapy are useful in selected patients. It is encouraging that sleep disordered breathing can be effectively treated in the vast majority of individuals provided they are correctly diagnosed and willing to cooperate with an appropriate therapeutic program. More detailed reviews of the current status of therapy for sleep apnea as well as the nonapneic mechanisms leading to oxyhemoglobin desaturation during sleep are available (22,44,70).

TABLE 3. Treatment of obstructive sleep apnea

MILD	MODERATE	SEVERE
(Asymptomatic)	(Symptomatic)	(Symptomatic + Arrhythmia)
Avoid CNS depressants (alcohol)	Medical (nasal CPAP[a])	Tracheostomy (if not corrected by CPAP or upper airway surgery)
Sleep position (side)	Surgical (UPP,[b] tonsillectomy, septoplasty, other)	
Weight reduction		
Treat associated medical conditions: Nasal congestion, hypothyroidism, hypertension, etc.		

[a]UPP, uvulopalatopharyngoplasty
[b]CPAP, continuous positive airway pressure

Because of the high prevalence of sleep apnea in the elderly population, sedative-hypnotics should not be routinely prescribed. A reasonable approach is to evaluate elderly patients for the presence of risk factors for sleep apnea. In individuals with a history of excessive daytime sleepiness, cyclical snoring or observed nocturnal pauses in breathing, sedative-hypnotics are best avoided. Diagnostic polysomnography should be considered as sleep apnea is probably present. While the presence of obesity, hypertension, and male sex all increase the probability of sleep apnea, their presence alone or in combination does not contraindicate the use of sedative-hypnotics.

In patients who are clinically symptomatic or have significant cardiopulmonary sequelae attributable to their sleep apnea, therapy is clearly indicated. However, the majority of elderly subjects will have only mild to moderate sleep apnea. If clinically asymptomatic, the indications for therapy are unclear and a conservative approach recommended. Advice to avoid central nervous system depressants including alcohol should be given along with dietary instructions for weight loss if the subject is overweight. Avoidance of the supine sleep position is generally helpful along with pharmacological therapy to maintain nasal patency if this is a problem. Surgical therapy for asymptomatic patients with mild apnea should be discouraged. Nasal continuous positive airway pressure (CPAP) can be tried; but if the patient is truly asymptomatic, no clinical benefit will be perceived and compliance will be a major problem. Carefully designed studies will be required to determine the long-term health effects of mild sleep apnea in clinically asymptomatic patients.

CLOSING COMMENTS

Each of us has experienced the unpleasant effects of transiently disrupted sleep. Those of us who have raised young children, completed medical housestaff training or worked nights on a rotating work schedule can more fully appreciate the effects of more chronic sleep disruption. Daytime fatigue, sleepiness, irritability, and difficulty in concentrating are the chronic companion of the sleep apneic and many elderly. The extent to which sleep apnea contributes to morbidity and premature mortality in the elderly is not known. Fortunately for individuals with sleep apnea, relief may be only a polysomnographic sleep study and therapeutic intervention away. For others, members of the scientific/ medical community must continue to probe the secrets of the night to help elucidate problems of the day. The rapid progress made over the past decade in identifying and treating sleep apnea has been gratifying. Continued exploration of the relationships between sleep, health, and aging will hopefully help each of us to awaken refreshed, followed by more tranquil sleep in the twilight of our lives.

REFERENCES

1. Altose, M.D., Leitner, J., and Cherniack, N.S. (1985): J. Gerontol., 40:147-153.
2. Ancoli-Israel, S., Kripke, D.F., Mason, W., and Kaplan, O.J. (1985): J. Gerontol., 40:419-425.
3. Ancoli-Israel, S., Kripke, D.F., Mason, W., and Messin, S. (1981): Sleep, 4:349-358.
4. Berthon-Jones, M., and Sullivan, C.E. (1982): Am. Rev. Respir. Dis., 125:286-289.
5. Berthon-Jones, M., and Sullivan, C.E. (1984): J. Appl. Physiol., 57:59-67.
6. Bixler, E.O., Kales, A., Cadieux, R.J., Vela-Bueno, A., Jacoby, J.A., and Soldatos, C.R. (1985): J. Appl. Physiol., 58:1597-1601.
7. Bliwise, D.L., Carey, E., and Dement, W.C. (1983): Exp. Aging Res., 9:77-81.
8. Block, A.J., Wynne, J.W., and Boysen, P.G. (1980): Am. J. Med., 66:75-79.
9. Carskadon, M.A., and Dement, W.C. (1981): J. Gerontol., 36:420-423.
10. Cartwright, R.D., Lloyd, S., Lilie, J., and Kravitz, H. (1985): Sleep, 8:87-94.
11. Catterall, J.R., Calverley, P.M., Shapiro, C.M., Flenley, D.C., and Douglas, N.J. (1985): Am. Rev. Respir. Dis., 132:86-88.
12. Clark, R.W., Boudoulas, H., Schaal, S.F., and Schmidt, H.S. (1980): Neurology, 30:113-119.
13. Cohn, M., Hesla, P.E., Kiel, M., and Nay, K.N. (1986): Chest, 89:529S.
14. Coleman, R.M., Miles, L.E., Guilleminault, C.C., Zarcone, V.P., Jr., van den Hoed, J., and Dement, W.C. (1981): J. Am. Geriatr. Soc., 29:289-296.
15. Dement, W., Richardson, G., Prinz, P., Carskadon, M., Kripke, D., and Czeisler, C. (1985): In: Handbook of The Biology of Aging, edited by C.E. Finch and E.L. Schneider, pp. 692-717. Van Nostrand Reinhold Company, New York.
16. Dempsey, J.A., and Skatrud, J.B. (1986): Am. Rev. Respir. Dis., 133:1163-1170.
17. Dolly, F.R., and Block, A.J. (1982): Am. J. Med., 73:239-243.
18. Douglas, N.J., White, D.P., Weil, J.V., Pickett, C.K., Martin, R.J., Hudgel, D.W., and Zwillich, C.W. (1982): Am. Rev. Respir. Dis., 125:286-289.
19. Elsner, R., Franklin, D.L., Van Citters, R.L., and Kenney, D.W. (1966): Science, 153:941-949.

20. Findley, L.J., Ries, A.L., Tisi, G.M., and Wagner, P.D. (1983): J. Appl. Physiol., 55:1777-1783.
21. Fishman, A.P. (1976): Circ. Res., 38:221-231.
22. Fletcher, E.C. (1986): In: Abnormalities of Respiration During Sleep, edited by E.C. Fletcher, pp. 95-154. Grune and Stratton, Orlando.
23. Fletcher, E.C., DeBehnke, R.D., Lovoi, M.S., and Gorin, A.B. (1985): Ann. Intern. Med., 103:190-195.
24. Fletcher, E., Miller, J., Schaaf, J., and Fletcher, J. (1985): Sleep Res., 14:154.
25. Guilleminault, C., Connolly, S.J., and Winkle, R.A. (1983): Am. J. Cardiol., 52:490-494.
26. Guilleminault, C., Motta, J., Mihm, F., and Melvin, K. (1986): Chest, 89:331-334.
27. Guilleminault, C., Silvestri, R., Mondini, S., and Coburn, S. (1984): J. Gerontol., 39:655-661.
28. Issa, F.G., and Sullivan, C.E. (1982): J. Neurol. Neurosurg. Psychiatry, 45:353-359.
29. Kales, A., Bixler, E.O., Cadieux, R.J., Schneck, D.W., Shaw, L.C., III, Locke, T.W., Vela-Bueno, A., and Soldatos, C.R. (1984): Lancet, 2:1005-1008.
30. Koskenvuo, M., Kaprio, J., Partinen, M., Langinvainio, H., Sarna, S., and Heikkila, K. (1985): Lancet, 1:893-896.
31. Kripke, D.F., and Garfinkel, L. (1984): Lancet, 1:99.
32. Kripke, D.F., Simons, R.N., Garfinkel, L., and Hammond, E.C. (1979): Arch. Gen. Psychiatry, 36:103-116.
33. Krol, R.C., Knuth, S.L., and Bartlett, D., Jr. (1984): Am. Rev. Respir. Dis., 129:247-250.
34. Kronenberg, R.S., and Drage, C.W. (1973): J. Clin. Invest., 52:1812-1819.
35. Krumpe, P.E., and Cummiskey, J.M. (1980): Am. Rev. Respir. Dis., 122:797-801.
36. Kryger, M., Quesney, L.F., Holder, D., Gloor, P., and MacLeod, P. (1974): Am. J. Med. 56:531-539.
37. Lavie, P. (1983): In: Sleep/Wake Disorders: Natural History, Epidemiology, and Long-Term Evolution, edited by C. Guilleminault and E. Lugaresi, pp. 127-135. Raven Press, New York.
38. Lavie, P., Fischel, N., Zomer, J., and Eliaschar, I. (1983): Acta Otolaryngol., 95:161-166.
39. Lavie, P., Gertner, R., Zomer, J., and Podoshin, L. (1981): Acta Otolaryngol., 92:529-533.
40. Lavie, P., and Rubin, A.E. (1984): Acta Otolaryngol., 97:127-130.
41. Leiter, J.C., Knuth, S.L., and Bartlett, D., Jr. (1985): Am. Rev. Respir. Dis., 132:1242-1245.
42. Leiter, J.C., Knuth, S.L., Krol, R.C., and Bartlett, D., Jr. (1985): Am. Rev. Respir. Dis., 132:216-219.
43. Leznoff, A., Haight, H.S., and Hoffstein, V. (1986): Am. Rev. Respir. Dis., 133:935-936.

44. Lombard, R.M., Jr., and Zwillich, C.W. (1985): Med. Clin. North Am., 69:1317-1336.
45. Lugaresi, E., Coccagna, G., and Cirignotta, F. (1978): In: Sleep Apnea Syndromes, edited by C. Guilleminault and W.C. Dement, pp. 13-22. Alan R. Liss, Inc., New York.
46. McGinty, D., Littner, M., Beahm, E., Ruiz-Primo, E., Young, E., and Sowers, J. (1982): Neurobiol. Aging, 3:337-350.
47. Miles, L.E., and Dement, W.C. (1980): Sleep, 3:119-220.
48. Miller, W.P. (1982): Am. J. Med., 73:317-321.
49. Orr, W.C., Martin, R.J., Imes, N.K., Rogers, R.M., and Stahl, M.L. (1979): Chest, 75:418-422.
50. Peirick, J., and Shepard, J.W., Jr. (1983): Med. Biol. Eng. Comput., 21:632-635.
51. Peterson, D.D., Pack, A.I., Silage, D.A., and Fishman, A.P. (1981): Am. Rev. Respir. Dis., 124:387-391.
52. Phillipson, E.A. (1978): Am. Rev. Respir. Dis., 118:909-939.
53. Prinz, P.N., Peskind, E.R., Vitaliano, P.P., Raskind, M.A., Eisdorfer, C., Zemcuznikov, N., and Gerber, C.J. (1982): J. Am. Geriatr. Soc., 30:86-93.
54. Remmers, J.E., deGroot, W.J., Sauerland, E.K., and Anch, A.M. (1978): J. Appl. Physiol., 44:931-938.
55. Reynolds, C.F., III, Coble, P.A., Black, R.S., Holzer, B., Carroll, R., and Kupfer, D.J. (1980): J. Am. Geriatr. Soc., 28:164-170.
56. Reynolds, C.F., III, Kupfer, D.J., Taska, L.S., Hoch, C.C., Sewitch, D.E., Restifo, K., Spiker, D.G., Zimmer, B., Marin, R.S., Nelson, J., Martin, D., and Morycz, R. (1985): J. Clin. Psychiatry, 46:257-261.
57. Reynolds, C.F., III, Kupfer, D.J., Taska, L.S., Hoch, C.C., Sewitch, D.E., and Spiker, D.G. (1985): Sleep, 8:20-29.
58. Scharf, S.M. (1984): In: Sleep and Breathing, edited by N.A. Saunders and C.E. Sullivan, pp. 221-240. Marcel Dekker, Inc., New York.
59. Schiffman, P.L., Trontell, M.C., Mazar, M.F., and Edelman, N.H. (1983): Chest, 84:695-698.
60. Schroeder, J.S., Motta, J., and Guilleminault, C. (1978): In: Sleep Apnea Syndromes, edited by C. Guilleminault and W.C. Dement, pp. 177-196. Alan R. Liss, Inc., New York.
61. Shepard, J.W., Jr. (1985): Med. Clin. North Am., 69:1243-1264.
62. Shepard, J.W., Jr. (1986): In: Abnormalities of Respiration During Sleep, edited by E.C. Fletcher, pp. 39-62. Grune and Stratton, Orlando.
63. Shepard, J.W., Jr., Garrison, M.W., Grither, D.A., and Dolan, G.F. (1985): Chest, 88:335-340.

64. Shepard, J.W., Jr., Garrison, M.W., Grither, D.A., Evans, R., and Schweitzer, P.K. (1985): Am. J. Med., 78:28-34.

65. Smallwood, R.G., Vitiello, M.V., Giblin, E.C., and Prinz, P.N. (1983): Sleep, 6:16-22.

66. Smolensky, M., Halberg, F., and Sargent, F., II (1972): In: Advances in Climatic Physiology, edited by S. Itoh, K. Ogata, and H. Yoshimura, pp. 281-318. Igaku Shoin Ltd., Tokyo.

67. Suratt, P.M., Truner, B.L., and Wilhoit, S.C. (1986): Chest, 90:324-329.

68. Taasan, V.C., Block, A.J., Boysen, P.G., and Wynne, J.W. (1981): Am. J. Med., 71:240-245.

69. Taasan, V., Wynne, J.W., Cassisi, N., and Block, A.J. (1981): Laryngoscope, 91:1163-1172.

70. Thawley, S.E. (1985): Med. Clin. North Am., 69:1337-1358.

71. White, D.P., Douglas, N.J., Pickett, C.K., Weil, J.V., and Zwillich, C.W. (1983): J. Appl. Physiol., 54:874-879.

72. White, D.P., Douglas, N.J., Pickett, C.K., Zwillich, C.W., and Weil, J.V. (1983): Am. Rev. Respir. Dis., 128:984-986.

73. Zepelin, H., McDonald, C.S., Wanzie, F.J., and Zammit, G.K. (1980): Sleep Res. 9:109.

74. Zepelin, H., McDonald, C.S., and Zammit, G.K. (1984): J. Gerontol., 39:294-300.

75. Zwillich, C., Devlin, T., White, D., Douglas, N., Weil, J., and Martin, R. (1982): J. Clin. Invest., 69:1286-1292.

76. Zwillich, C.W., Pickett, C., Hanson, F.N., and Weil, J.V. (1981): Am. Rev. Respir. Dis., 124:158-160.

Central Nervous System Disorders of Aging: Clinical Intervention and Research, edited by Randy Strong et al. Raven Press, New York © 1988.

INTERVENTION IN ACUTE STROKE

John B. Selhorst, M.D.

Department of Neurology,
St. Louis University School of Medicine
St. Louis, Missouri 63110

Stroke is clinically manifested as a sudden focal neurologic deficit that is caused by impaired vascular supply to the nervous system. Afflicted patients are often those with disease, particularly atherosclerosis, within the cerebrovasculature. Consequently, in an aging population, the magnitude of cerebrovascular disease is substantial. The number of strokes annually occurring in the United States exceeds 500,000, and deaths from stroke approximate 200,000. This incidence ranks stroke next to heart disease and cancer as the third most common cause of natural death in the United States. For those who survive, suffering from severe disability is common. In an analysis of 991 patients, nearly three-quarters were unable to return to an independent lifestyle (65). In 1982, the economic impact of stroke on our society was estimated by Yatsu and Coull (71). The direct cost of health care for acute stroke was 2 billion dollars, and indirect costs approached an additional 6 billion dollars. Undoubtedly, these sums are now higher.

Care for patients with stroke is traditionally directed toward compassionate rehabilitation. Realization of the high mortality, morbidity and economic burden justifies a more concentrated effort toward the prevention and amelioration of acute ischemic neurologic deficits. In recent years, much attention has been given to stroke prevention. Risk profiles for stroke have been identified. Statistical significance is definable in those older than 58 years of age, especially 68 years of age, with heart disease, peripheral vascular disease and a residual neurological deficit (3). Suspected and manageable, but unproven, factors are diastolic hypertension, diabetes and smoking; systolic hypertension is a risk factor in the presence of heart disease. One careful epidemiologic study spanning two recent decades shows success in stroke prevention with a 45% decline in the incidence of stroke (65). This

achievement is largely attributed to better treatment of
hypertension and more careful management of patients with a
stroke-prone profile. Many misconceptions and controversies in
stroke prevention, however, still abound.

Sparked by advances in basic research, an interest is
developing in the direct intervention upon acute ischemia of
the brain. A graded relationship between cerebral blood flow
and reversible and irreversible cell damage has been defined.
Loss of cerebral autoregulation is recognized with focal brain
ischemia. Intracellular biochemical changes have been
identified during ischemia. These discoveries have opened
avenues for a number of clinical trials involving manipulations
upon the clotting mechanism, the micro-circulation and the
ischemic cell.

The following discussion briefly classifies the various
types of strokes. Attention is then focused on ischemic stroke
involving large and medium-sized arteries. Recent studies that
assist in clarifying previous misunderstandings in the
prevention of these strokes are outlined, and current
techniques for direct intervention in ischemic processes within
the nervous system are reviewed.

CLASSIFICATION

Impaired cerebral blood flow results either from
extravasation of blood from a vessel or obstruction of flow
within it, hence, the terms hemorrhagic or ischemic stroke.
Most often this interrupted flow occurs in the arterial rather
than the venous bed. A hemorrhagic stroke occurs in
approximately 15% of patients suffering from cerebrovascular
disease. CT scanning has greatly improved the diagnosis of
hemorrhagic forms of stroke, and, thereby, indirectly clarified
the identification of ischemic insult to the central nervous
system. Intracranial bleeding is caused mostly by
intraparenchymal hemorrhages (10%) or ruptured berry aneurysms
(5%). Intraparenchymal bleeding is thought to occur from
rupture of microaneurysms that form on the distal portion of
deeply penetrating arterioles. These microaneurysms are found
mostly in hypertensive patients. The berry aneurysm is
generally located on the basal cerebral arteries forming the
circle of Willis. Consequently, its rupture is from a much
higher head of arterial pressure. This accounts for ruptured
aneurysms having the highest of mortality rates among the
subsets of stroke.

A large majority of strokes (85%) are due to ischemic
insults. Some 20% of these are caused by small or "lacunar"
infarcts. These result from obstruction of arterioles by a
lipohyalinoid deposition that, like microaneurysms, is also a
consequence of sustained hypertension. Because these
arterioles supply a relatively small amount of neural tissue, a
lacunar infarct has a limited size and, as a result, a more

favorable prognosis than other strokes (51). The greater number of ischemic strokes (65%) are caused by either a thrombus or embolus in major cerebral arteries or their immediate branches; these infarcts are largely responsible for the devastation of public health attributed to stroke. Consequently, in the name of prevention, considerable effort is expended toward recognizing the early signs of embolization and determining the potential source of an embolus. However, even with a careful search, including angiography, a plausible site for a thrombus or embolus is not identifiable in 40% of patients (29). Thus, an impact upon stroke must involve a means toward reducing the destruction of tissue caused by ischemia.

PREVENTION

Fisher (22) in 1952 proposed that atherosclerotic disease of the extracranial vessels was responsible for transient ischemia and cerebral infarction. In the ensuing decade, platelet and cholesterol fragments, similar to those found in carotid atheromas, were described in the fundi of patients experiencing transient monocular loss of vision. Understandably, the notion developed that transient ischemic attacks (TIAs) of the eye or brain were warning clues for the surgical removal of carotid atheromas. Prophylactic removal of carotid atherosclerosis is now widespread. Recently, the larger medical implications of (TIAs) have become more fully appreciated, and the risks of carotid endarterectomy have been acknowledged. A broader role for medical management is evolving, and warrants being placed in the perspective of current data regarding asymptomatic bruits and symptomless retinal emboli, amaurosis fugax and retinal infarcts, TIAs and prophylactic medical and surgical therapy.

Asymptomatic Bruit

Revelant to the significance of bruits is the prevalence of carotid atherosclerosis. In an evaluation of 178 unselected autopsies, Fisher and colleagues (23) found 9% with an extracranial carotid artery occluded. Just over half were judged symptomatic. Intracranial occlusions were noted in another 4%. Atherosclerotic stenosis was present in 40%, 14% being greater than 75% stenotic. This study corresponds to earlier reports of greater than 50% stenosis in one or more extracranial arteries in 40% of the patients over 50 years of age (47).

Given the frequency with which atherosclerosis is found in the carotid system, how common are carotid bruits? From a random sampling of Olmstead County, Minnesota, residents over 45 years of age, Sandok and associates (59) detected cervical murmurs in 12.6%. In this survey, 4.3% of the bruits were midcarotid in location, being distinguished from venous hums, supraclavicular and vertebral artery bruits, and 2.9% were asymptomatic. As expected, the incidence of bruits increased with age. Given the prevalence of stroke or TIAs in 600/100,000 of the American population (45), a symptomless state of carotid atherosclerosis and carotid bruit are clearly predominant. How significant then is carotid atherosclerosis to the occurrence of stroke when advanced carotid atherosclerosis is found in a large minority of the older half of the general population? Does the chief clinical manifestation of carotid atherosclerosis, the bruit, indicate added risk? Is this risk dependent on the degree of stenosis? Are there any situations in which the risk of stroke is increased?

These questions have been addressed in a series of publications. In 1980, Heyman et al. (38) carried out a survey of 1,620 persons, 45 years of age or older. Asymptomatic bruits were detected in 4.4%, and nearly 2.5% were auscultated over the carotid. Bruits increased with age and were more often found in women and those with hypertension. In patients followed over 6 years, stroke occurred in 14% of the patients [10] with a bruit versus 3% of patients who did not have a bruit. Stroke was more common in men having a bruit (28%) than in women (9%). Most importantly, the vascular territory of the stroke correlated with the cervical bruit in only 3 of the 10 patients developing a stroke! Additionally, in patients with bruits there was a significant increase in mortality from heart disease. In the Framingham, Massachusetts, epidemiologic study of cardiovascular disease (68), 105 women and 66 men who had a cervical bruit were identified. Monitored over 8 years, TIAs occurred in 8 (4.6%), and stroke in 21 (12.3%) of the study subjects. This was twice the expected stroke rate. Once again, the majority of strokes were located in a vascular territory that differed from that of the bruit. There was also a two-fold increase in myocardial infarction. Another study includes 70 subjects with asymptomatic bruits followed over a mean of 4 years (25). Four transient ischemic events were experienced without subsequent infarction. Three strokes occurred, but only 1 was associated with 50% or greater carotid stenosis. Myocardial infarction developed in 6 patients. Carotid bruits appear, therefore, to be a very significant sign of cardiovascular disease and a less significant and nonfocal sign of cerebrovascular disease.

Durward and colleagues (16) have further expanded the recommendations for patients with carotid atherosclerosis. They reported on 73 patients followed for more than 4 years with greater than 50% stenosis proven by angiography; these were patients in whom angiography was performed during evaluation of TIAs involving the contralateral carotid territory. An ipsilateral stroke occurred in 2 patients (3%), and TIAs in 10 patients (14%). These researchers advise that patients be followed more closely until appropriate ischemic symptoms appear. In another report that included 124 patients with asymptomatic, ulcerated or stenotic carotid arteries, no increased risk of stroke was found (30). These studies have strong implications toward the current application of sensitive ultrasonographic techniques. With favorable results reported with the use of aspirin in a Canadian study of TIAs (12), it is likely that many patients will now be placed on aspirin before TIAs develop. Furthermore, because ischemic stroke probably has heterogeneous causes, the widespread use of aspirin therapy may delay the appearance of stroke in the population, but it is not expected to reverse the process of atherosclerosis.

The importance of bruits in patients undergoing surgery has also been investigated. In one study, only 1 stroke occurred among 104 patients with bruits, while 3 patients experienced a stroke among 631 who did not have a bruit (58). The importance of a carotid bruit has been questioned more often in patients having induced hypotension with surgery, especially those undergoing coronary artery bypass. An audible bruit is detected in 10% to 20% of these patients. Furlan and Craciun (26) did not find a greater incidence of perioperative stroke in patients with 50% to 90% stenotic carotid arteries than in those patients without carotid atherosclerosis. In fact, 8 perioperative strokes (7%) occurred in the ipsilateral hemisphere among 115 patients having a carotid endarterectomy with a coronary bypass. From this study, the number of patients with greater than 90% atherosclerotic plaques was insufficient to draw conclusions, but it certainly appears that less stenotic lesions do not increase the risk for stroke during surgery.

Retinal Emboli

Occasionally, a cholesterol embolus is discovered at the bifurcation of a retinal artery. The embolus may be recent or the residue of a fragment lodged in the retina many years before. Sometimes its discovery is prompted by the evaluation of a retinal infarct. There is only a single report regarding asymptomatic cholesterol emboli in the retina (55). This study included patients who already had retinal infarcts (12%), amaurosis fugax (AF) (12%) and strokes (38%). Of the 205 patients followed over 8 years, 16% developed a stroke, two-thirds in the ipsilateral cerebral hemisphere. The mortality, however, was much greater, involving 72% of the patients versus an expected mortality rate of 35%. Thus, cholesterol emboli suggest a greater risk for the ipsilateral stroke than a carotid bruit. But, more like carotid bruits, they indicate an increased mortality risk, and this risk was most often associated with heart disease.

Amaurosis Fugax and Transient Ischemic Attacks

AF, "fleeting blindness," or transient monocular blindness typically lasts only several minutes, but visual loss persisting for hours is known to occur. Patients complain of either a complete loss of vision or a temporary obscuration resembling a fog, mist, cloud or blur. Dimness is as much a quality of the visual loss as is the loss of contrast. Recurrent episodes are common. Onset is marked by a sudden and progressive reduction in the central field in the majority, and characterized in a few by a collapse of the peripheral field similar to a slowly closing shutter of a camera. In some patients, vision is lost in an altitudinal fashion that corresponds to impaired flow in the upper and lower branch of the central retinal artery. Thus, the classic complaint of a shade or curtain coming over the eye is given, although it happens infrequently. Concurrent cerebrovascular or cardiac symptoms are rare. However, a highly stenotic [6] or occluded [2] carotid artery was found in an angiographic study of patients with separately occurring, transient symptoms of the ipsilateral eye and brain (54).

Recognized causes of AF include local disorders in the central retinal artery, disease of the carotid system, cardiac disorders, and emboli from the systemic circulation. Vasospasm is known to cause AF in association with migraine, Raynaud's phenomenon and polyarteritis nodosa. Migrainous events are characterized by scintillations, positive visual phenomena, and subsequent headache or orbital pain. It is worth noting that positive visual phenomena and associated headache, but not scintillations, have been observed in patients with AF and atheromatous carotid disease. Giant cell arteritis and thrombosis of the posterior ciliary arteries are sometimes heralded by monocular loss of vision. A platelet of cholesterol embolus is assumedly the cause of AF in patients with atherosclerotic disease of the carotid bifurcation or siphon, carotid dissection or fibromuscular dysplasia of the carotid artery. AF associated with atherosclerosis of the ophthalmic artery is very infrequently diagnosed. Cardiac emboli reaching the retinal vasculature are described in patients with valvular heart disease, arrhythmias, myxomas, myopathies, ventricular aneurysms and endothelial disturbances. Cardiac emboli are especially identified in younger patients with central retinal artery occlusions (4). Systemic emboli reaching the eye constitute an amazing and surprising number of fragments, e.g., air, amniotic fluid, lipid soluble contrast agents, fat, talc and sheared-off pieces of intravenous tubing.

Examination of the eye of a patient who earlier had AF is normal or shows highly refractile, yellowish cholesterol emboli. The crystalline cholesterol embolus usually lodges at an arterial bifurcation, the point at which the lumen suddenly is reduced by one half. In many patients, the retinal arteries appear nearly normal. However, slight tactile pressure upon the globe reduces intraocular flow, and sometimes causes a partially obscured plaque to reflect synchronously with the pulse as it is exposed in diastole and washed over in systole. These cholesterol deposits obviously originate from an atheromatous source more proximal to the heart, and the carotid bifurcation is the most common. In rare instances, small white emboli are observed during an attack of AF. These are generally believed to be platelet emboli. They move rapidly from arterial bifurcation to bifurcation, and they are so friable that they quickly fragment and become too small to see. In other instances of AF, the retinal arteries were observed to pulsate, but an embolus was not observed (18).

In patients with retinal infarcts from either central retinal artery (CRA) or branch CRA occlusion, the retina shows varying degrees of whitish haze that reflects an infarcted ganglion cell layer. The retinal arteries are normal, focally narrow, thread-like, obstructed by platelet aggregates or cholesterol, or have a segmented "boxcar" or "cattle-track" like flow. A visual field defect corresponds to the zone of retinal infarction. If the macula is involved, central visual acuity and color vision are impaired. Often an afferent pupillary defect is found. Due to preservation of the underlying receptor cells, the electroretinogram (ERG) is normal. With occlusion of the ophthalmic artery, the retina has a bright white appearance due to concurrent choroidal infarction, the ERG is abnormal, and the patient may complain of ocular pain.

TIAs are temporary neurologic symptoms of 24 hours or less that are referable to insufficient blood supply of the carotid or vertebral-basilar circulation. The duration of a TIA may extend over 5 to 10 minutes or last up to 1 hour or more (54). Those TIAs that are longer are more often associated with open carotids and intracranial branch artery occlusions. TIAs involving small areas of the cerebral cortex and having ischemic symptoms limited to an arm or leg or to dysphasia are more often associated with carotid stenosis (36). Between 25% to 40% of patients with TIAs are reported to have a subsequent stroke (52). In one careful study, nearly one-third of the patients with TIAs had a cerebral infarction within 6 months; and 6 months after the infarct, over one-half were dead or bedridden (13), thus, the potential seriousness of a TIA. A more favorable prognosis holds for younger populations (52) and for patients with normal angiograms (50). As important as the occurrence of stroke are the observations of a 20% cumulative rate over 5 years of myocardial infarction or sudden death in patients with TIAs.

The main issue for a patient with AF, retinal infarction or TIA is whether or not an embolus was responsible and, if it was, what is the risk for stroke and overall health. In a retrospective study of 140 patients presenting with AF, 15% had

evidence of a cerebral infarct, 17% had TIAs, and 10% had a
retinal infarction (unpublished). Among 85 patients presenting
with partial retinal infarcts or CRA occlusion, those with
evidence of carotid atherosclerosis had signs of a stroke (18%)
or experienced TIAs (15%). Interestingly, a recent
retrospective study showed that carotid bruits and angiographic
evidence of atherosclerosis were more likely in patients with
AF (71%) than in patients with TIAs (36%). Not surprisingly,
intracranial disease was greater in patients with TIAs (27%)
than in those with AF (11%). A recent prospective report of 93
patients with AF and 212 patients with TIAs had similar
findings (41). Operative carotid atherosclerosis was more
common in AF patients (66%) than in those with cerebral TIAs
(51%). However, over 7 years, the cumulative stroke rate was
lower in those with AF (14%) than in those with TIAs (27%).
TIAs occurred more often in those patients who were
hypertensive and black. Recurrent TIAs, myocardial infarctions
(MIs) or sudden death occurred nearly equally in the 2 groups
(28% vs. 33%). In summary, the risk for stroke (2% year) is
increased four-fold among patients with AF, but is much less
than that for patients with TIAs. More importantly, there is a
four- to five-fold greater mortality from heart disease in
patients with both AF and TIAs. In another report of 110
patients, patients with AF again had a lower incidence of
stroke than patients with TIAs (56). Clearly, however, those
patients with AF and a stenotic carotid had a greater risk for
stroke than those with a normal carotid. There was a similar
mortality rate for patients with AF and TIAs, most of which was
again attributable to cardiac disease. Another report shows
that intracranial internal carotid artery stenosis poses a much
greater cardiovascular risk for mortality than a
cerebrovascular one (48). Thus, a noninvasive cardiovascular
evaluation is indicated in all patients with AF as well as
those with TIAs.

    The viewpoint has emerged that AF is more often associated
with carotid embolization, in fact the leading indicant, than
TIAs, which have a more heterogeneous etiology in the
intracranial as well as extracranial vasculature. Small emboli
from the carotid system cause amaurosis in the very sensitive
and symptomatic retina, where the vessels are the caliber of
penetrating meningeal vessels. Obstruction of meningeal
vessels on the cortical surface by similarly sized emboli may
result in only a minute and, probably, symptomless infarct or
reversible ischemic deficit. TIAs in the cerebral circulation
more likely result from larger systemic emboli that are swept
into the higher flow of the middle cerebral artery or originate
from local intracranial atherosclerotic lesions (54).
Alternatively, some TIAs last a short duration or have very
limited ischemic symptoms, which are associated with carotid
stenosis and, perhaps, temporary impairment of cerebral flow.

Interventional Medical and Surgical Therapy

Hemostasis is supported by the products of the prostaglandins found in the walls of all blood vessels, particularly prostacyclin (PGl_2), a powerful vasodilator and platelet antiaggregant (35). An alteration in this process is suggested by in vitro tests that show increased platelet aggregation in blood samples from patients with TIAs and strokes (66). This finding is assumed, but never shown in vivo, to play a role in the pathophysiology of cerebrovascular disease. Studies of fluid dynamics demonstrate the migration of red blood cells toward the center of the blood column, while platelets are found on its edge. Mechanical distortions in flow, especially ulcerations or stenosis that promote a vortex, bring the platelet membrane into contact with collagen in disrupted endothelial surfaces. The contact releases phospholipases from the platelet membrane. Liberated phospholipids are hydrolyzed into arachidonic acid. The usual predominance of PGl_2 is briefly overcome by the production of thromboxane (A_2), a vasoconstricting and potent aggregating agent. Aspirin impedes the prostaglandin pathway by interfering with the oxygenation of arachidonic acid through the irreversible acetylation of cyclooxygenases. Intermittent dosing with aspirin has been proposed to diminish the tendency for platelet aggregation in patients with vascular disease, while allowing for sufficient activity of the platelet prostaglandin pathway to maintain hemostasis. In a Canadian cooperative study of 585 subjects that used a placebo and sulphinpyrazone, a reversible cyclooxygenase inhibitor, findings showed a 50% reduction in stroke or death with 1300 mg aspirin over 26 months (12). To date, this is the most important study on the value of aspirin. This report has been criticized, however, because the results applied only to men and because of the relatively limited numbers of subjects. Another study of 604 patients with TIAs or strokes, showed a protective effect of 100 mg of aspirin on the occurrence of fatal and nonfatal strokes and MIs over a 3-year period (10). Other studies have also suggested a beneficial effect of aspirin in reducing stroke, and a much larger study on the value of aspirin is now under way in the United Kingdom. In addition, Garde et al. (27) have subsequently reported that aspirin was equally as effective as coumadin toward reduction of stroke and TIAs. Dipyridamole, a platelet anti-aggregant differing in its action from aspirin, has not been found to have any additive effect when combined with aspirin (2,10).

Carotid endarterectomy (CE) is the third most commonly performed procedure in the United States. This is an astonishing development considering that the indications for the procedure were no further defined or accepted in 1971 when 15,000 CEs were performed than in 1985 when well over 110,000 were anticipated. A majority of the increase in CEs is

attributed to surgery for asymptomatic carotid artery disease.
This is ironic given less than 2% risk of stroke per year for
these patients and the results of the Joint Study reported in
1970 (20).   A 4.5% incidence of stroke following CE and a 25%
perioperative morbidity and mortality rate were reported.   Only
those patients with ipsilateral, symptomatic carotid stenosis
benefited from the procedure.   From a survey of American
hospitals over 13 years, Dyken and Pokras (17) recently found
an operative mortality rate of 2.8% among 491,000 CEs.   Another
review of 3,328 CEs from 48 institutions has shown a 6% risk of
stroke and death (24).   Complications were fewer in patients
complaining of AF, having vein patch grafting and undergoing
electroencephalographic monitoring, and more numerous in
patients with a progressing stroke or having a concurrent
coronary artery bypass.   From a specialized center, perhaps,
better results are obtainable.   A Mayo Clinic series had an
operative mortality of less than 1% and a perioperative stroke
rate of 3% (67).   The value of the procedure, given its
immediate risks, has to be weighed against the reduction over
3.5 years in the Joint Study of stroke and death of 15.4% for
those having surgery versus 24.5% for patients not having a CE.
The combined risks for CE and angiography have raised serious
questions about the justification for so many CEs, even though
there is a long-term effect in stroke prevention (8).   Most
recently, the value of multicenter, randomized trials has been
acknowledged in showing the efficacy of simple mastectomy and
irradiation over radical mastectomy for patients with cancer of
the breast and the absence of benefit from intracranial bypass
procedures in reducing stroke following carotid occlusion.
Thus, a call for a randomized trial of medical (aspirin) versus
surgical (CE) therapy has risen for patients with TIAs and
carotid atherosclerosis.   This study is soon to commence.

DIRECT INTERVENTION

The potential for successful intervention in the course of
acute neurologic deficits is clinically suggested by the
reversibility of TIAs and the often observed improvement and
sometimes nearly full resolution of major neurological
deficits.   Additionally, patients with acute ischemia
frequently have a rapidly sputtering onset of increasing
neurologic deficit.   Only recently, however, has ischemia of
the central nervous system undergone careful investigation at
the cellular level.   These studies are opening avenues for
therapeutic intervention that are currently receiving much
attention.

Pathophysiology of Ischemic Infarction

Active intervention in acute stroke requires an
understanding of the anatomy and control of the cerebral

circulation and the consequences of impaired blood supply upon
the electrophysiology, cellular metabolism and structural
integrity of the brain. Cerebral circulation is closely
coupled to cerebral metabolism, which is very demanding. The
average brain weighs 1400 gm and accounts for 2% of total body
weight, but it requires 14% of the cardiac ouptut or an average
blood flow of 750 ml/min. The high cellular and electrical
activity of the brain creates a demand that necessitates a
delivery of 57 ml/min of oxygen or 23% of the total oxygen
consumption. Surprisingly, the required cerebral blood flow
and large delivery of oxygen is accomplished through a
capillary network that is only half as dense (100 mm/mm3) as
that found in muscle (200 mm/mm3). The delivery of vital
nutrients to maintain energy stores through this vascular bed,
therefore, requires a very dynamic regulation of cerebral blood
flow (49). Under physiologic conditions, variation in vascular
resistance of the large and medium-sized arterioles is minimal.
The regulation of cerebral blood flow is determined principally
by the arteriolar (diameter<70 microns) and capillary bed (44).
There, normal cerebral blood flow averages 55 ml/100 gm/min,
with a higher distribution, 75 ml/100/gm, being directed to the
gray matter versus the white matter, which receives 25 ml/100
gm/min (7). This flow is regulated by the regional production
of pCO2.

Before considering the physiological and biochemical
events occurring with limitations in microvascular flow, there
are 2 important features regarding obstruction of large or
medium-sized vessels and stroke that deserve attention. They
are the extent of the anastomotic supply and the degree of
obstruction in a vessel. Variations in the collateral supply
about the cervical vasculature, the circle of Willis and
anastomotic connections over the cortical surface are well
recognized as having the potential for providing full
compensation for occlusion of one or more major arteries. The
variable degree of obstruction of an embolus or thrombosis is,
however, less well recognized. Frequently, a sudden
obstruction is construed as total when it is just as likely
incomplete. For example, a cholesterol embolus in the retina
is often observed without signs of retinal infarction; the
crystalline material is wedged in the arterial lumen, but only
partly obstructs it. The different rates of flow that are
determined by the anastomotic supply and degree of obstruction
result in graded zones of blood supply within the acute
ischemic area. These zones are given terms borrowed from
astronomy. The umbra, or area of total darkness in an eclipse,
refers to a region with little flow and irreversibly infarcted
tissue; the penumbra, a dim area of partial darkness during an
eclipse, symbolizes a zone of incomplete flow and potentially
reversibly damaged brain tissue (5).

As blood flow is compromised, energy stores fall. In the
nervous system, the neuron's ability to generate an electrical

potential is first affected. Continued deprivation of energy stores results in the cells's inability to maintain an osmotic pump and an ionic gradient that are essential for the stability of the cell membrane. Laboratory investigations have shown separate thresholds of cerebral blood flow necessary for electrical and ionic functon. Similar findings in man show slowing of the electroencephalogram at 16-17 ml/100 gm/min (60,64). Experimental studies have demonstrated a failure in the ionic gradient to occur with flows below 10 ml/100 gm/min (6,11). In awake monkeys, Jones and colleagues (43) have shown a threshold of 23 ml/100 gm/min for the onset of paralysis and 8 ml/100 gm/min for hemiplegia. Most importantly, the development of infarction was dependent upon the degree and duration of ischemia. Reductions in cerebral blood flow below 10 ml/100 gm/min were well tolerated for 15 to 20 minutes. Similar reductions for 2 to 3 hours resulted in infarction. Infarction also occurred with permanent reductions in regional blood flow 17-18 ml/100 gm/min.

As perfusion fails, a rise in pCO_2 induces vasodilation of the microvascular bed and an increase in regional blood flow. When the cerebral circulation falls between 25-50 ml/100 gm/min, increased oxygen extraction from the blood stream maintains the cerebral metabolic rate of oxygen and energy production by the cell. As mentioned, cerebral blood flow below 23 ml/100 gm/min alters the electrical activity of the cell. A reduction in cellular adenosine triphosphatase stores and a rise in intracellular osmolarity have been found. Below 10 ml/100 gm/min, a number of cellular events occur which are associated with infarction. The ionic pump fails and leads to potassium efflux and calcium influx. Anaerobic metabolism results in an increase in lactic acid and a fall in intracellular pH. The acidic millieu favors ionization of calcium, which affects membrane permeability and contributes to the breakdown of phospholipid in the cell membrane. A rise in intracellular ionized calcium is possibly responsible for the massive release in neurotransmitters that occurs with ischemia. The liberation of free fatty acids triggers the formation of thromboxanes, leukotrienes, endobroxides and free radicals. Vacuoles appear in the mitochondria, and eosinophilic staining is seen in histologic preparations. As mentioned above, the onset of necrosis and its severity depends on the duration of these biochemical changes.

Several systemic factors also affect the outcome of impaired cerebral blood flow. With focal ischemia, there is a rise in the lactic acid. The increase in tissue pH apparently blunts the responsiveness of the microvasculature to pCO_2. Regional autoregulation is lost, and local perfusion becomes passively dependent upon systemic perfusion pressure (21). Uptake of ionized calcium by arterioles induces vasospasm which also compromises perfusion. Clumping of intravascular elements is observed. In the absence of oxygen, hyperglycemia is also thought to potentiate ischemic damage to cells, possibly by supporting anaerobic metabolism and augmenting lactic acid accumulation (40).

Assessment

The goals of an interventional program are to arrest the progression of infarction and to restore function to all reversibly damaged ischemic tissue. A practical strategy for successful stroke intervention necessarily involves three phases to accomplish these goals: 1) rapid assessment of the patient; 2) prompt pharmacologic treatment of ischemic processes; and 3) restoration of the impaired circulation.

The presentation of a patient with an acute neurologic deficit confronts the clinician with the dilemma of whether reversible or irreversible damage has occurred. The acute ischemic episode represents either a TIA, reversible ischemic neurologic deficit (RIND), stroke-in-evolution or completed stroke. TIAs are generally considered as deficits enduring for less than 24 hours, although they often last only a few minutes or occasionally several hours. RINDs are deficits of minimal degree that have entirely remitted within 3 weeks; their natural history parallels TIAs. Completed strokes are mild to severe, with fixed neurologic deficits for 24 hours or longer. Although ischemic cell change is known to begin within 5 minutes after total arrest of the circulation, Hossmann and Kleiheus (40) have pointed out that the functional magnitude of this neuronal loss is not known. Rather, they have demonstrated that a number of neurons are unaffected after 1 hour. This study has now been confirmed in a number of animal experiments. This work and that of Jones and others (43) suggest to many observers that in the early hours after onset there is a temporary window for therapeutic intervention in acute stroke. During this period, however, the current lack of a sensitive marker of ischemic tissue prevents the clinician from distinguishing between a TIA, RIND, stroke-in-evolution or a completed stroke. Due to the potentially devastating consequences of a completed stroke and depending upon the risks involved, in the early phase of stroke the patient's condition may be assumed to be passing through this therapeutic window.

Rapid assessment of stroke patients includes an immediate and complete examination and acquisition of standard laboratory tests. This includes cranial tomography to exclude a mass lesion that occasionally mimics a stroke, e.g., hemorrhage, tumor or abscess. Medical management begins by maintenance of the blood pressure and control of hemodynamically significant arrhythmias. Signs of congestive heart failure should be reduced in order to augment cardiac output. Oxygenation needs to be supported, because hypoxia, like hypotension, has devastating effects upon ischemic tissue. Renal function and balanced electrolytes need to be established. Hyperglycemia is

best reduced to levels less than 125 mg%. Hydration should be
sufficient to prevent volume depletion.

Pharmacologic Protection

     Studies on the protective effect of pharmacological agents
against cerebral ischemia have involved both intraneuronal
metabolism and the microvasculature of laboratory animals. The
first efficacious effect was reported with the use of
barbiturates (53,72). This was attributed to a suppression of
energy utilization and a reduction of the sodium and potassium
fluxes needed to generate action potentials. A blunting of
potassium efflux after an ischemic challenge is also proposed
for hypothermia, phenytoin and lidocaine (70). Propranolol is
reported to decrease experimentally produced infarction, but
the mechanism is unclear. Several studies have also
investigated the effects of indomethacin and prostacyclin
(PGI2) on cerebral infarction (15,32). Indomethacin blocks
prostaglandin turnover in the arachidonic cascade by impeding
formation of thromboxane A_2. Prostacyclin antagonizes
thromboxane A_2 and, as noted previously, produces an
anti-aggregating and vasodilating effect. In the laboratory, a
significant reduction in platelet aggregation, improvement in
regional blood flow, and restoration of cortical sensory evoked
potentials occurred with a combination of indomethacin and
PGI_2. One study, however, employed epoprostenol (PGI_2) in 36
patients with cerebral infarcts less than 48 hours old and
found no benefit over controls (46).
     Faden (19) showed rapid improvement in sensory cortical
evoked potentials and cerebral blood flow in animals with a
cerebral infarct receiving high dosages of naloxone, the opiate
antagonist. Many conflicting clinical reports about the
benefits of naloxone for the treatment of acute stroke have
since been published. Naloxone (.8-1.2 mg every 10 minutes)
has been given to 13 patients; 10 of 11 nonfatal patients
eventually showed improvement, 3 immediately, and 7 recovered
to their pre-admission status (42). The degree of neurologic
deficit and the timing between the onset of the stroke and the
beginning of treatment were not stated; the results are
nonetheless encouraging, especially because of the expected
development of more specific opiate receptor antagonists. More
recently, Adams and colleagues (1) have demonstrated the safety
and efficaciousness of large dose-escalation trials (52.3 to
4978 mg) of naloxone in 5 of 12 patients and 9 of 15 patients.
These preliminary findings corroborate the observations about
naloxone made in the laboratory, where higher dosages are often
employed. At dosages exceeding opiate receptor antagonism,
naloxone alters membrane transport of calcium, reduces lipid
peroxidation, increases cerebral blood flow, and improves
cardiac performance.
     Blockade of calcium entry into cells by nimodipine was

investigated because of the potential for reducing the deleterious effects of intracellular calcium accumulation occurring with ischemia (34). The calcium channel blocker may also reduce the degree of vasospasm in the microvasculature that is associated with ischemia. In animal studies, nimodipine increases cerebral blood flow and has fewer systemic and cardiac effects than other calcium channel blockers. In human trials, similar effects have been observed. In a preliminary double-blind Dutch study (28), nimodipine significantly reduced the death rate (6 of 79) in 8% of treated patients versus 21% of controls (18 of 85). A double-blind, placebo and multiple dose trial of nimodipine for use within the first 48 hours of acute infarction is expected to begin soon.

Human trials of other pharmacologically protective agents on the ischemic brain are limited and poorly controlled, mostly because of the difficulty in immediate quantification of the injury. A study using sodium thiopental (2 gm every 8 hours) reported a one-third reduction in mortality. This benefit, however, was not substantiated in a double-blind study of 26 patients (61). Aminophylline is reported to diminish cerebral energy states and mortality in another poorly controlled study (9). Numerous reports regarding the application of steroids in stroke have not demonstrated any conclusive benefit.

Restoration of the Circulation

By the Hagen-Poiseuille equation, blood flow is directly proportional to blood pressure and the radius of the vessel and inversely proportional to blood viscosity (69). With the loss of autoregulation following an acute infarct, viscosity is the one variable that is easily manipulated in an attempt to restore flow. The viscosity of blood is largely determined by the red cell mass. Optimal rheological flows occur with hematocrits of 33%, a point at which oxygen transport is still at a high level. Experimental reduction of the hematocrit by 30% to 50% improves regional cerebral blood flow by 10-20 ml/100 gm/min. This finding is in contrast to the effect of simple volume expansion; whole blood transfusions do not increase cerebral blood flow. Volume expansion bears considering in stroke patients, however, because chronic volume contraction is not infrequent in patients using diuretic agents, and in such patients volume replacement will augment cardiac output through improved end diastolic filling. Hypervolemic hemodilution is most likely to be effective in infarcts with adequate collateral supply and unlikely to help improve infarcts with poor collateral flow such as lacunar infarcts. Patients with initial hematocrits below 39% are unlikely to have substantial improvement in cerebral blood flow with added manipulations that bring the hematocrit to 33%.

Currently, hypervolemic hemodilution is achieved by use of dextrans, 5% albumin or the fibrinogen synthesis inhibitor, pentoxifylline. If venesection is employed to rapidly lower the hematocrit, it is important to avoid volume depletion. Dextrans were reported in a preliminary Swedish study of acute stroke to improve neurologic scores in 85% of patients versus 64% of controls (62). Interim results, however, of a larger multicenter study have not shown a similar benefit. A trial of a low molecular weight hydroxyethyl starch is currently being conducted in the United States. With plasma expansion, pressor agents are also proposed to increase regional perfusion in the dysautoregulated zones that are passively dependent on systemic pressure for added flow. There are no current studies on the value of pressor agents in the treatment of acute stroke, probably because of the inherently high rate of cardiac disease in stroke patients.

Reports of hemorrhagic stroke following revascularization procedures have limited attempts to restore the circulatory defect causing an acute neurologic deficit. In the Joint Study, mortality was 42% in patients who had an endarterectomy within 2 weeks of the onset of an acute stroke (20). Surgery was often performed, however, several days or more after a major infarction was established. With respect to the development of hemorrhagic infarction and immediate surgery, the experimental work of Crowell and associates is important (14). They found that one- to two-hour clippings of the middle cerebral artery were associated with mild neurologic deficit and ischemic injury. Clippings over 6 hours caused severe neurological deficit and extensive infarction with hemorrhage. They surmised that intervention prior to 4 hours would avoid hemorrhagic infarction. Thrombosis of the microvasculature and generation of an active inflammatory response over several days probably potentiate development of a hemorrhagic infarct from a necrotic vascular bed. The work of Jones and associates (43) suggests that intervention in acute ischemia is more feasible if under 2 to 3 hours, depending on the extent of impaired regional blood flow. Practical matters of transportation and necessary differential diagnosis of stroke patients limit the regular application of revascularization procedures of large or medium-sized vessels in acute stroke.

Ringelstein et al. (57) have advised on current surgical practice for emergency carotid surgery. They stated that CE is applicable to 3 groups of patients: 1) those with fluctuating symptoms; 2) those with stuttering but limited neurological deficits; and 3) those in the early stage of a rapidly progressive stroke. The benefit of surgery in these groups is not established, and the concerns for hemorrhagic infarction and demonstrated experimental limitations after 4 hours must be considered. Pertinent, perhaps, is the report of Hafner and Tew (31), who described a successful emergency CE in 3 patients developing acute neurologic deficits during hospitalization.

An alternate technique for restoration of the circulation is angioplasty. This procedure was used on the basilar artery by Sundt and colleagues (63) in 2 patients with intractable vertebral-basilar insufficiency. Focal atherosclerotic lesions are cracked by expansion of a flotation balloon. A few recent reports have described application of this technique to a whole range of cerebrovascular lesions, including fibrous dysplasia and atherosclerotic lesions of the carotid arteries, atherosclerotic vertebral arteries, post-surgical carotid stenosis, and Takayasu's disease. Currently, the potential for distal embolization has discouraged, however, wider use of angioplasty in the cerebral circulation.

The increasing access to cerebral vessels by catheterization with balloon flotation devices is likely to renew interest in thrombolysis of acutely occluded vessels. Current developments in acutely occluded peripheral and coronary arteries are encouraging. Streptokinase injected into the cerebral circulation was investigated in the laboratory years ago. Unfortunately, success was limited by a high incidence of hemorrhagic infarction. Perhaps more rapid assessment and early administration of pharmacologic protective agents will allow this technique to become more feasible. There is greater promise for the development of thrombolytic drugs, such as tissue plasminogen activator, which has fewer of the untoward reactions of streptokinase or urokinase.

REFERENCES

1. Adams, H.P., Olinger, C.P., Barson, W.G., Butler, M.J., Graff-Radford, N.R., Brott, T.G., Biller, J., Damasio, H., Tomsick, T., Goldberg, M., Spilker, J.A., Berlinger, E., Dambrosia, J., Biros, M., and Hollern, R. (1986): Stroke, 17:404-409.
2. American-Canadian Co-Operative Study Group (1985): Stroke, 16:406-415.
3. American-Canadian Co-Operative Study Group (1985): Stroke, 17:12-18.
4. Appen, R.E., Wray, S.H., and Cogan, D. (1975): Am. J. Ophthalmol., 79:374-377.
5. Astrup, J., Siesjo, B.K., and Symon, L. (1981): Stroke, 12:723-725.
6. Astrup, J., Symon, L., Branston, N.M., and Lassen, N.A. (1977): Stroke, 8:51-57.
7. Austin, G., Laftin, D., Vasudevan, R., Lichter, E., and Hayward, W. (1974): In: Microvascular Anastomosis for Cerebral Ischemia: Cerebral Blood Flow in Stroke Type Patients, edited by J.M. Fein and H.O. Reichman, pp. 241-265. Springer-Verlag, New York.
8. Barnett, H.J.M., Plum, F., and Walton, J.N. (1984): Stroke, 15:941-943.

9. Blaisdell, W.F., Clauss, R.H., Galbraith, J.G., Imparato, A.M., and Wylie, E.J. (1969): JAMA, 209:1889-1895.

10. Bousser, M.G., Eschwege, E., Haguenau, M., Lefaucconnier, J.M., Thibault, N., Touboul, D., and Touboul, P.J. (1983): Stroke, 14:5-14.

11. Branston, N.M., Strong, A.J., and Symon, L. (1977): J. Neurol. Sci., 32:305-321.

12. Canadian Cooperative Study Group (1978): N. Engl. J. Med., 299:53-59.

13. Cartlidge, N.E.F., Whisnant, J.P., and Elveback, L.R. (1977): Mayo Clin. Proc., 52:117-120.

14. Crowell, R.M., Olsson, Y., Klatzo, I., and Ommaya, A. (1970): Stroke, 1:439-448.

15. Dougherty, J.H., Levy, D.E., Rawlinson, D.G., Ruff, R., Weksler, B.B., and Plum, F. (1982): Neurology, 32:970-974.

16. Durward, Q.J., Ferguson, G.G., and Barr, H.W.K. (1982): Stroke, 13:459-464.

17. Dyken, M.L., and Pokras, R. (1985): Stroke, 15:948-950.

18. Ellenberger, C., and Epstein, A.D. (1986): Semin. Neurol., 6:185-193.

19. Faden, A.I. (1983): Stroke, 14:169-172.

20. Fields, W.S., Maslenikov, V., Myers, J.S., Hass, W.K., Remington, R.D., and McDonald, M. (1970): JAMA, 211:1993-2003.

21. Fieschi, C., Agnoli, A., Battistini, N., and Bozzao, L. (1986): Neurology, 18:1166-1179.

22. Fisher, C.M. (1952): Arch. Ophthalmol., 47:167-203.

23. Fisher, C.M., Gore, I., Okabe, N., and White, P.D. (1965): J. Neuropathol. Exp. Neurol., 24:455-476.

24. Fode, N.C., Sundt, T.M., Robertson, J.T., Perless, S.J., and Shields, C.B. (1986): Stroke, 17:370-376.

25. Ford, C.S., Frye, J.L., Toole, J.F., and Lefkowitz, D. (1986): Arch. Neurol., 43:219-222.

26. Furlan, A.J., and Craciun, A.R. (1985): Stroke, 16:797-799.

27. Garde, A., Samuelsson, K., and Fahlgren, H. (1983): Stroke, 14:677-681.

28. Gelmers, H.J., Gorter, K., de Weerdt, C.J., Wiezer, J.H.A., Prinses, I., and Ziekenhuis, A. (1986): Stroke, 17:145.

29. Gross, C.R., Kase, C.S., Mohr, J.P., Cunningham, S.C., and Baker, W.E. (1984): Stroke, 15:249-255.

30. Grotta, J.C., Bigelow, R.H., and Hu, H. (1984): Neurology, 34:437-442.

31. Hafner, C.D., and Tew, J.M. (1981): Surgery, 89:710-717.

32. Hallenbeck, J.M., Leitch, D.R., Dutka, A.J., Greenbaum, L.J., and McKee, A.E. (1982): Ann. Neurol., 12:145-156.

33. Harbison, J.W., Selhorst, J.B., and Waybright, E.A. (1982): Ann. Neurol., 12:74.

34. Harris, R.J., Branston, N.M., Symon, L., Bayhan, M., and Watson, A. (1982): Stroke, 13:759-766.

35. Harrison, M.J.G. (1983): In: Cerebrovascular Disease:
    Thromboembolism, edited by M.J.G. Harrison and M.L. Dyken,
    pp. 171-196. Butterworths, London.
36. Harrison, M.J.G., Inasek, R., and Marshall, J. (1986):
    Stroke, 17:391-392.
37. Harrison, M.J.G., and Marshall, J. (1985): Stroke,
    16:795-797.
38. Heyman, A., Wilkerson, W.E., Heyden, S., Helms, M.J.,
    Bartel, A.G., Karp, II.R., Tyroller, H.A., and Hames, C.G.
    (1980): N. Engl. J. Med., 302:838-841.
39. Heyman, A., Wilkerson, W.E., Hurwitz, B.J., Haynes, C.S.,
    Utley, C.M., Rosati, R.A., Burch, J.G., and Gore, T.B.
    (1984): Neurology, 34:626-630.
40. Hossman, K.A., and Kleiheus, P. (1973): Arch. Neurol.,
    29:375-384.
41. Hurwitz, B.J., Heyman, A., Wilkerson, W.E., Haynes, C.S.,
    and Utley, C.M. (1985): Ann. Neurol., 18:698-704.
42. Jabily, J., and Davis, J.N. (1983): Stroke, 15:36-39.
43. Jones, T.H., Morawetz, R.B., Crowell, R.M., Marcoux, F.W.,
    FitzGibbons, S.I., DeGirolami, U., and Ojemann, R.G.
    (1981): J. Neurosurg., 54:773-782.
44. Kanzow, E., and Dieckhoff, D. (1969): In: Cerebral Blood
    Flow: On the Location of Vascular Resistance in the
    Cerebral Circulation, edited by M. Brock, C. Fieschi,
    D.H. Ingvar, N.A. Lassen, and K. Schurmann, pp. 96-97.
    Springer, Berlin.
45. Kurtzke, J.F. (1982): Neurology, 32:1207-1214.
46. Linet, O, Hsy, C.Y., Faught, R.E., Hogan, A.J.,
    Furlan, B.M., Coull, D.C., Huang, and Yatsu, F.M. (1985):
    Stroke, 16:149.
47. Martin, M.J., Whisant, J.P., and Sayre, G.P. (1960): Arch.
    Neurol., 3:530-538.
48. Marzewski, D. (1982): Stroke, 13:821-824.
49. McHenry, L.C. (1978): Cerebral Circulation and Stroke.
    Greenhouse & Co., New York.
50. Mendelowitz, D.S., Kimmins, S., and Evans, W.E. (1981):
    Arch. Surg., 116:1587-1591.
51. Mohr, J.P. (1982): Stroke, 13:3-11.
52. Muuronen, A., and Kase, M. (1982): Stroke, 13:24-31.
53. Nemoto, E.M. (1978): Crit. Care Med., 6:203-214.
54. Pessin, M.S., Duncan, A.W., Mohr, J.P., and Poskanzer, D.C.
    (1977): N. Engl. J. Med., 296:358-362.
55. Pfaffenbach, D.D., and Hollenhorst, R.W. (1973): Am. J.
    Ophthalmol., 75:66-72.
56. Poole, C.J.M., and Ross Russell, R.W. (1985): J. Neurol.
    Neurosurg. Psychiatry, 48:902-905.
57. Ringelstein, E.B., Zeumer, H., and Angelou, D. (1983):
    Stroke, 14:867-875.
58. Ropper, A.H., Wechsler, L.R., and Wilson, L.S. (1982):
    N. Engl. J. Med., 307:1388-1401.
59. Sandok, B.A. (1982): Mayo Clin. Proc., 57:227-230.

60. Sharbrough, F.W., Messick, Jr., J.M., and Sundt, Jr., T.M. (1973): Stroke, 4:674-683.
61. Shinhoj, E., and Paulson, O.B. (1970): Acta Neurol. Scand., 46:129-133.
62. Strand, T., Splund, K., Eriksson, S., Hagg, E., Lithner, F., and Wester, P. (1984): Stroke, 15:980-989.
63. Sundt, T.M., Smith, H.C., Campbell, J.K., Vlietstra, R.E., Cucchiara, R.G., and Stanson, A.W. (1980): Mayo Clin. Proc., 55:673-680.
64. Trojaborg, W., and Boysen, G. (1973): Electroencephalogr. Clin. Neurophysiol., 34:61-69.
65. Turney, T.M., Garraway, W.M., and Whisant, J.P. (1984): Stroke, 15:790-794.
66. Walsh, P.N., Kansu, T.A., Corbett, J.J., Savino, P.J., Goldberg, W.P., and Schatz, N.J. (1981): Circulation, 63:552-559.
67. Whisnant, J.P., Sandok, B.A., and Sundt, T.M. (1983): Mayo Clin. Proc., 58:171-175.
68. Wolf, P.A., Kannel, W.B., Sorlie, P., and McNamara, P. (1981): JAMA, 245:1442-1445.
69. Wood, J.H., and Kee, D.B. (1985): Stroke, 16:756-772.
70. Yatsu, F.M. (1983): Neurol. Clin., 1:37-53.
71. Yatsu, F.M., and Coull, B.M. (1981): In: Current Neurology, edited by S.H. Appel, pp. 159-203. Wiley Medical Publication, New York.
72. Yatsu, F.M., Diamond, I., Graziano, C., and Lindquist, P. (1972): Stroke, 3:726-732.

Central Nervous System Disorders of Aging:
Clinical Intervention and Research, edited by
Randy Strong et al. Raven Press, New York
© 1988.

THE FAMILY AS AN INTEGRAL PART OF THE MANAGEMENT

OF CENTRAL NERVOUS SYSTEM DISORDERS

Peggy A. Szwabo

Division of Geriatric Psychiatry
St. Louis University Medical Center
St. Louis, Missouri 63104

Progressive cognitive impairment of loved ones represent a
frequent and profound challenge to families. Families provide
80 percent of the care for impaired elderly with gradual
assumption of decision-making activities and increased physical
demands in providing activities of daily living (ADL) (8).
Approximately one-third of care providers spend more than 40
hours per week in personal care activities (13). Many articles
have demonstrated the need for home health and have identified
specific activities of daily living that require outside assistance. Shanas and others (20,6) have found that approximately
one-third to one-fourth of older adults require home help
services.
   The National Center for Health Statistics (NCHS) estimates
that 10 percent of the noninstitutional elderly are as severely
disabled as those who live in extended care facilities (17,24).
   It is predicted that with rising health care costs the
responsibility of care will increasingly fall upon the
shoulders of families (12). Despite the debilitating aspects
of the disease, patients with dementing illnesses reside at
home until late in their illness. The U.S. Comptroller General
Office Survey (1977) noted that 90 percent of home help

services were provided by family members (23). Only recently have we begun to look at the psychologic, social, and physical effects on family members or caregivers.

In assuming more caretaking and management responsibilities, families react in various ways such as with anger, guilt, conflict, and stress. Many of these reactions are similar to those noted in grieving (22). These feelings can impede the caregiver from being able to function in a realistic quality way. There is also the potential for increasing stress and tension even leading to verbal and physical abuse (3).

Much has been written about the burden of caring for impaired elderly relatives. Besides the physical and emotional needs of the impaired individual, many of the caretakers feel "sandwiched" by care demands of the elder and by the needs of their offspring. Middle-aged children look forward to their own time as their children grow up, but now they are forced to change their plans to care for impaired relatives. This results in a variety of emotional reactions (2).

There are many issues that must be addressed in order for health care professionals to assist families. In this chapter, we will explore issues and problems for the health provider, identify common themes and problems family members experience, describe stages of burden and review treatment approaches.

CLINICIAN ISSUES

One of the frequent problems which families encounter is emotional stress during the diagnostic process (2). Family members are acutely aware that something is seriously wrong and are often frustrated when their physicians can give them no answers. In the early stages of the disease, the diagnosis is difficult. By the completion of the evaluation, family members may be increasingly anxious, angry and mistrustful of their physicians. When the diagnosis has been confirmed, spouses complain of the way in which results were conveyed to them and of lack of helpful direction, e.g., "Put him in a nursing home...". Even when the disease process was explained in great detail, Barnes and his group (2) found that family members could not "hear"; their anxiety and denial was so great that family members could not understand or accept the explanation.

Lack of Therapy Options

In studies of psychotherapeutic options for the aged, the Group for the Advancement of Psychotherapy (9) found that many therapists dislike working with the older patient because they must confront their own fears of growing older. The older patient forces one to address aging issues. More importantly, unresolved conflicts with the therapist's own family may prevent him from working effectively or aggressively with the patient and his family.

Meyer and others (15) have observed that most health care providers do not have adequate family therapy skills or do not feel comfortable in providing ongoing family support.

The reality is that the family is the primary resource for the patient. They are the first to call with a concern or to report a change. Since they provide the majority of care, they are a necessary part of treatment and management of the patient.

Many clinicians have very limited knowledge of the community resources available to assist families who provide in-home care. As a result, they fail to provide adequate direction. Unfortunately, unless the family is resourceful, this lack of direction may necessitate earlier institutionalization.

Treatment Concerns

Treatment and management poses ethical issues for the clinician. The management of impaired patients is not technologically oriented but rather emphasizes social environmental approaches, safety surveillance, and observation for changes in physical and emotional states. These approaches are not as challenging and require labor intensive investment and creative management by caregivers.

There is no cure for progressive cognitive impairment. The concept of chronicity presents a problem for the medical model. The medical model focuses on curing diseases. When a cure is not possible, clinicians react in a variety of ways: limiting treatment options, backing away from the patient, total abandonment of the patient, referral to other professionals, or recommendations for nursing home placement. Confronting these concerns on the part of the clinician will do much to open the doors of communication with the patient's family and ultimately help provide better care and support for the cognitively-impaired patient.

FAMILY ISSUES

Caretaking of an impaired elderly relative demands a balancing act. The effect of the emotional and physical demands on the caregiver will temper the way they care for their elderly parent.

Overall, most families are genuinely concerned and care about their aging parents. The stress of caretaking and other life demands may effect their efforts and quality of caretaking.

The conflict between these demands and the family's life style, personality and needs may evoke certain reactions. These reactions are common to most families though not all experience or are able to identify them.

Common Themes

Family members often feel guilty about not being able to do enough for the elderly patient. They may feel guilt-ridden because they did not identify the problem early enough or feel badly that they did not seek help sooner.

Some are angry at themselves (though they may never be able to identify it) for not being able to do more, angry at their situation and feel trapped. These feelings may be cyclical, e.g., guilt which turns to anger which, in turn, intensifies the guilt. They may be angry with the medical system for having no answers, no definitive diagnosis, no direction, and no cures. Anger and frustration may escalate with the up and down course of "good" and "bad" days. They may have difficulty seeing these behaviors as part of the course of the disease but feel that the behavior is manipulative and purposeful.

Additional unresolved conflicts with the parent may surface, exacerbating emotional responses and intensifying the situation. This additional conflict may increase the caregiver's anger and burden of care.

Conflicts between siblings may surface over distribution of caregiving responsibilities. For example, one child may be the primary caretaker with others absent, involved from afar or critical of the caretaker's efforts and decisions (16). In some families, bitter struggles erupt regarding aggressiveness of care, financial responsibility, living arrangements, need for respite and family help in care giving.

An often voiced concern is the prolonged grief over the loss of the person of the loved one long before his physical demise, an experience some have described as a "never ending funeral." A host of physical and emotional symptoms may be experienced by the caregiver, e.g., depressive symptoms to a full blown major depression, neglect of one's own health, and problems with sleeplessness and irritability.

As the older adult's problems become more apparent, other relationships may suffer. The spouse of the caregiver, spouse of the elder, and grandchildren may all become enmeshed in trying to help and create a tense situation as their own issues emerge. Whatever affects the caregiver eventually affects their spouse, children and others. Brody (5) has demonstrated that middle-aged women are the primary caregivers. Sons become caregivers when the daughter is not available, but sons are usually assisted by a wife and generally experience less stress.

Many families mention the problem of isolation. Social supports, which are now a necessity, may diminish because of the increased supervision required by the impaired spouse but also because of his socially inappropriate behavior. A commonly voiced problem at support groups is that friends do not understand what is going on and, therefore, avoid contact with the affected family. In contrast, caregivers may send out subtle signals that they prefer to be alone for reasons of exhaustion or embarrassment. The symptoms need to be assessed and gently discussed as a normal part of the ramifications of the disease process.

Disease-Related Problems

Lack of understanding of the disease and the progressive nature of the illness may occur due to caregiver's anxiety and denial. They may not be able to "hear" or understand what is happening. This may cause the caretaker to make frequent phone calls for assistance, complaints or other veiled attempts for support. They may also "doctor shop" for a prognosis that sounds more favorable. The search for cures, medications and other treatments may be sought unremittingly as they become more anxious and upset over their relative's deterioration.

Coping abilities may be unduly tested as more socially unacceptable behavior and mood changes occur in the impaired person. The caretaker and family members have increasingly greater difficulty in coping with accusatory, hostile and wandering behavior. Physical changes such as incontinence often necessitate institutionalization (18).

Respite Issues

Eventually, the clinician will have to address the concerns of respite and institutionalization. Respite services, which provide periodic relief, on a temporary or intermittent basis, to caregivers of the chronically ill living at home (14), are often lacking even in metropolitan areas. Informal systems can be developed within family networks, neighbors, churches and home health agencies. The issue is one of identifying the fact that caregivers need respite. Incorporating respite treatment into the plan is part of the management of the cognitively impaired. The clinician may only need to give the caretaker permission for self care. Unfortunately, one person is often overburdened with caretaking. The role of the clinician is to identify the need for respite and try to coordinate (or delegate coordination of) family members, home health and community support to provide care without detriment to the caregiver and patient. The caregiver's emotional state and subsequent reactions seen in anxiety, guilt and over-involvement may seem to prevent planning of respite. Family conflict may erupt even when others observe that one is overburdened and others are viewed as not doing their fair share. Clinicians need to be as supportive and kind with gentle suggestions on how to manage the patient and preserve the caretaker. Other alternatives such as day-care programs may serve as respite for the caretaker.

Placement

At some point in the progression of the illness, institutionalization may be needed. The vow "I'll never place my..." will have to be addressed. Concrete suggestions such as how to choose a nursing home, guidelines on looking at facilities, and predicting their reactions to their first visit to the home can be very helpful. Understanding and reinforcement regarding the good care they have provided is paramount. Discussing the pros and cons of placement with the family is indicated (Table 1) (19). Families need help working through the psychological struggle associated with the decision to place. The clinician must be cognizant that families sometimes need to fail. That is, they must try everything first before considering placement (19,21). With this in mind, one can review with the family, reinforce all they have done, and suggest it is now time to consider long-term placement.

TABLE 1. Family hopes in hospitalization
                 or long-term care

---

1. Maximum humanization of care.
2. Commitment to maintenance and enhancement of resident's dignity.
3. Encouragement of as much independence in ADL as possible.
4. Tolerance of difficult behaviors, and competence in the management of catastrophic reactions.
5. Imaginative program of activities for stimulation and maximization of resident's physical, mental and social capabilities.
6. Room to roam--protected areas for walking and rummaging.
7. Staff availability for discussion of issues of patient care.
8. Ways to stay involved and to "do" for their loved one.

Bretscher & Szwabo, 1986 (4)

For the reasons addressed above, family focused treatment is the treatment of choice for the cognitively impaired patients. The family provides the assistance and care but is also the barometer of the patient's course. The emotional reactions and stresses of the caregiver can help or hinder the patient's situation.

STAGES OF BURDEN

There are four stages of burden that families experience: crisis, separation, reinvolvement and reassessment. In this section these stages will be explored.

Crisis

Initially, families are in "crisis" and are just beginning to acknowledge that something is wrong with their relative. They may be ambivalent about their involvement and experience a wide range of feelings and frustrations. They seek hopeful answers and solutions. The future is uncertain, and they are justifiably fearful and anxious (Table 2). The role of the health professional is to be cognizant of the crisis and to assist the family in negotiating the health care system. They want information, direction, resources, and, above all, support from their clinicians. This affords the clinician the opportunity to build an alliance to provide that care and communication.

TABLE 2. <u>Family needs</u>

---

1. Recognition of their involvement with the patient and their input regarding patient's history and successful approaches.
2. Understanding on the part of staff of what the family has been through and is presently feeling.
3. Patience with their questions, concerns, fears.
4. Streamlining, as much as possible, the evaluation process.
5. Welcome and encouragement to frequently visit their loved one, with assurances of the availability of staff for family concerns.
6. Give practical, concrete suggestions on interacting and visiting with elder.
7. Warm and eager acceptance of their loved one, and demonstration of understanding.
8. Reaffirmation and encouragement of their involvement in treatment decisions and opportunities to discuss possible institutional decisions.
9. Assurance at this facility that the illness of their loved one is a known entity and that the staff are comfortable, confident and unafraid of assuming the responsibility for his/her care.

Bretscher & Szwabo, 1986 (4)

Separation

As the family's involvement increases, the "separation" phase begins. They may react either by withdrawing or becoming over-involved. As the situation stabilizes and resources have been instituted, the caregiver may temporarily withdraw from the picture and experience a sense of relief. This is a normal response to the exhausting prelude to the crisis of recognition of the relative's decline. Individuals need to be allowed to

restabilize. The clinician can be instrumental in preventing
feelings of guilt and abandonment by predicting the need for
restabilization and begin to reinvolve the caregiver after
respite. Over-involvement occurs when the caregivers' own
stress is so high that they cannot let others help. This individual may not be able to separate and becomes increasingly
anxious and highly critical of others' efforts. This caregiver
needs firm guidance and support, and usually responds well when
information about the patient's progress is shared on a regular
basis. In this stage, the key is to meet the family's needs
rather than waiting for the family's request for help.

Reinvolvement

Reinvolvement of the family should be initiated soon after
separation to avert increased anxiety or increased avoidance of
the impaired relative. This avoidance is usually secondary to
feelings of guilt and abandonment. Short periods of respite
have the potential of evoking guilt and feelings of abandonment
on the part of the caregiving child. To encourage this self
care, diplomacy and sensitivity is required on the part of the
clinician.

Expecting family involvement cannot be seen as a demand but
as a way to stay involved in providing quality care. The
clinician may need to clarify roles: e.g., who does what and
when; define expectations of the disease process; what is realistic; what treatment can be offered; and identify ways to give
the family control. The clinician will need to demonstrate
practically and concretely how the family can be involved; for
example, teach the family how to do reality orientation, bowel
and bladder routines, and provide good nutrition (2).

Reassessment

The goal of the family approach is defining and reinforcing
ways the family can be therapeutic. The family caregiver must
be viewed as an integral part of evaluation, treatment and
management of the impaired elder. It is the health provider
that must support and identify ways that the family can continue their help in providing more quality care. As the
patient and his needs change, the process of reassessment is
crucial. The professional must identify potential difficulties
before there is a crisis and assist the family in working
through the physical and emotional burden of caring for their
deteriorating loved one.

THERAPEUTIC APPROACHES

Recent reports in the literature reflect the growing concern
for providing approaches and programs for caretakers
(1,10,11,25). The underlying assumptions of the programs

reflect the importance of establishing communication, concern for the family and acknowledgment of their efforts and need for information.

Professionals and family members need to be collaborators in encouraging the elder's independence, as well as treatment and rehabilitative efforts. Initially, the generalist can offer support in a variety of ways by demonstrating their concern for their patient and by acknowledging the family's caregiving efforts.

Knowledge of and referral to appropriate community resources such as home health services, day care, senior citizens programs, and the Alzheimer's Disease and Related Disorders Association (ADRDA) is a necessity (Table 3). More importantly, support can be provided by assisting the family in the day-to-day caregiving by suggesting practical approaches.

TABLE 3. Support services for families

---

1. Creative and flexible care.
2. Information and participation in treatment planning.
3. Support groups for family members of non-institutionalized dementia patients.
4. Day care services for dementia patients in the community.
5. Respite care.
6. Support groups for spouses and/or children of hospitalized/ill/elderly and extended care facility (ECF) residents.
7. Sponsorship or provision of space for local ADRDA Chapter or similar services.

Bretscher & Szwabo, 1986 (4)

Use of reminiscence or life review techniques in encouraging integration of remote memories with the present can help defuse potentially exasperating situations that occur when there is repetitive speech (7). Helping family members identify pre-disease hobbies and activities can be beneficial in encouraging quality interaction, for example, grandmother loves flowers. The family members can bring the flowers to stimulate a discussion of grandma's past involvement with flowers thereby incorporating her past memories with present conversations with the family. Bringing objects promotes interaction and sharing but also involves stimulation of the senses. These kinds of approaches model ways to interact with an impaired relative in a therapeutic manner. It diverts the tendency of families to note how much the impaired person has deteriorated since the last visit. Approaches like this channel the family into a more productive activity.

Family caregivers may require referral for more intense psychotherapy. The generalist needs to identify and refer the overloaded caregiver to a specialist.

Support groups, such as the ADRDA, relieve some of the stress through education and peer sharing. Support groups developed under the auspices of the treatment facilities have demonstrated their effectiveness. These programs are usually cost free and are a service of the facility to patients and their families. Reports indicate their success by near perfect attendance at meetings, high level of participation and informal networking among the families outside of the group. Another benefit is the ability to help members make institutional placement and view it as necessary. Families participating in these programs report greater enthusiasm and better care for the loved ones; in some cases, it was also observed by the patient (22,25). It has been observed that the caregiver is able to resume some personal activities with positive carryover from the group experience (1). Lastly, Kahan and his group (7) found that educating family members about dementia and providing opportunities to discuss problems in a supportive environment had a positive effect in reducing the perception of burden and levels of depression in caregivers.

CONCLUSION

Professionals can do a great deal to help families through a very difficult experience. There is no cure for the dementias at the present, but the family-focused approach can assist families to continue to provide quality care for their loved ones. Professionals can make a tremendous contribution to the family's caregiving efforts by helping them cope with what is for them a very frightening, difficult experience.

REFERENCES

1. Aronson, M., Levin, G., and Lipkowitz, R. (1984): Gerontologist, 24:339-342.
2. Barnes, R., Raskind, M., Scott, M., and Murphy, C. (1981): J. Am. Geriatr. Soc., 29:80-85.
3. Beck, C., and Phillips, C. (1983): J. Gerontol. Nurs., 9:97-101.
4. Bretscher, C., and Szwabo, P. (1986): An unpublished handout, Geriatric Psychiatry, St. Louis University, St. Louis, Missouri.
5. Brody, E. (1981): In: Clinical Aspects of Alzheimer's Disease and Senile Dementia, edited by N.E. Miller and G.D. Cohen, pp. 310-331, Raven Press, New York.
6. Brody, E. (1985): Mental Health and Physical Health Practices of Older People, Springer Publishing Co., New York.
7. Butler, R. (1963): Am. J. Psychiatry, 26:65-76.

8. Ebersole, P., and Hess, E. (1979): Toward Healthy Aging, pp. 359-362, C.V. Mosby Co., St. Louis, Missouri.
9. Group for the Advancement of Psychotherapy (1981): GAP, pp. 17-81, New York.
10. Kahan, J., Kemp, B., Staples, F., and Brummel-Smith, K. (1985): Am. Geriatr. Soc., 33:664-670.
11. Lansky, M. (1984): Psychiatr. Ann., 14:126-129.
12. Levine, N., Gendron, C., Dastoor, D., Poitras, L., Sirota, S., Barza, S., and Davis, J. (1984): Am. J. Psychother., 27:215-223.
13. Mace, N., and Rabins, P. (1981): In: The 36-Hour Day: A Family Guide to Caring for Persons with Alzheimer's Disease, Other Dementing Illness, and Memory Loss in Later Life, pp. 139-154, Johns Hopkins, Baltimore.
14. Meltzer, J.W. (1982): Center for Study of Social Policy, pp. 2-5, Washington, D.C.
15. Meyers, A. (1984): In: Mental Health Assessment and Therapeutic Intervention with Older Adults, edited by C.D. Whanger and A.C. Meyers, pp. 3-11, Aspen Systems Corporation, Rockville, Maryland.
16. Moss, M., Moss, S., and Moles, S. (1985): Gerontologist, 25:134-140.
17. National Center for Health Statistics (1981). Health Characteristics of Persons with Chronic Activity Limitations: United States, 1979. Data from the National Health Survey, Series 10, No. 137, Hyatesville, Maryland.
18. Ouslander, J., Urman, H., and Uman, G. (1986): J. Am. Geriatr. Soc., 34:83-90.
19. Sancier, B. (1984): National Association of Social Workers, Inc., 1-2:63-65.
20. Shanas, E. (1962): The Health of Older People: A Social Survey, Harvard University Press, Cambridge, Massachusetts.
21. Stewart, R. (1984): National Association of Social Workers, Inc., 7-8:386-390.
22. Teusink, J., and Mahler, S. (1984): Hosp. Community Psychiatry, 2:152-156.
23. U.S. Comptroller General of the U.S., April 1977, p. 29, Washington, D.C.
24. U.S. Department of Health and Human Services (1982): White House Conference on Aging (1982), p. 92, Bethesda, Maryland.
25. Wasow, M. (1986): National Association of Social Workers, Inc., 3-4:93-97.

Central Nervous System Disorders of Aging: Clinical Intervention and Research, edited by Randy Strong et al. Raven Press, New York © 1988.

MOLECULAR BIOLOGY OF NERVE DEGENERATION

Tong H. Joh and Harriet Baker

Laboratory of Molecular Neurobiology
Cornell University Medical College
New York, New York 10021

Is there an abnormal and selective gene expression in degenerating neurons?

Some aging disorders of human brain, such as Alzheimer's and Parkinson's diseases, are associated with massive degeneration of specific neuronal populations. Alzheimer's disease (AD) and senile dementia of the Alzheimer's type are known to be associated with progressive deterioration of memory and cognitive function (5,18). Postmortem studies have demonstrated profound reduction in the cholinergic markers of the nucleus basalis of Meynert of patients with these diseases (10,42). Parkinson's disease, on the other hand, is a degenerative disease of the dopaminergic neuronal group, A9, in the substantia nigra. The causes of specific neuronal degeneration in each of these diseases are not known. Generalized age-related degeneration of neurons does not appear to account for these disorders, but both diseases are known to develop primarily in aging subjects.

Over the years, we and others (14,39-41) observed that many proteins are selectively and transiently expressed in certain types of neurons and cells during development. Mechanisms underlying this kind of transient expression and the functions of these proteins are unknown. However, it is parsimonious to think that these proteins have distinct functions in these cells during development. For example, one can hypothesize that these transiently expressed proteins may play important roles, such as inducing or regulating other proteins, or maintaining developmentally specific cellular activities.

Selective changes in the expression of certain proteins may also occur in aging neurons. One hypothesis proposes that many aspects of aging may be a consequence of cells drifting away from their normal state of differentiation (11,25). Accordingly, neurodegeneration associated with aging and age-related diseases could be a consequence of neurons ceasing to be highly differentiated. This can occur in two ways. First, there may be altered expression of genes that is responsible for the highly differentiated properties of neurons. The decrease of particular neurotransmitter specific synthetic enzymes, the loss of neurotransmitter receptors (13,26,29,38) and the increase in the frequency of abnormal neuronal morphology (23,36) are examples of dysdifferentiation in the aging brain. Secondly, dysdifferentiation may be manifested as a derepression of endogenous genes in tissue in which they are not normally expected to be expressed. For example, Ono and Cutler (25) reported an increase in the mRNA related to globin, a protein usually associated with erythrocytes, in the brain of mice during aging. In addition, they found an age-associated elevation in mRNA related to murine leukemia virus in mouse brain. It may not be too much a stretch of the imagination to think that the abnormal expression of certain proteins interferes with normal cellular functions, and eventually leads to degeneration of neurons.

Recent extraordinary findings of Wolozin et al. (44) may represent excellent examples of our hypothesis. They showed that a specific protein, molecular weight 68,000, is expressed in Alzheimer's brain (44). Histological studies of Alzheimer's brain show that this protein is present both in neurons exhibiting neuritic plaques and neurofibrillary tangles, and in some morphologically normal neurons. These results suggest that the appearance of this protein may be related to the degeneration of neurons in AD. Although the function of this protein, its detailed structure, and relationships to other existing proteins are not yet known, their findings parallel our own line of thinking, the possibility that selective expression of certain proteins occurs in degenerating neurons.

One of the most interesting subjects in modern molecular biology is to study tissue specificity of gene expression, the expression of certain proteins that is normally restricted to particular cell types. A proper review of phenotypic and genotypic expression is beyond the scope of this chapter. However, the above findings indicate that there is a selective, specific and abnormal gene expression of a certain protein in degenerating neurons in AD brains. It is not known whether this type of selective gene expression occurs in degenerating neurons in other brain disorders such as Parkinson's disease. Furthermore, we have to consider the possibility that some proteins cease to be expressed in degenerating neurons.

In the following sections, we summarize our findings of biochemical phenomena occurring in the cell bodies, axon terminals and postsynaptic cell bodies of injured neurons in the central nervous system of rat. Expression of phenotype specific proteins and enzymes in neurons can be manipulated by lesions of presynaptic neurons. Although these phenomena may not be exact models of degenerative disorders of aging brains, we hope they provide some basic biochemical insight into neuronal plasticity, especially when neurons degenerate, regenerate or sprout in the central nervous system.

TISSUE SPECIFICITY OF CATECHOLAMINE NEURONS

Catecholamines, dopamine (DA), norepinephrine (NE) and epinephrine are synthesized from tyrosine in vivo by four enzymatic reactions (Fig. 1). Tyrosine hydroxylase (TH) is the first and rate limiting enzyme in the pathway which catalyzes the reaction of L-tyrosine to 3,4-dihydroxyphenyl-alanine (L-DOPA). L-DOPA is converted to DA by the catalytic reaction of aromatic L-amino acid decarboxylase (AADC). The third enzyme, dopamine beta-hydroxylase (DBH), catalyzes the reaction of DA to NE which is converted to epinephrine by phenylethanolamine N-methyltransferase (PNMT).

An interesting feature of this pathway is that the expression of these enzymes is tissue specific. As shown in Fig. 1, all four enzymes are expressed only in epinephrine neurons. In NE neurons, the first three enzymes, TH, AADC and DBH, but not PNMT, are expressed. DBH and PNMT are not expressed in DA neurons. Thus, the general marker protein of catecholamine neurons is TH since AADC is present not only in monoaminergic neurons but also in non-neuronal cells in kidney, liver and thymus (8).

Dramatic and predictable changes in the levels of catecholamine enzyme proteins occur in neurodegenerative diseases and in experimentally induced neuronal degeneration. An increase in PNMT has been found in the cell bodies of degenerating neurons in the C1 and C2 regions of the brain stem in AD (6). In contrast, there is a decrease in this enzyme in the axon terminal regions of these neurons (6). There is also evidence for an increase in TH in surviving neurons in the substantia nigra of patients who died of Parkinson's disease (4,9,16,21,31). That phenomenon has been reproduced in an experimental model of Parkinson's disease in which partial lesions of the rat substantia nigra pars compacta are made with 6-hydroxydopamine, a neurotoxin that is specific for catecholamine containing neurons (1,37,45). One question that we ask is, does altered expression of catecholamine enzymes contribute to degeneration of neurons? For example, increased synthesis of catecholamines is one possible consequence of increases in biosynthesis of enzymes such as PNMT and TH, both of which are rate limiting with respect to catecholamine synthesis. Increases in cellular levels of epinephrine depress the biosynthesis of the PNMT protein (7). Is it possible that other proteins critical to normal cellular function may be similarly affected? Conversely, if cell

specific enzymes such as TH and PNMT cease to be expressed, do
these cells degenerate? By examining the behavior of specific
gene products after neuronal injury, general principles may be
discovered concerning the role that gene expression plays in
degenerating neurons and what factors govern gene expression
during neuronal degeneration. We and others have developed
experimental models of neuronal injury to answer some of these
questions. The findings are discussed in the following
sections.

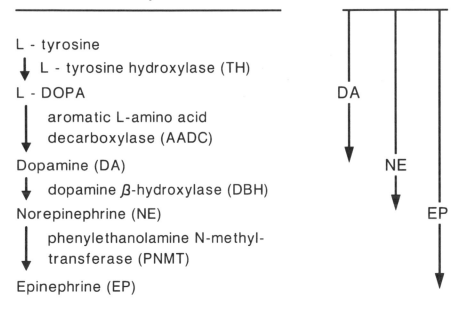

FIG. 1. Catecholamine biosynthetic pathway and phenotype
specific expression of enzymes.

BIOCHEMICAL CHANGES OF CENTRAL
CATECHOLAMINE NEURONS TO INJURY

Our previous publications (17,27,28,30,32-34) have
discussed this subject in detail and, thus, only a short
summary will be presented in this section.
    Following transection of central axons of both DA and NE
neurons in the brain, the activities and amounts of TH, both
distally and caudally to the transection, change. Distally,
TH and DBH activity in NE neurons decline over 10 to 12 days
(the anterograde reaction) (30,32-34). In contrast, in DA
neurons, TH activity rapidly, within 24 hours, falls distal to

the lesions in a manner comparable to that seen in peripheral sympathetic ganglia.

During the retrograde reaction elicited by axonal lesions, a characteristic pattern of changes in TH activity occurs within the cell bodies of DA and NE neurons. Initially, there is a substantial increase of enzyme activity, followed within the first 24 to 48 hours by a gradual decline, reaching about 50% of control by day four. Both TH and DBH activities remain depressed for approximately two weeks and then gradually return to normal. The reduction of enzyme activity during the retrograde reaction in DA and NE neurons is produced by a reduction in the amount of enzymes (27,33). In the DA system, the reversibility of the changes of enzyme accumulation depends upon the proximity of the lesion to the cell body (27,28). Lesions placed within the nigrostriatal pathway close to the cell bodies in the substantia nigra result in cell death and, thereby, in permanent loss of some enzyme activity. However, lesions placed distally elicit reversible changes.

The reversible accumulation of neurotransmitter synthetic enzymes during the retrograde reaction in central catechol-amine neurons, therefore, at least after distal lesions, is comparable in both NE and DA neurons. The time course of the changes appears to parallel that of the sprouting phenomenon and, as Ross and Reis (35) have suggested, represents a reordering of the priorities of protein biosynthesis, favoring the increased accumulation of proteins involved in the regeneration of cell surface at the expense of those required for neurotransmission. However, it has never been considered whether any abnormal gene expression occurs during either the retrograde reaction or irreversible neuronal death. Expression or inhibition of other important proteins and enzymes which are essential for axonal transport or membrane lipid biosynthesis should be carefully examined. However, it should be recognized that either abnormal expression or inhibition of certain genes may have a great deal of influence on the cell death or survival. Although these phenomena may or may not be important to the etiology of AD, Parkinson's disease or other aging disorders, the molecular mechanisms governing neuronal degeneration may be similar in both cases.

OLFACTORY AFFERENT REGULATION OF CATECHOLAMINE ENZYME GENE EXPRESSION

In a recent series of experiments, the peripheral afferent innervation arising from the olfactory receptor neurons has been shown to transneuronally regulate the expression of neurotransmitters in the juxtaglomerular cell population of the olfactory bulb (3,19,24). Following lesion, receptor axons and terminals degenerated with a consequent decrease in the size of the olfactory glomeruli and a reduction in weight of the olfactory bulb. There were also significant changes in transmitter biosynthesis and degradation in intrinsic juxtaglomerular DA neurons with decreases in the activity of TH, the levels of transmitter, DA, and the levels of its major metabolite, 3,4-dihydroxyphenylacetic acid. At the same post-lesion times when TH activity was reduced, juxtaglomerular DA neurons were no longer demonstrable with antibodies to TH, indicating that the decrease in activity was attributed to a loss of TH protein.

There was, however, evidence that the juxtaglomerular DA neurons, although deficient in TH, were still present. For example, the numbers of juxtaglomerular neurons did not appear to decrease (12,15,22); they retained the ability to take up DA (22) and to synthesize transmitter from L-DOPA. In subsequent experiments, we found that both AADC activity and immunostaining were maintained at about 65% of control levels in the same animals where TH activity was reduced to about 20 to 25% of control levels (2), indicating that a large percentage of the DA neurons did not degenerate. Using a similar protocol, Kream et al. (20) demonstrated that substance P as well as TH expression were transneuronally regulated in the hamster. The olfactory system is unique as it retains many properties only expressed during development in other central nervous system regions (43). Thus, alteration in phenotypic expression may reflect unique expression of trophic factors which may impact on neuronal survival. These findings directly demonstrated a selective-afferent transneuronal influence on transmitter synthetic capacity of a target cell that may be mediated through specific access to subcellular genetic machinery necessary for phenotypic expression.

CONCLUDING REMARKS

The recent rapid development of molecular genetic research has contributed to the understanding of gene structure, regulation and expression. Further, these new techniques will probably allow an understanding of specific, selective and abnormal gene expression during neuronal degeneration, regeneration and survival. Advanced technology for the production of monoclonal antibodies to specific proteins, preparation of DNA probes for the characterization and identification of genes and their products, and manipulation of these genes for the modification of gene expression will certainly be utilized for multidisciplinary research efforts to find the mechanisms underlying the neuronal degenerative diseases, especially in aging brains.

REFERENCES

1. Agid, Y., Javoy, F., and Glowinski, J. (1973): Nature, 245:150-151.
2. Baker, H., Kawano, T., Albert, V., Joh, T.H., Reis, D.J., and Margolis, F.L. (1984): Neuroscience, 11:605-615.
3. Baker, H., Kawano, T., Margolis, F.L., and Joh, T.H. (1983): J. Neurosci., 3:69-78.
4. Bernheimer, H., and Hornykiewicz, O. (1965): Klin. Wochenschr., 43:711-715.
5. Blessed, G., Tomlinson, B.F., and Roth, M. (1968): Br. J. Psychiatry, 114:797-811.
6. Burke, W.J., Chung, H.D., Strong, R., Marshall, G.L., Davis, W.L., and Joh, T.H. (1987): In: Geriatric Clinical Pharmacology, edited by W.G. Wood and R. Strong, pp. 47-69. Raven Press, New York.
7. Burke, W.J., Davis, J.W., and Joh, T.H. (1983): Endocrinology, 113:1102-1110.
8. Christenson, D.G., Diarman, W., and Udenfriend, S. (1970): Arch. Biochem. Biophys., 141:356-367.
9. Davidson, J., Lloyd, K., Dankova, J., and Hornykiewicz, O. (1971): Experientia, 27:1048-1049.
10. Davies, P., and Maloney, A.J. (1976): Lancet, 2:1403.
11. Dean, R.G., Socher, S.H., and Cutler, R.G. (1985): Arch. Gerontol. Geriatr., 4:43-51.
12. Estable-Puig, J.F., and DeEstable, R.F. (1980): Exp. Neurol., 24:592-602.
13. Finch, C.E., Randall, P.K., and Marshall, J.F. (1981): Annu. Rev. Gerontol. Geriatr., 2:49-87.
14. Gershon, M.D., Rothman, T.P., Joh, T.H., and Teitelman, G. (1984): J. Neurosci., 4:2269-2280.
15. Graziadei, P.P.C., and Moti-Graziadei, G.A. (1980): J. Neurocytol., 9:145-162.
16. Hornykiewicz, O. (1973): Fed. Proc., 32:183-190.
17. Joh, T.H., and Reis, D.J. (1978): In: Colrgium Internationale Neuropsychopharmacology, edited by P. Denicer, C. Raudouce-Thomas, and A. Villeneuve, pp. 1457-1465. Pergamon Press, Oxford.
18. Kaufman, D.M. (1984): Clinical Neurology for Psychiatrists. Grune & Stratton, Inc., New York.
19. Kawano, T., and Margolis, F.L. (1982): J. Neurochem., 39:342-348.
20. Kream, R.M., Davis, B.J., Kawano, T., Margolis, F.L., and Macrides, F. (1984): J. Comp. Neurol., 222:140-154.
21. Lloyd, K.G., Davidson, L., and Hornykiewicz, O. (1975): J. Pharmacol. Exp. Ther., 195:453-464.
22. Margolis, F.L., Roberts, N., Ferriero, D., and Feldman, J. (1974): Brain Res., 81:469-483.
23. McNeill, T.H. (1983): In: Review of Biological Research in Aging, Vol. 1, edited by M. Rothstein, pp. 163-178. Alan R. Liss, Inc., New York.

24. Nadi, N.S., Head, R., Grillo, M., Hempstead, J., Grannot-Reisfield, N., and Margolis, F.L. (1981): Brain Res., 213:365-371.
25. Ono, T., and Cutler, R.G. (1978): Proc. Natl. Acad. Sci. USA, 75:4431-4435.
26. Pradhan, S.N. (1980): Life Sci., 26:1643-1656.
27. Reis, D.J., Gilad, G., Pickel, M., and Joh, T.H. (1978): Brain Res., 144:325-342.
28. Reis, D.J., Ross, R.A., Gilad, G., and Joh, T.H. (1978): In: Neuronal Plasticity, edited by C.W. Cottman, pp. 197-226. Raven Press, New York.
29. Reis, D.J., Ross, R.A., and Joh, T.H. (1977): Brain Res., 64:345-353.
30. Reis, D.J., Ross, R.A., Pickel, M., and Joh, T.H. (1977): In: Neurotransmitter Function: Basic and Clinical Aspects, edited by W.S. Fields, pp. 143-161. Symposia Specialists, Florida.
31. Rinne, U.K., Sonninen, V., and Hyyppa, M. (1971): Life Sci., 10:549-557.
32. Ross, R.A., Joh, T.H., and Reis, D.J. (1975): Brain Res., 89:380-386.
33. Ross, R.A., Joh, T.H., and Reis, D.J. (1975): Brain Res., 92:57-72.
34. Ross, R.A., Joh, T.H., and Reis, D.J. (1979): Brain Res., 160:174-179.
35. Ross, R.A., and Reis, D.J. (1974): Brain Res., 73:161-166.
36. Scheibel, M.E., Tomiyosa, U., and Scheibel, A.B. (1977): Exp. Neurol., 56:598-609.
37. Snyder, A.M., Stricker, E.M., and Zigmond, M.J. (1985): Ann. Neurol., 18:544-551.
38. Strong, R. (1985): In: Review of Biological Research in Aging, edited by M. Rothstein, pp. 181-196. Alan R. Liss, Inc., New York.
39. Teitelman, G., Baker, H., Joh, T.H., and Reis, D.J. (1979): Proc. Natl. Acad. Sci. USA, 776:509-513.
40. Teitelman, G., Joh, T.H., Grayson, L., Park, D., Reis, D.J., and Iacovitti, L. (1985): J. Neurosci., 5:29-39.
41. Teitelman, G., Reis, D.J., and Joh, T.H. (1981): Proc. Natl. Acad. Sci. USA, 78:5225-5229.
42. Whitehouse, P.J., Price, D.L., Clark, A.W., Coyle, J.P., and DeLong, M.R. (1980): Ann. Neurol., 10:122-126.
43. Whittemore, S.R., Evendal, T., Larkfors, L., Sieger, A., Suromberg, I., and Persson, H. (1986): Proc. Natl. Acad. Sci. USA, 83:817-821.
44. Wolozin, B.L., Pruchnicki, A., Dickson, D.W., and Davies, P. (1986): Science, 232:648-650.
45. Zigmond, M.J., and Stricker, E.M. (1984): Life Sci., 35:5-18.

Central Nervous System Disorders of Aging: Clinical Intervention and Research, edited by Randy Strong et al. Raven Press, New York © 1988.

THE EFFECT OF AGING ON THE

EXPRESSION OF SPECIFIC GENES BY RAT BRAIN

Carol T. Wismer, Kathleen A. Sherman,* Mary Zibart, and Arlan Richardson

Department of Chemistry,
Illinois State University, Normal, Illinois 61761;
*Department of Pharmacology
Southern Illinois University Medical School,
Springfield, Illinois 62766

Although gene expression has been studied in a variety of tissues, only within the last decade have studies on gene expression focused on the aging brain. The mammalian brain is not only the most complex organ in terms of function and structure, but it is also the most complex tissue in terms of the diversity of its RNA transcripts. For example, there are some 30,000 genes that are expressed uniquely within the brain (25).

TRANSLATION

The expression of genetic information can be divided into two phases: translation and transcription. Prior to 1980, most of the studies on aging and gene expression focused on translation, i.e., protein synthesis. A decline in protein synthesis has been reported with increasing age in various tissues from a wide variety of living organisms (20).

Many investigators have reported that the protein synthetic activities of the brain change during development (20); however, only a few investigators have studied brain protein synthesis during senescence. Kanungo et. al. (16) found a progressive increase in the in vivo incorporation of [^{14}C]-leucine into protein by rat brain between 11 and 89 weeks of age. However, Gordon and Finch (11) found no change in the incorporation of leucine in vivo between mature (9-12 months) and senescent (26-28 months) mice. In a related study in which mice were used, McMartin and Schedlbauer (18) reported that the incorporation of

[^{14}C]-leucine into acid insoluble material by brain slices decreased less than 10% between 5 and 25 months of age. Several investigators (2,9,15) have reported an age-related decline in the cell-free protein synthetic activity of the brain *in vitro*. Ekstrom et al. (8) reported that a significant decrease in the cell-free protein synthetic activity of the brain occurred after the brain reached maturity. A decrease of 56% was reported between 6 and 32 months of age. Fando et al. (9) measured the effect of age on brain protein synthesis using three assay systems: *in vivo*, slices, and cell-free. The rates of protein synthesis were measured in the forebrain and cerebellum of Fischer F344 rats. Their results showed that the rate of protein synthesis declined significantly between 1 and 24 months of age in all three assay systems.

Dunlop et al. (7) observed a decrease in the *in vivo* synthesis of proteins by the cerebral hemispheres and the cerebellum between 2 and 10 months of age. Fando et al. (9) reported that *in vivo* protein synthesis by various regions of the brain decreased between 3 and 23 months of age. Recently, Ingvar et al. (14) compared the rates of protein synthesis in rat brain as a function of age. *In vivo* protein synthesis of the whole brain decreased 17% between 6 and 23 months of age; this decrease was significant. However, when they measured the *in vivo* protein synthesis of specific brain regions, they found that a significant decrease in protein synthesis was observed in some, but not all, brain regions. The largest decreases in protein synthesis were found in the inferior olivary nucleus and the red nucleus. Protein synthesis by these brain regions decreased 25% between 6 and 23 months of age. Thus, a decrease in brain protein synthesis appears to occur after maturation; however, the age-related changes in protein synthesis appear to vary considerably from one brain region to another.

Senescent changes in brain structure and function are well-known; however, the underlying cause(s) of these changes is poorly understood. The changes in morphology, structural maintenance, and remodeling in the nervous system are possibly related to the long-term effects of the age-related changes in protein synthesis.

TRANSCRIPTION

RNA Synthesis

A change in protein synthesis could be due to changes in transcription. The expression of mRNA is the primary site of control of gene expression in eukaryotes. However, only a few studies on the transcriptional activity of the brain have been conducted. Zs-Nagy and Semsei (29) measured total and poly(A)$^{+}$ RNA syntheses in senescent rats. They reported a considerable decrease in the rates of synthesis of both types of RNA between 1.5 and 29 months of age in the brain cortex. In a related study, Semsei et al. (23) reported a slight decrease in RNA synthesis after 13 months of age; however, this decrease was not statistically significant. Although it appears that the synthesis of poly(A)$^+$RNA decreases with age, Coleman et al. (6) reported that the levels of poly(A)$^+$ RNA did not change with age in rat brain. In addition, they found no age-related change in the complexity of the RNA.

Levels of Specific mRNAs

In the studies cited above, only the amount or the synthesis of total or poly(A)$^+$RNA was measured. These data do not provide any information on the changes that may occur with age in specific mRNAs. For example, does the age-related decline in RNA synthesis result from a decline in the genetic potential of the cell to synthesize all mRNA species? An understanding of the mechanism responsible for the change in poly(A)$^+$RNA synthesis is complicated by the fact that specific genes appear to be affected differentially by the aging process. To gain a better understanding of how aging affects gene expression at the level of transcription, it is necessary to study age-related changes in specific mRNAs. Studies within this area are difficult because mRNA is a very heterogenous population, and it makes up only about 2% of the total cellular RNA. The age-related changes in mRNA synthesis would have dramatic effects on the gene expression in the aging organism due to the central role that mRNA plays in the transfer of genetic information. With the development of recombinant DNA technology, it is possible to study the effect of aging on the expression of specific genes in the brain. In this report, the effect of aging on the levels of β-actin and β-tubulin mRNA in brain from male Fischer F344 rats was determined by hybridization to cDNA probes.

Total RNA was isolated from the brain of male Fischer F344 rats ranging from 5 to 37 months of age as described by Chirgwin et al. (4). Fig. 1 shows the Northern blot analysis of RNA pooled from 5-, 12-, 23-, and 37-month-old rats with cDNA probes to β-tubulin and β-actin. It in apparent from Fig. 1 that each probe hybridized to specific mRNA species. Based upon migration of rRNA standards, β-tubulin cDNA hybridized to mRNA species of 2.4 kb and 1.9 kb. These sizes are in agreement with the sizes of 2.5 kb and 1.8 kb reported by Bond and Farmer (3) for β-tubulin mRNA in poly(A)$^+$RNA from the brain of Sprague-Dawley rats, and the sizes of 2.6 kb and 1.8 kb for β-tubulin mRNA in human HeLa cells (13). The β-actin probe hybridized to a mRNA species of 2.2 kb. This agrees with the values for β-actin mRNA obtained by Bond and Farmer (3) and Waters et al. (28) of 2.2 kb and 2.1 kb, respectively. Fig. 1 also shows that the migration of β-tubulin and β-actin did not change as a function of age. In addition, there was no evidence for an

age-related change in the degradation of these two mRNAs.
   The relative levels of β-tubulin and β-actin were determined
by dot blot hybridization, and the data are given in Tables 1
and 2. As shown in Fig. 2, a linear increase in the amount of
the cDNA probe that hybridized to the RNA was found with RNA
concentrations between 2 and 16 μg. Virtually no radioactivity
was associated with control samples that had tRNA applied to the
filters. Therefore, little non-specific binding of the probes
was detected under the conditions used for hybridization. Using
8 μg per dot, the relative levels of β-tubulin and β-actin mRNA
were measured in brain RNA isolated from 5- to 37-month-old
rats. The data in Table 1 indicates that the level of β-tubulin
mRNA changed very little with increasing age. Using
autoradiography/densitometry to measure the mRNA levels, no
significant change was observed. However, the level of
β-tubulin mRNA for 37-month-old rats was significantly lower
than the other ages when the hybridization was measured using a
scintillation counter. We conclude that levels of β-tubulin mRNA
do not change appreciably with age. The data in Table 2 give
the relative levels of β-actin in total RNA isolated from brains
of 5- to 37-month-old rats. No significant change in the levels
of β-actin mRNA was observed.

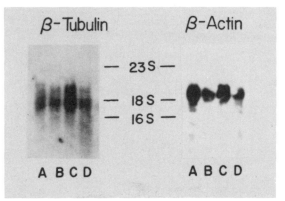

   FIG. 1. <u>Northern blot analysis of RNA isolated from the
brain of rats of various ages.</u> Total RNA from 5-(A), 12-(B),
23-(C) and 37-(D) month-old rats was fractionated by gel
electrophoresis using 1.2% agarose (19), transfered to
nitrocellulose membranes by the method of Southern (24), and
hybridized to radioactively-labelled cDNA probes to either
β-tubulin or β-actin as described by Thomas (26). The migration
of rRNA from <u>E. coli</u> and brain are shown.

   Because the brain is a complex organ and the different regions have different functions as well as different molecular
components, the levels of β-tubulin and β-actin mRNAs in

various regions of the brain were studied in 4-month-old rats. Fig. 3 shows the Northern blot analysis of RNA extracted from the brain stem, cerebellum, cortex, hippocampus, hypothalamus, and the striatum.

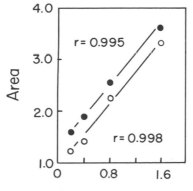

μg RNA

FIG. 2.   The hybridization of the cDNA probes to various levels of brain RNA. The hybridization of the cDNA probe to β-tubulin (O) and β-actin (●) to various amounts of RNA isolated from the brain of a 5-month-old rat was conducted using the dot blot technique described by Thomas (26). The cDNA probes were labeled with [^{32}P]-radioactivity by nick translation (17), and the levels of mRNA in each RNA dot blot were determined by measuring the relative spot intensities on the autoradiographs with a scanning densitometer. The correlation coefficients (r) for the hybridizaion of each probe are shown.

TABLE 1.   Levels of β-tubulin mRNA in rat brains of various ages[a]

	Relative levels of β-tubulin mRNA			
Age (mos)	Area	Percentage	cpm	Percentage
5	1.44 ± 0.04	100	1,517 ± 50	100
12	1.30 ± 0.16	90	1,398 ± 17	92
23	1.36 ± 0.04	94	1,370 ± 162	90
37	1.29 ± 0.05	90	1,239 ± 48	82[b]

[a]The data were obtained with 8 µg of RNA per blot. The level of each mRNA species was determined as described by Rutherford et al. (21). Each value represents the mean ± SEM of data from four animals for each age. The percentage is expressed on the basis of the 5-month-old group as 100%. [b]This value is significantly (p < 0.05) lower than the value for 5 months of age.

TABLE 2. Levels of β-actin mRNA in rat brains of various ages[a]

	Relative levels of β-actin mRNA			
Age (mos)	Area	Percentage	cpm	Percentage
5	1.74 ± 0.21	100	2,218 ± 127	100
12	1.61 ± 0.19	93	2,053 ± 286	93
23	1.63 ± 0.03	94	2,095 ± 52	95
37	1.61 ± 0.16	93	2,015 ± 100	91

[a]The data were obtained with 8 μg of RNA per blot. Each value represents the mean ± SEM of data from four animals for each age. The percentage is expressed on the basis of the 5-month-old group as 100%.

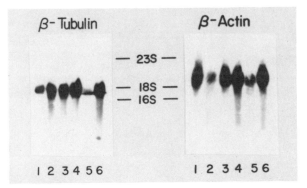

FIG. 3. Northern blot analysis of RNA isolated from various regions of rat brain. Total RNA was isolated from the brain stem (1), cerebellum (2), cortex (3), hippocampus (4), hypothalmus (5), and striatum (6) pooled from six 4-month-old rats. The RNA was fractionated and hybridized to radioactively-labelled cDNA probes to either β-tubulin or β-actin as described in Fig. 1. The migration of rRNA from E. coli and brain are shown.

The cDNA probe to β-tubulin hybridized to RNA species of 1.9 kb in all regions of the brain studied. The larger RNA species (2.4 kb) was not found in any of the regions, even after longer exposure. The failure to locate the 2.4 kb RNA species in the brain regions shown in Fig. 3 might be due to the fact that the species is located in a region of the brain not studied. It is also possible that the 2.4 kb RNA species may have been degraded during the time it took to dissect the regions. It should be noted that Bond and Farmer (3) also observed only the 1.8 kb RNA species in the cerebrum and cerebellum of Sprague-Dawley rats. The Northern blot analysis also shows that the levels of β-tubulin mRNA are different for the various brain regions. The levels of β tubulin mRNA in brain stem and hypothalamus are lower than in the other four regions. Bond and Farmer (3) reported that the β-tubulin mRNA was less for the cerebellum than the cerebrum. In our analysis, these two regions appeared to be similar.

The cDNA probe of β-actin hybridized to a RNA species of 2.2 kb. This is in agreement with the 2.2 kb reported by Bond and Farmer (3) for β-actin in the cerebrum and cerebellum in Sprague-Dawley rats. The migration of the mRNA was similar for all brain regions studied. Northern blot analysis also shows that the cerebellum and the hypothalamus have much lower levels of β-actin than the other four regions. Bond and Farmer (3) reported that the levels of β-actin mRNA in the cerebellum were greater than in the cerebrum.

CONCLUSIONS

In this study the expression of tubulin and actin genes was studied as a function of age in the brain. Tubulin and actin genes are expressed in all eukaryotic cells. In the central nervous system, the expression of these genes appears to be related to the development of neurons.

It has been recognized for some time that tubulin is composed of two similar subunits, α and β (28). Although these subunits can be separated, the α- and β-tubulins have a molecular weight of approximately 53,000 (5,28). Brain β-tubulin shows evidence of microheterogenicity and the proportion of the various subspecies of β-tubulin change during early development (12,27). This implies a heterogenetic nature of tubulin, which may be post-transcriptional or artifactual. The tubulins from a wide variety of eukaryotic sources migrate with comparable motility rates on one- and two-dimensional gel electrophoresis and, therefore, are assumed to be an evolutionary conserved proteins (5).

β-Tubulin is one of the principle components of microtubules, and it is a major component of all eukaryotic cells. Several studies have suggested that microtubules and microfilaments both act to transmit serum growth factor signals that stimulate the initiation of DNA synthesis in fibroblasts (3). In the central nervous system, a characteristic feature of the differentiation of neurons is an extensive neurite outgrowth involving the mobilization of large pools of cytoskeleton proteins into the various structural elements of the axons and dendrites (22).

Bond and Farmer (3) found that β-tubulin represented 20 to 25% of the total protein synthesized in rat brain at birth; however, this amount decreases to 2 to 5% by 33 days of age. Using a cDNA probe to β-tubulin, they showed that the decrease in tubulin synthesis was paralleled by a decrease in the level of β-tubulin mRNA. Bond and Farmer (3) reported that β-tubulin mRNA levels increased after birth in the cerebrum, peaked at day 8, and decreased 95% by day 80. The cerebellar pattern does not show an increase in β-tubulin mRNA levels. However, β-tubulin mRNA levels decreased 80% by day 80.

There are two cytoplasmic forms of the actin gene, β and γ (28). The β-actin sequence is present in the genome only once while the γ-actin sequence occurs, at most, three times (5). The actins have similar molecular weights and both are coded for 2.1 kb mRNA (5,28). There are six distinct gene products known for actin, which were discovered through protein sequencing (5).

The synthesis of β-actin is characteristic of normal rat brain. β-Actin is one of the most abundant proteins synthesized by the neonatal rat brain, but its synthesis decreases dramatically after birth (3). β-Actin is believed to play major roles in cell division, cell-shape changes, secretory processes, phagocytosis, cell and organelle motility, and muscle contraction (5,22,28).

Anderson (1) reported that the β-actin content of fibroblasts increases in relation to total cell protein during in vitro aging. Farmer et al. (10) demonstrated that β-actin mRNA expression changes dramatically during cell configuration changes accompanying cell growth. Bond and Farmer (3) reported that β-actin mRNA levels are regulated during the development of the cerebrum and cerebellum; however, the overall result is a dramatic decline in mRNA levels, which accompanies nerve cell differentiation. Bond and Farmer (3) found that the developmental changes which occurred in the cerebrum and cerebellum were similar to that which occurred in the whole brain. The β-actin mRNA levels increased after birth, peaked at day 8, and declined 50% by day 80.

This study represents the first information on the effect of aging and senescence on the expression of the genes for β-tubulin and β-actin. Although the levels of these mRNAs change dramatically during brain development, the levels of these mRNA species remain relatively constant between 5 and 37 months of age in whole rat brain. In addition, there is no evidence for any change in the size or degradation of the β-actin and β-tubulin mRNAs. However, we observed marked differences in the levels of β-tubulin and β-actin mRNA in various regions of rat brain. Therefore, it is possible that the levels of these two mRNA species might change with age within specific brain regions.

ACKNOWLEDGMENT

This work was supported in part by NIH grant AG 01548. We thank Dr. Marc W. Kirschner of the University of California, San Francisco, for the cDNA probes to β-tubulin and β-actin.

REFERENCES

1. Anderson, P.J. (1978): Biochem. J., 169:169-172.
2. Bobillier, P., Sakai, F., Sequin, S., and Jouvet, M. (1974) J. Neurochem., 22:23-31.
3. Bond, J.F., and Farmer, S.R. (1983): Mol. Cell. Biol., 3:1333-1342.
4. Chirgwin, J.M., Przybylia, A.E., MacDonald, R.J., and Rutler, W.J. (1979): Biochemistry, 18:5294-5299.
5. Cleveland, D.W., Lopata, M.A., MacDonald, R.J., Cowan, N.J., Rutter, W.J., and Kirschner, M.W. (1980): Cell, 20:95-105.
6. Coleman, P.D., Kaplan, B.B., Osterburg, H.H., and Finch, C.E. (1980): J. Neurochem., 34:335-345.
7. Dunlop, D.S., van Elden, W., and Lajtha, A. (1977): J. Neurochem., 29:939-945.
8. Ekstrom, R., Liu, D.S.H., and Richardson, A. (1980): Gerontology, 26:121-128.
9. Fando, J.L., Salinas, M., and Wasterlain, C.G. (1980): Neurochem. Res., 5:373-383.
10. Farmer, S.R., Van, K.M., Seev, A.B., and Penman, S. (1983): Mol. Cell. Biol., 3:182-189.
11. Gordon, S.M., and Finch, C.E. (1974): Exp. Gerontol., 9:264-273.
12. Gozes, I., and Littauer, U. (1978): Nature, 276:411-413.
13. Hall, J.L., Dudley, L., Dobner, P.R., Lewis, S.A., and Cowan, N.J. (1983): Mol. Cell. Biol., 3:854-862.
14. Ingvar, M.C., Maeder, P., Sokoloff, L., and Smith, C.B. (1985): Brain, 108:155-170.
15. Johnson, T.C. (1976): J. Neurochem., 22:17-23.
16. Kanungo, M.S., Joul, O., and Ready, K.R. (1970): Exp. Gerontol., 5:261-269.
17. Maniatis, T. (1982): In: Molecular Cloning, edited by T. Maniatis, E.F. Fritsch, and J. Sambrook, pp. 466-467. Cold Spring Harbor Laboratory, New York.
18. McMartin, D.N., and Schedlbauer, L.M. (1975): J. Gerontol., 30:132-136.
19.. McMaster, G.K., and Carmichael, G.C. (1977): Proc. Natl. Acad. Sci. USA, 74:4835-4838.
20. Richardson, A. (1981): In: CRC Handbook on Aging, edited by R.C. Adelman and R.J. Florin, vol. 1, pp. 79-101. CRC Press, Ohio.
21. Rutherford, M.S., Baehler, C.S., and Richardson, A. (1986): Mech. Aging Dev., 35:245-254.

22. Schmitt, H., Gozes, I., and Littauer, U. (1977): <u>Brain Res.</u>, 121:327-342.
23. Semsei, I., Szeszak, F., and Zs.-Nagy, I. (1982): <u>Arch. Gerontol. Geriatr.</u>, 1:29-42.
24. Southern, E.M. (1975): <u>J. Mol. Biol.</u> 98:503-517.
25. Sutcliffe, J.G., Milner, R.J., Gottesfeld, J.M., Reynolds, W. (1984): <u>Science</u>, 225:1308-1315.
26. Thomas, P.S. (1980): <u>Proc. Natl. Acad. Sci. USA</u>, 77:5201-5205.
27. van Hungen, K., Chin, R.C., and Baxter, C.F. (1981): <u>J. Neurochem.</u>, 37:511-514.
28. Waters, S.H., Distal, R.J., and Hecht, N.B. (1985): <u>Mol. Cell. Biol.</u>, 5:1649-1654.
29. Zs-Nagy, I., and Semsei, I. (1984): <u>Exp. Gerontol.</u>, 19:171-178.

Central Nervous System Disorders of Aging:
Clinical Intervention and Research, edited by
Randy Strong et al. Raven Press, New York
© 1988.

MEMBRANE STRUCTURE IN AGED HUMANS AND ANIMALS

W. Gibson Wood*† and Friedhelm Schroeder §+

*Geriatric Research, Education and Clinical Center,
Veterans Administration Medical Center;
†Departments of Neurology and Internal Medicine,
St. Louis University School of Medicine,
St. Louis, Missouri 63125; and
§Departments of Pharmacology and Medicinal Chemistry,
College of Pharmacy; and †Departments of Pharmacology
and Cell Biophysics, College of Medicine,
University of Cincinnati, Cincinnati, Ohio 45267-0004

Biological membranes are a key component of cell structure and function. Membranes partition the cell into different functional compartments, are involved in regulation of enzyme activity and ion transport, and provide a matrix for receptors and antigenic sites (24,36,49). Membranes, as proposed by Singer and Nicolson (42), consist of a lipid bilayer with proteins immersed at different depths. The principal lipids are phospholipids and their fatty acids and cholesterol. The phospholipids are located at the surface of the extracellular and cytoplasmic leaflets of the membrane. Fatty acids are attached to the phospholipids and extend into the hydrophobic area of each leaflet. Cholesterol, the predominant sterol in membranes, affects membrane physical properties by acting on the phospholipids and acyl groups (15).

Two classes of membrane proteins have been described. Peripheral proteins are associated with the membrane surface (18). Actin, myosin, fibronectin, and spectrin are examples of peripheral proteins. The second class of proteins is the integral proteins that are either embedded in the membrane or transverse it. Examples of integral proteins are Na^+,K^+-ATPase and adenylate cyclase. Proteins are thought to affect membrane structure by interacting with lipids (28). This effect of proteins has not received much attention in aging studies (5).

Changes in membrane structure have been linked to various diseases (24,28). For example, membrane structure is altered in myocardial ischemia, liver disease, certain hematological disorders such as sickle cell disease, and neoplasia. Erythrocyte membranes of alcoholic patients are more rigid and show a diminished response to alcohol in vitro as compared to membranes of control subjects (4,51). Not only have membrane changes been found in well-defined pathological conditions, but changes have also been observed in older as compared to younger organisms. One hypothesis is that pathological changes in membranes are a principal factor of the aging process (44). Age changes in membrane structure may explain age differences in cellular function. This chapter will review studies on membrane structure in aged organisms and consider the utility of the hypothesis that changes in membranes are an important component of the aging process. Age differences in membrane structure will be examined from the standpoint of changes in membrane fluidity and lipid composition. While the emphasis of this volume is on brain, this chapter will include discussion of membranes of other organs because of the relatively small number of studies on brain membranes of aged humans and animals.

MEMBRANE FLUIDITY

Cellular function is regulated by the fluidity of the membrane lipid environment (28). Membrane fluidity is a general term that has been used to describe the movement of lipids in the membrane. Fluidity can be affected by what has been described as intrinsic and extrinsic factors (28). Examples of intrinsic factors are lipid composition, integral proteins, and hydration. Extrinsic factors would be anesthetics including alcohol as well as other drugs. It has been argued that an "optimal" membrane fluidity is required for efficient membrane function such as enzyme activity, transport and other functions (36).

Generally, fluidity has been used to describe the degree of rigidity of the membrane. However, it is important to point out that fluidity actually consists of two components that have been described as rate of motion, a dynamic component, and extent of motion, a static component (37,39). Parameters such as limiting anisotropy, rotational rate, order parameter and rotational correlation time refer to different physical properties of the membrane. Most aging studies have used fluidity without distinguishing between the dynamic and static components. Therefore, in this chapter, membrane fluidity will be used in the broadest sense to describe motion in the bulk lipid environment of the membrane.

Two methods that are commonly used for measuring physical properties of membranes are electron spin resonance (ESR) and fluorescence spectrometry (see 13 and 26 for reviews of these methods). ESR uses a spin-labeled probe that reports on motion at different depths within the membrane. The majority of studies report an order parameter that is a measure of the extent of probe motion. A common probe used in fluorescence studies is diphenylhexatriene (DPH) that reports on the hydrophobic core of the membrane. The parameter that is usually reported is fluorescence polarization that consists of both rate of motion and extent of motion (39).

Listed in Table 1 are some of the studies using ESR and fluorescence spectrometry that have examined membrane fluidity in membranes of different age groups of animals and humans. Of the nineteen studies listed, nine reported a decrease in fluidity with increasing age, nine found no age differences, and one study reported more fluid membranes in aged animals. Of the nine studies that found age differences, six used the fluorescent probe DPH and measured steady state polarization. The other three studies used ESR and spin-labeling. Seven studies using ESR and two studies using fluorescence reported no age differences in membrane fluidity.

At first glance, it would appear that fluorescence spectrometry may be a more sensitive indicator of membrane physical properties than ESR. An alternative explanation is that the two techniques are measuring separate properties of the membrane. As discussed above, most fluorescence studies use DPH and measure steady state polarization that consists of both a dynamic component and a static component. The preponderance of ESR studies use the order parameter that is comparable to the static component. A dynamic parameter that can be measured in ESR studies is rotational correlation time (13), but it is rarely used. Greater consistency between the two methods might be found if both compared dynamic components and static components. Aging may have a greater effect on one as compared to the other. Another consideration when comparing the two methods is where in the membrane the probes are reporting. DPH reports on the hydrophobic core of the membrane. Most of the ESR studies use the 5-doxyl stearic acid that reports on motion close to the surface of the membrane. A better comparison would be to use the fluorescent fatty acid, transparinaric acid, that reports on motion close to the membrane surface. It is possible that age differences in membrane structure are greater in the hydrophobic core than close to the hydrophilic surface. Support for this interpretation is shown by the study of Cimino et al. (10) that is listed in Table 1. Effects of age were significantly different with the 16-doxyl probe that reports on the hydrophobic core as compared to the 5-doxyl probe that reports close to the membrane surface. Such a distinction with respect to probe location has been seen for ethanol and dolichol (8,25).

Another consideration is that the approach has been to examine the bulk membrane environment. However, most agree that the membrane consists of "patches" of lipids that differ in their physical properties and, in some instances, are

tightly bound to proteins (22,23). These lipid micro-
environments would not be detected using techniques that report
on bulk membrane properties and, perhaps, such microdomains
change with increasing age. Moreover, the membrane bilayer is
actually two monolayers whose physical properties and lipid
distribution are not the same (31,41; see 40 in this volume).
Future studies will need to examine membrane structure from
the perspective of lipid domains in order to fully understand
the connection between structure and function in aged humans
and animals.

TABLE 1. Age differences in membrane fluidity

Membrane	Species	Age	Method	Fluidity	Ref.
RBC[a]	Human	15-70 yr	ESR	↓[b]	20
RBC	Human	< 25,65+ yr	ESR	ND	5
RBC	Mouse	3-24 mo	ESR	ND	3
Platelet	Human	17-86 yr	FS	↓	11
Lymphocyte	Human	10-80 yr	FS	↓	34
Prostate	Rat	1-30 mo	FS	↓	14
Adipocyte	Rat	6,24 mo	ESR	ND	33
LPM	Rat	6-30 mo	FS	↓	30
LM	Rat	3-24 mo	ESR	↑	2
LM	Mouse	4-28 mo	ESR	ND	50
LM	Rat	3-27 mo	ESR	↓	38
Striata	Rat	3,30 mo	FS	↓	10
Striata	Rat	3,30 mo	ESR	↓	10
Striata	Rat	3-25 mo	FS	ND	21
Cortex	Rat	3,30 mo	FS	ND	10
SPM	Rat	3,24 mo	FS	↓	6
SPM	Mouse	3-24 mo	ESR	ND	3
SPM	Mouse	4-28 mo	ESR	ND	50
BM	Mouse	3-24 mo	ESR	ND	3

[a]Abbreviations: BM, brain microsome; ESR, electron spin
resonance; FS, fluorescence spectrometry; LM, liver microsome;
LPM, liver plasma membrane; ND, no age differences; RBC, red
blood cell membrane; SPM, synaptic plasma membrane.
[b]Increase (↑) or decrease (↓) in fluidity with age.

LIPID COMPOSITION

Membrane lipids directly determine the fluidity of the
membrane. There has been some indication that proteins may also
have an effect on membrane structure, although, most would agree
that lipids are the primary component involved. In addition to
their effects on membrane structure, lipids have recently been
shown to be involved in signal transduction and as recognition
sites for macrophages (1,12,16). These effects have not been

well-studied with respect to aging and will not be discussed
here. Instead, this section will examine the extent of changes
in the major lipids of membranes with increasing age.

Table 2 summarizes various studies that have examined lipid
composition of membranes in relation to age. This table is not
inclusive but is representative of studies that have used
different membranes from humans and animals. Five parameters
are listed: 1) cholesterol; 2) total phospholipid; 3) the ratio
of cholesterol to phospholipid; 4) individual phospholipids;
and 5) fatty acids.

Cholesterol

Cholesterol content was found to increase in brush border,
liver microsomes, myelin, SPM and brain microsomes. The
increase with age ranged approximately between 23 and 46%. One
study reported a decrease in SPM cholesterol; and no age
differences were seen in red blood cell membranes (RBC),
adipocyte, liver plasma membranes (LPM) or liver microsomes.

The studies which found that cholesterol did increase with
age showed rather large differences between young and old
membranes. However, an age-related increase in cholesterol
content does not appear to be a consistent finding. An obvious
explanation for the inconsistency among studies might be
methodology. Procedures for membrane preparations, cholesterol
analysis, and species could all have an effect on the final
result. It would seem that the most parsimonious conclusion is
that it has not been clearly determined as to whether membrane
cholesterol content increases with age.

Total Phospholipid Content

Table 2 shows phospholipid content of membranes from
different organs. An increase in phospholipid content with
age is seen in human RBC, brush border, LPM, liver microsomes,
myelin, SPM, and brain microsomes. Although significant,
these age differences were generally small. No age differences
were seen in mouse RBC, adipocyte membranes or mouse liver
microsomes. One study reported a decrease in total phospholipid
content of SPM in old as compared to young rats.

Even if total phospholipid content changes with age, such
data do not reveal which phospholipid is changing. Another
drawback is that one phospholipid might increase and another
phospholipid decrease with age which would not be reflected in
total content. While total phospholipid content by itself may
not provide much information on age differences, it is
important in relation to cholesterol content in membranes. An
increase in the cholesterol to phospholipid ratio has been
found to be associated with increased membrane rigidity (9,20).
An age-related increase in the cholesterol to phospholipid
ratio has been reported in human RBC, adipocyte, brush border,

TABLE 2. Age differences in lipid composition

Membrane	Source	Age	Cholesterol	Phospholipid	C/P	Phospholipids	FA	Ref.
RBC[a]	Human	15-70+ yr	ND	↑[b]	↑		ND	20
RBC	Mouse	3-24 mo	ND	ND	ND			2
Adipocyte	Rat	6,24 mo	ND	ND	↑			33
Brush Border	Rat	10-30 mo	↑	↑	↑		16.0↑	32
LPM	Rat	3-24 mo	ND	↑	↑	PC↓	20.4↓	43
LM	Macaque	2-21 yr	↑	↑	ND	PC↑,CL↓		48
LM	Mouse	6,28 mo	ND	↑	ND	ND		52
LM	Rat	3-27 mo		ND	↑	ND		38
Myelin	Human	14-84 yr	↑	↑	↑	ND	ND	44
Myelin	Mouse	3-26 mo	↓	↓	ND		ND	45
SPM	Rat	3,24 mo	↑	↑	ND			6
SPM	Mouse	3-24 mo	↑	↑	ND			2
BM	Mouse	3-24 mo		ND				2
Myelin	Rat	3-19 mo	ND	ND	↑	PE↑		29

aAbbreviations: BM, brain microsome; CL, cardiolipin; C/P, ratio of cholesterol to phospholipid; FA, fatty acid; LM, liver microsomes; LPM, liver plasma membranes; ND, no age differences; PC, phosphatidylcholine; PE, phosphatidylethanolamine; RBC, red blood cell membrane; SPM, synaptic plasma membrane.
bIncrease (↑) or decrease (↓) in fluidity with age.

LPM, liver microsomes, and myelin. Age differences were not found in mouse RBC, macaque liver microsomes, SPM, or brain microsomes.

Individual Phospholipids and Fatty Acids

Phospholipids are the main lipid class in the membrane (27). The phospholipids commonly found in membranes are phosphatidylcholine, phosphatidylethanolamine, phosphatidylserine, phosphatidylinositol and sphingomyelin. Few studies on membranes have examined individual membrane phospholipids among different age groups of either humans or animals. An extensive study emphasizing whole brain lipid composition of different species and age groups has been reported by Rouser et al. (35).

Table 2 shows that of the six studies listed on membrane phospholipids, three found no age differences of individual phospholipids. Phosphatidylcholine increased in liver microsomes and decreased in LPM with age. Phosphatidylethanolamine was found to be higher in myelin of older rats.

Fatty acids are another important lipid component of the membrane. Changes in fatty acid composition, such as an increase or decrease in the ratio of saturated to unsaturated fatty acid, can affect membrane structure. Four studies in this review examined fatty acids of phospholipids. Three studies described no age differences, and one study found an increase in the saturated fatty acid palmitic and a decrease in arachidonic acid in rat kidney brush border membranes. The unsaturated index was also lower in aged animals of which would be reflective of a more rigid membrane environment.

CONCLUSIONS

It would appear that no firm conclusions can be made regarding age changes in membrane structure. Age differences in membrane fluidity of the bulk lipid are not consistently observed. Greater consistency, however, is seen with fluorescent probes as compared to spin-labels. This difference between the two methods may reflect differences in where the probes align themselves in the membrane and not that fluorescent probes are more sensitive than are spin-labels. Generally, most studies have used the fluorescent probe DPH or the 5-doxyl stearic acid spin-label. Fluorescent probes such as 1-(4-trimethylammoniumphenyl)-6-phenyl-1,3,5-hexatriene and transparinaric acid would provide data concerning the membrane surface and, in the case of parinaric acid, report in a similar manner as the 5-doxyl stearic acid spin-label. ESR studies could use the deeper reporting probes such as the 12- and 16-doxyl stearic acids.

Another consideration in studies of membrane fluidity among different age groups is that attempts should be made to distinguish between the dynamic and static properties of the probe. Aging studies have, for the most part, used fluorescence polarization and order parameter. Additional data on membranes could be gained by delineating the dynamic and static membrane properties.

It is not apparent whether there are appreciable changes in membrane lipid composition with increasing age. Generally, studies report either an increase in lipid content or no age differences. Part of this inconsistency may be due to differences in procedures for membrane preparation and lipid analysis. Problems in examining age differences in lipid composition are discussed by Rouser et al. (35). Certainly, data on individual phospholipids and fatty acids in membranes of different age groups have not been forthcoming and need to be determined. Moreover, other compounds in addition to cholesterol and phospholipids may affect membrane structure. To this end, the chapter by Sun et al. (46) discusses how dolichol might affect both membrane structure and function. Other membrane components that need to be examined are gangliosides, polyphosphoinositide lipids, and both peripheral and integral proteins.

The status of changes in membrane structure with increasing age is similar, in some respects, to ethanol-induced changes in membranes. Ethanol both in vitro and in vivo affects membrane fluidity, but consistent changes are not observed in lipid composition (47). It has been suggested that ethanol may have a more specific effect on certain lipid domains or boundary lipids (19). Recent data from our laboratory and others (7,40) show that ethanol and benzyl alcohol have an asymmetric effect on membranes, i.e., one monolayer is more affected than the other. Membrane asymmetry and aging is discussed in the next chapter.

Studies on membrane structure of aged humans and animals have progressed to the point where the most current approaches to studying membrane structure should be incorporated. Such approaches range from separating the dynamic and static properties of membranes to looking at different membrane components such as dolichol. An emerging area in the study of membranes is the capacity of membranes to develop a nonbilayer form (17). This transformation can be induced or inhibited by various factors, e.g., drugs, temperature, specific lipids. What effect aging may have on nonbilayer forms in membranes has not been examined.

ACKNOWLEDGEMENTS

The excellent editorial assistance of Sandy Melliere and Sharon Smith was much appreciated. This work was supported in part by USPHS, NIAAA Grant 02054 (to W.G.W.), the Medical Research Service, the Geriatric Research, Education and Clinical Center of the Veterans Administration, and USPHS, NIH Grant GM31651 (to F.S.).

REFERENCES

1. Abdel-Latif, A.A. (1983): In: Handbook of Neurochemistry, edited by A. Lajtha, pp. 91-131. Plenum Press, New York.
2. Armbrecht, H.J., Birnbaum, L.S., Zenser, T.V., and Davis, B.B. (1982): Exp. Gerontol., 17:41-48.
3. Armbrecht, H.J., Wood, W.G., Wise, R.W., Walsh, J.B., Thomas, B.N., and Strong, R. (1983): J. Pharmacol. Exp. Ther., 226:387-391.
4. Beauge, F., Stibler, H., and Borg, S. (1985): Alcoholism: Clin. Exp. Res., 9:322-326.
5. Butterfield, D.A., Ordaz, F.E., and Markesbery, W.R. (1982): J. Gerontol., 37:535-539.
6. Calderini, G., Bonetti, A.C., Battistella, A., Crews, F.T., and Toffano, G. (1983): Neurochem. Res., 8:483-492.
7. Chabanel, A., Abbott, R.E., Chien, S., and Schachter, D. (1985): Biochim. Biophys. Acta, 816:142-152.
8. Chin, J.H., and Goldstein, D.B. (1981): Mol. Pharmacol., 19:425-431.
9. Chin, J.H., Parsons, L.M., and Goldstein, D.B. (1978): Biochim. Biophys. Acta, 513:358-363.
10. Cimino, M., Vantini, G., Algeri, S., Curatola, G., Pezzoli, C., and Stramentinoli, G. (1984): Life Sci., 34:2029-2039.
11. Cohen, B.M., and Zubenko, G.S. (1985): Life Sci., 37:1403-1409.
12. Costello, P.B., and Green, F.A. (1987): Biochim. Biophys. Acta, 896:52-56.
13. Curtain, C.C., and Gordon, L.M. (1984): In: Membranes, Detergents, and Receptor Solubilization, edited by J.C. Venter and L.C. Harrison, pp. 177-213. Alan R. Liss, Inc., New York.
14. Dave, J.R., and Witorsch, R.J. (1984): Biochim. Biophys. Acta, 772:321-327.
15. Demel, R.A., and DeKruyff, B. (1976): Biochim. Biophys. Acta, 457:109-132.
16. Green, F.A., and Costello, P.B. (1987): Biochim. Biophys. Acta, 896:47-51.
17. Gruner, S.M. (1985): Proc. Natl. Acad. Sci. USA, 82:3665-3669.
18. Guidotti, G. (1980): In: Membrane Physiology, edited by T.E. Andreoli, J.F. Hoffman, and D.D. Fanestil, pp. 49-60. Plenum Press, New York.
19. Harris, R.A. (1984): Lab. Invest., 50:113-114.
20. Hegner, D. (1980): Mech. Ageing Dev., 14:101-118.
21. Henry, J.M., and Roth, G.S. (1987): Life Sci. (in press).
22. Jost, P.C., Griffith, O.H., Capaldi, R.A., and Vanderkooi, G. (1973): Proc. Natl. Acad. Sci. USA, 70:480-484.
23. Jost, P.C., Nadakavukaren, K.K., and Griffith, O.H. (1977): Biochemistry, 16:3110-3114.

24. Kummerow, F.A. (1983): Ann. NY Acad. Sci., 414:29-43.
25. Lai, C.S., and Schutzbach, J.S. (1986): FEBS Lett., 203:153-156.
26. Lakowicz, J.R. (1986): Principles of Fluorescence Spectroscopy. Plenum Press, New York.
27. Le, A.V., and Doyle, D. (1984): In: Membranes, Detergents, and Receptor Solubilization, edited by J.C. Venter and L.C. Harrison, pp. 1-25. Alan R. Liss, Inc., New York.
28. Lenaz, G., and Castelli, G.P. (1985): In: Structure and Properties of Cell Membranes, Vol. 1, edited by G. Benga, pp. 93-136. CRC Press, Boca Raton, Florida.
29. Malone, M.J., and Szoke, M.C. (1982): J. Gerontol., 37:262-267.
30. Nokubo, M. (1985): J. Gerontol., 40:409-414.
31. Op den Kamp, J.A.F. (1979): Annu. Rev. Biochem., 48:47-71.
32. Pratz, J., and Corman, B. (1985): Biochim. Biophys. Acta, 814:265-273.
33. Rifkind, J.M., Suda, T., Wang, J.T., Heim, J., and Roth, G.S. (1985): Exp. Gerontol., 20:99-105.
34. Rivnay, B., Bergman, S., Shinitzky, M., and Globerson, A. (1980): Mech. Ageing Dev., 12:119-126.
35. Rouser, G., Kritchevsky, G., Yamamoto, A., and Baxter, C.F. (1971): Adv. Lipid Res., 10:261-361.
36. Sanderman, H. (1978): Biochim. Biophys. Acta, 515:209-237.
37. Schachter, D., Abbott, R.E., Cogan, U., and Flamm, M. (1983): Ann. NY Acad. Sci., 414:19-28.
38. Schmucker, D.L. (1986): In: Geriatric Clinical Pharmacology, edited by W.G. Wood and R. Strong, pp. 159-177. Raven Press, New York.
39. Schroeder, F. (1985): In: Subcellular Biochemistry, Vol. 11, edited by D.B. Roodyn, pp. 51-101. Plenum Press, New York.
40. Schroeder, F., Gorka, C., and Wood, W.G. This volume.
41. Seigneuret, M., Zachowski, A., Hermann, A., and Devaux, P.F. (1984): Biochemistry, 23:4271-4275.
42. Singer, S.J., and Nicolson, G.L. (1972): Science, 175:720-731.
43. Spinedi, A., Rufini, S., and Luly, P. (1985): Experientia, 41:1141-1143.
44. Sun, A.Y., and Sun, G.Y. (1979): In: Interdisciplinary Topics in Gerontology, Vol. 15, edited by H.P. von Hahn, pp. 34-53. S. Karger, New York.
45. Sun, G.Y., and Samorajski, T. (1972): J. Gerontol., 27:10-17.
46. Sun, G.Y., Schroeder, F., Williamson, L.S., Gorka, C., Sun, A.Y., and Wood, W.G. This volume.
47. Sun, G.Y., and Sun, A.Y. (1985): Alcoholism: Clin. Exp. Res., 9:164-180.

48. Sutter, M.A., Wood, W.G., Williamson, L.S., Strong, R., Pickham, K., and Richardson, A. (1985): <u>Biochem. Pharmacol.</u>, 34:2983-2987.
49. Tanaka, Y., and Schroit, A.J. (1983): <u>J. Biol. Chem.</u>, 258:11335-11343.
50. Wood, W.G., Gorka, C., Armbrecht, H.J., Williamson, L.S., and Strong, R. (1986): <u>Life Sci.</u>, 39:2089-2095.
51. Wood, W.G., Lahiri, S., Gorka, C., Armbrecht, H.J., and Strong, R. (1987): <u>Alcoholism: Clin. Exp. Res.</u> (in press).
52. Wood, W.G., Williamson, L.S., Rocco, D., and Strong, R. (1986): <u>Exp. Gerontol.</u>, 21:195-201.

Central Nervous System Disorders of Aging: Clinical Intervention and Research, edited by Randy Strong et al. Raven Press, New York © 1988.

NEURONAL MEMBRANE ASYMMETRY AND AGING

Friedhelm Schroeder,*† Chris Gorka,† and W. Gibson Wood†§

*Departments of Pharmacology and Medicinal Chemistry, College of Pharmacy, and the †Departments of Pharmacology and Cell Biophysics, College of Medicine, University of Cincinnati, Cincinnati, Ohio 45267-0004; †Geriatric Research, Education and Clinical Center, Veterans Administration Medical Center; and §Departments of Neurology and Internal Medicine, St. Louis University School of Medicine, St. Louis, Missouri 63125

It is now well-recognized that lipids have not only a structural role but are also important dynamic molecules involved in the physiology of man and animal. Lipids such as prostaglandins, thromboxanes, leukotrienes, diglycerides, and polyphosphoinositides are recognized as important cellular messenger molecules and are the forms of intense research efforts. In the past, most investigators of membrane lipid structure determined only the bulk structure. However, more exciting evidence uncovered recently indicates that not only are biological membranes composed of a bilayer lipid membrane with embedded proteins, but that this bilayer consists of an exofacial leaflet and a cytofacial leaflet that are neither identical nor coupled. It has been found that the lipid content of the two leaflets differs (23). Differences between the two leaflets have also been reported for membrane fluidity (24). In erythrocyte membranes, the exofacial leaflet is less fluid as compared to the cytofacial leaflet, whereas, just the opposite results are seen in the murine fibroblast (LM) plasma membrane (Table 1). The transbilayer distribution of cholesterol may be the primary determinant of this fluidity difference. For brain membranes, very little is known regarding transbilayer membrane lipid distribution or structure (23). The transbilayer distribution of cholesterol in myelin has been variously reported as enriched in the outer leaflet (1) or equally distributed (29). The transbilayer structure of neural cell surface membranes has heretofore not been reported.

211

TABLE 1. Correlation of plasma membrane individual leaflet fluidity and cholesterol content

Method	More Rigid		Sterol Enriched		Ref.
	Inner Leaflet	Outer Leaflet	Inner Leaflet	Outer Leaflet	
Red Blood Cell					
Fluorescence				+	9,18,22,40
EM				+	5
Fluorescence		+			18,40
ESR		+			31,37
DSC		+			3
Fluorescence			+		9,14,22,25
LM Fibroblast					
Fluorescence	+				14,20,21,25, 27,33–36
ESR	+				41

Abbreviations used: EM, electron microscopy; ESR, electron spin resonance; DSC, differential scanning calorimetry; LM, murine fibroblast.

It has been proposed that membrane asymmetry is required for membrane function and that a decrease in asymmetry may result in diminished function (23). A reduction in membrane asymmetry for fluidity and lipid distribution has been observed in erythrocytes from patients with sickle cell disease and acanthocytosis (16). Age changes in membrane function may result, in part, from a decrease in membrane asymmetry (23). We used a new method to examine membrane fluidity of the two leaflets of synaptic plasma membranes (SPM) from three different age groups of mice (6, 18, 28 months). Differential polarized phase fluorometry indicated that the exofacial leaflet was more fluid than the cytofacial leaflet in SPM of young animals. This difference in membrane fluidity between the two leaflets was significantly less in SPM of older animals.

LATERAL ORDER OF DOMAINS IN MEMBRANES

There is increasing evidence (reviewed in ref. 35) that in the plane of the membrane, the biological membranes are composed of patches or domains differing sharply in lipid composition, structure, and function. However, with the exception of the hepatocyte, kidney, and microvillus membrane lateral domains, isolation and characterization of such lateral domains have been difficult and will not be dealt with further here.

TRANSMEMBRANE ORDER OF DOMAINS IN MEMBRANES

Transbilayer domains, the cytoplasmic (inner) and exofacial (outer) leaflets, can be readily detected and characterized. The individual leaflets of cell surface membranes have been characterized by a host of methods including chemical-labelling, phospholipases, cholesterol oxidase, exchange proteins, fluorescence, electron spin resonance, nuclear magnetic resonance, differential scanning calorimetry, etc. (reviewed in refs. 23 and 24).

In order to examine the transbilayer phospholipid and fatty acid distribution of brain synaptic plasma membranes, we have utilized the trinitrobenzenesulfonic acid (TNBS) labelling technique (detailed in ref. 24). Only 11 ± 3% of phosphatidylethanolamine and less than 1% of the phosphatidylserine were located in the extracellular leaflet (Table 2). A similar observation was recently reported for rat brain synaptic plasma membranes (13). Likewise, the inner leaflet aminophospholipids contained most of the unsaturated fatty acyl chains. The transbilayer distribution of cholesterol in the SPM is not known.

TABLE 2. <u>Mouse brain synaptic plasma membrane individual leaflet aminophospholipid and unsaturated fatty acid distribution[a]</u>

Parameter	Transbilayer Distribution	
	Outer Leaflet	Inner Leaflet
Phosphatidylethanolamine	11 ± 3	89 ± 3[b]
Phosphatidylserine	< 1	> 99[b]
Phosphatidylethanolamine U/S	0.3 ± 0.1	1.9 ± 0.1[b]
Phosphatidylserine U/S	–	3.6 ± 0.3

[a]Transbilayer aminophospholipid asymmetry and fatty acid chain asymmetry of brain SPM from 6-month-old male C57BL/6NNIA mice were determined as described earlier (6,7,28). Values represent the mean ± SEM (n = 3).
[b]$p < 0.05$ by Student's t-test.

The TNBS labelling procedure was also used to examine the transbilayer structure of the synaptic plasma membrane (28). 1,6-Diphenyl-1,3,5-hexatriene (DPH), a fluorescent probe molecule, and differential polarized phase fluorometry were used to examine the order (limiting anisotropy) and dynamics (rotational relaxation time) of membrane lipids sensed by DPH in the inner and outer leaflets of SPM (Fig. 1). The limiting anisotropy, a parameter dependent on the restriction to probe motion, of DPH was significantly greater in the inner versus

the outer leaflet. A similar trend was evident for the DPH
rotational relaxation time which was longer in the inner
leaflet. These data signify that DPH motion is more restricted
and slower (it takes more time for rotation) in the inner than
outer leaflet. Simply stated, the outer leaflet is more fluid
than the inner leaflet.

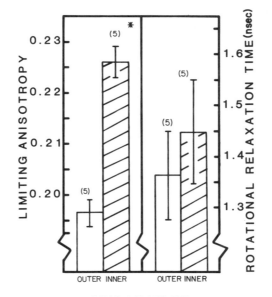

SPM LEAFLET

FIG. 1. Structure and dynamics of DPH motion in SPM
individual leaflets. SPM were isolated from 6-month-old male
C57BL/6NNIA mice, TNBS labelled under nonpenetrating
conditions, and individual leaflet parameters determined as
described elsewhere (28).

EFFECT OF AGING ON TRANSMEMBRANE ORDER

The fluorescence polarization of DPH, measured in the whole
membrane of the SPM, was also investigated as a function of
age (Fig. 2). Fluorescence polarization contains information
about both statics and dynamics of probe motion without
resolving the two. The data are presented to show that the
"bulk" properties (average of two leaflets and unresolved
static and dynamic parameters) also sense a change in SPM
membrane structured with age.

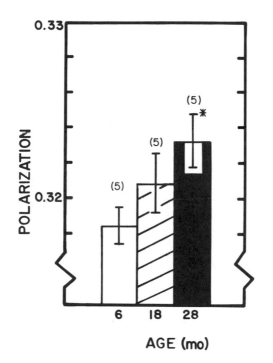

FIG. 2. Effect of age on SPM fluidity. SPM were isolated
from male C57BL/6NNIA mice as a function of age, and
fluorescence polarization was determined (28).

The major observation to be made from these data is that
the fluorescence polarization of DPH increased with age, a
finding consistent with that of others (26,42), indicating
that SPM membranes may become more rigid with age. Whether
this change in polarization is due to a change in structural
order or simply due to faster rotation of the probe without
change in structural order is not known. Neither is it known
whether one or both leaflets are affected. Therefore, the
effect of age on DPH individual leaflet limiting anisotropy
and rotational relaxation time was measured. The limiting
anisotropy of DPH increased much more rapidly in the outer
than in the inner leaflet (Fig. 3). The rotational relaxation
time of DPH motion in each leaflet was much less affected.

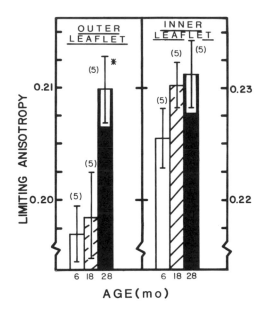

FIG. 3. <u>Effect of age on SPM individual leaflet fluidity.</u>
All procedures were performed as described for Fig. 1 except
that mice of varying ages were used.

The mechanism whereby the SPM outer leaflet becomes
relatively more rigid with increasing age is not known.
However, a survey of the literature on aging (reviewed in ref.
23) strongly implicates an involvement of free radical and/or
peroxidative damage to membranes. Lipid peroxidation, for
example, enhanced the transbilayer movement of phospholipids
in both model and mammalian cell membranes and altered the
transbilayer distribution of phospholipids in the surface
membranes of erythrocytes (reviewed in ref. 23). Polyunsaturated fatty acids present in high amounts of SPM
(Table 2) and other membranes are prime targets for oxidative
injury. Unsaturated fatty acids also appear to regulate the
transbilayer distribution of sterol. For example, when LM
fibroblasts were cultured in a defined medium, their plasma
membranes contained only monounsaturated fatty acids. In
contrast, when the cells were cultured in the presence of
linoleic acid (a diunsaturated fatty acid capable of being
peroxidized without production of malondialdehyde), this fatty
acid was rapidly incorporated into plasma membrane
phospholipids such that $5.1 \pm 0.2\%$ (n = 6) of the plasma
membrane total phospholipid acyl species were linoleate,
confirming earlier results of others (4). Peroxidation reduced
this amount to $4.4 \pm 0.3\%$ and concomitantly decreased the
double bond index from $2.57 \pm 0.10\%$ to $2.15 \pm 0.10\%$ (Fig. 4).

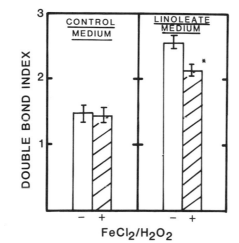

FIG. 4. Effect of linoleate supplementation and peroxidation with $FeCl_2/H_2O_2$ on LM fibroblast plasma membrane double bond index. This index was calculated as the sum of each percent unsaturated fatty acid x number of double bonds in that fatty acid/sum of each percent saturated fatty acid. Values represent the mean ± SEM (n = 6). An asterisk refers to $p < 0.05$ by Student's t-test.

This index was not changed in control membranes. The enrichment of LM plasma membrane phospholipids with linoleate dramatically shifted the transbilayer distribution of sterol from enrichment in the inner leaflet to enrichment in the outer leaflet (Fig. 5). However, peroxidation with $FeCl_2/H_2O_2$ did not alter the transbilayer distribution of sterol in either control or oleate enriched plasma membranes. The effects of oleate enrichment on membrane structure were equally dramatic (Table 3). Linoleate enrichment of LM cell plasma membrane phospholipids decreased the inner leaflet but not outer leaflet fluidity such that the transbilayer fluidity difference was essentially abolished. The effect of peroxidation was threefold: a) Peroxidation made the plasma membranes (inner and outer leaflet) more rigid, as measured by increased limiting anisotropy, in all cases. b) In control membranes (containing only monounsaturated fatty acids), peroxidation reversed the normal order of fluidity. That is, the outer leaflet became more rigid. c) Linoleate enriched plasma membranes had a more rigid outer leaflet after peroxidation without change in inner leaflet rigidity. Thus, peroxidation increased the rigidity of the outer but not inner leaflet, while polyunsaturated fatty acid incorporation affected the inner but not outer leaflet fluidity. These observations are pertinent to the other data shown above where the outer leaflet of SPM became more rigid with age, while the inner leaflet remained unaltered with increasing age of the donor animals. Perhaps, oxidative injury to membranes may also be contributary to the altered SPM transbilayer structure noted in aging.

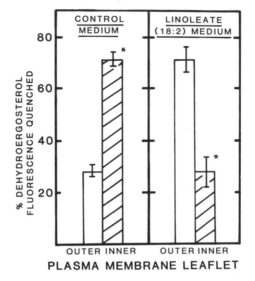

PLASMA MEMBRANE LEAFLET

FIG. 5. Effect of linoleate incorporation on LM fibroblast transbilayer sterol distribution. LM fibroblasts were cultured with dehydroergosterol and in the absence or presence of 5 μM linoleate-BSA (18:2). Cells were untreated or treated with TNBS; plasma membranes were isolated and dehydroergosterol fluorescence was determined. An asterisk refers to $p < 0.05$ (n = 3 to 5) by Student's t-test as compared to outer leaflet. All procedures for measuring transbilayer sterol distribution were as described in refs. 9 and 22.

TABLE 3. Effect of peroxidation on LM plasma membrane
individual leaflet fluidity[a]

Medium Fatty Acid	$H_2O_2/FeCl_2$	Leaflet limiting anisotropy		
		Outer	Inner	Inner + Outer
None	−	0.148 ± 0.008	0.194 ± 0.009[b]	0.171 ± 0.006
None	+	0.219 ± 0.011[c]	0.167 ± 0.011[b]	0.193 ± 0.006[c]
18:2	−	0.134 ± 0.007	0.133 ± 0.006	0.134 ± 0.006
18:2	+	0.171 ± 0.008[c]	0.131 ± 0.008[b]	0.151 ± 0.007[c]

[a]All conditions were described in legend to Fig. 5.
[b]$p < 0.05$ (n = 3 to 5) by Student's t-test as compared to outer leaflet.
[c]$p < 0.05$ as compared to $-H_2O_2/FeCl_2$.

ORIGIN OF LIPID ASYMMETRY

Although an asymmetric transbilayer distribution of lipids was first recognized over fifteen years ago, its origin is still unknown (reviewed in ref. 23). A number of mechanisms have been proposed. Only the most pertinent are discussed here. First, the de novo versus externally induced origin of lipid asymmetry was resolved using LM fibroblasts (10,14,19,22) and brain synaptosomes (6-8,13). Since both serum lipoproteins and the external leaflet of red blood cells are enriched in phosphatidylcholine, sphingomyelin, and cholesterol, and because these lipids are free to exchange, it seems possible that the lipid asymmetry could be induced by exchange processes. However, in the above experiments, neither LM fibroblasts nor mouse or rat brain synaptosomes were exposed to serum lipoproteins, yet both membranes had an asymmetric organization of membrane lipids.

Thus, it appears more likely that an asymmetric distribution of lipids in biological membranes arises de novo, that is, it is made by the cell. At least three mechanisms have been proposed. First, chemical equilibrium (polar head group packing) has been postulated to constrain the phosphatidyl-choline and sphingomyelin to be enriched in the external leaflet of biological membranes. For example, in model membranes phosphatidylethanolamine is known to pack more tightly and, therefore, segregate to the inner monolayer of phosphatidylcholine-phosphatidylethanolamine vesicles with a small radius of curvature (15). A similar logic has been invoked to the transbilayer distribution of cholesterol in small lipid vesicles (11,12,32). Such a mechanism for generating lipid asymmetry may be important to the small synaptic vesicles involved in release of neurotransmitters (17). Second, physical restraints (cytoskeleton, membrane proteins, or specific lipids) may constrain certain lipids to one leaflet. For example, cholesterol is thought to associate preferentially with lipids such as phosphatidylcholine and/or sphingomyelin (2,38,39). The attraction of these lipids for each other may aid in maintaining the asymmetry. However, this preference of cholesterol for specific phospholipids has not been demonstrated in the fluid phase (39). More importantly, in biological plasma membranes, fluorescent sterols do not associate preferentially with these lipids (10,14). Last, enzymatic mechanisms (phospholipase, base exchange, methylation, phospholipid exchange proteins, or "flippases") have been proposed. A particularly intriguing study reported the presence of a specific ATP requiring enzyme in the human red blood cell membrane for the transbilayer translocation of aminophospholipids (30,43). In summary, the origin and regulation of membrane lipid asymmetry are not known and remain the subject of active interest. In a few systems such as the red blood cell plasma membrane, transbilayer phospholipid asymmetry appears to be regulated by an energy requiring protein mediated process. However, a similar system has not been reported in other cells.

ACKNOWLEDGEMENTS

The helpful technical assistance of Ms. S. Lawrence and Mr. G. Hubert was much appreciated. This work was supported in part by USPHS, National Institute of Health Grant GM31651 (to F.S.), USPHS, NIAAA Grant 02054 (to W.G.W.), the Medical Research Service, and the Geriatric Research, Education, and Clinical Center of the Veterans Administration.

REFERENCES

1. Caspar, D.L.D., and Kirschner, D.A. (1971): Nature, 231:46–52.
2. Demel, R.A., Jansen, J.W.C.M., Van Dijck, P.W.M., and Van Deenen, L.L.M. (1977): Biochim. Biophys. Acta, 465:1–10.
3. Dijck, P.W., Zoelen, E.J., Seldenrijk, R., Van Deenen, L.L., and de Gier, J. (1976): Chem. Phys. Lipids, 17:336–343.
4. Ferguson, K.A., Glaser, M.A., Bayer, W.H., and Vagelos, P.R. (1975): Biochemistry, 14:146–151.
5. Fisher, K.A. (1976): Proc. Natl. Acad. Sci. USA, 73:173–177.
6. Fontaine, R.N., Harris, R.A., and Schroeder, F. (1976): Life Sci., 24:395–398.
7. Fontaine, R.N., Harris, R.A., and Schroeder, F. (1980): J. Neurochem., 34:269–277.
8. Fontaine, R.N., and Schroeder, F. (1979): Biochim. Biophys. Acta, 558:1–12.
9. Hale, J.E., and Schroeder, F. (1981): J. Lipid Res., 22:127–130.
10. Hale, J.E., and Schroeder, F. (1982): Eur. J. Biochem., 122:649–661.
11. Huang, C., Charlton, J.P., Shyr, C.T., and Thompson, T.E. (1970): Biochemistry, 9:3422–3426.
12. Huang, C.-H., Sipe, J.P., Chow, S.T., and Martin, R.B. (1974): Proc. Natl. Acad. Sci. USA, 71:359–362.
13. Kagan, V.E., Tyurin, V.A., Goburnov, N.V., Prilipko, L.L., and Chelomin, V.P. (1984): Zh. Evol. Biokhim. Fiziol. (J. Evol. Biochem. Physiol.), 20:9–16.
14. Kier, A.B., Sweet, W.D., Cowlen, M.S., and Schroeder, F. (1986): Biochim. Biophys. Acta, 861:287–301.
15. Lentz, B.R., and Litman, B.J. (1978): Biochemistry, 17:5537–5543.
16. Lubin, B., Chiu, D., Bastacky, J., Roelofsen, B., and Van Deenen, L.L. (1981): J. Clin. Invest., 67:1643–1649.

17. Michaelson, D.M., Barkai, G., and Barenholz, Y. (1983): Biochem. J., 211:155-162.
18. Rimon, G., Hanski, E., and Levitzki, A. (1980): Biochemistry, 19:4451-4460.
19. Sandra, A., and Pagano, R.E. (1978): Biochemistry, 17:332-338.
20. Schroeder, F. (1978): Nature, 275:528-530.
21. Schroeder, F. (1980): Eur. J. Biochem., 112:293-307.
22. Schroeder, F. (1981): FEBS Lett., 135:127-130.
23. Schroeder, F. (1984): Neurobiol. Aging, 5:323-333.
24. Schroeder, F. (1985): In: Subcellular Biochemistry, Vol. II, edited by D.B. Roodyn, pp. 51-101. Plenum Press, New York.
25. Schroeder, F. (1987): In: Advances in Membrane Fluidity, Vol. 1, edited by R.C. Aloia, C.C. Curtain, and L.M. Gordon (in press). Alan R. Liss, Inc., New York.
26. Schroeder, F., Goetz, I.E., and Roberts, E. (1984): Mech. Ageing Dev., 25:365-389.
27. Schroeder, F., and Kinden, D.A. (1980): Nature, 287:255-256.
28. Schroeder, F., Morrison, W.J., Gorka, C., and Wood, W.G. (1987): Biochim. Biophys. Acta (submitted).
29. Scott, S.C., Bruckdorfer, K.R., and Worcester, D.L. (1980): Biochem. Soc. Trans., 8:717-719.
30. Seigneuret, M., and Devaux, P.F. (1984): Proc. Natl. Acad. Sci. USA, 81:3751-3755.
31. Seigneuret, M., Zachowski, A., Hermann, A., and Devaux, P.F. (1984): Biochemistry, 23:4271-4275.
32. Smith, R.J.M., and Green, C. (1974): FEBS Lett., 42:108-111.
33. Sweet, W.D., and Schroeder, F. (1986): Biochem. J., 239:301-310.
34. Sweet, W.D., and Schroeder, F. (1986): Biochim. Biophys. Acta, 861:53-61.
35. Sweet, W.D., and Schroeder, F. (1987): In: Advances in Membrane Fluidity, Vol. 2, edited by R.C. Aloia, C.C. Curtain, and L.M. Gordon (in press). Alan R. Liss, Inc., New York.
36. Sweet, W.D., Wood, W.G., and Schroeder, F. (1987): Biochemistry (May 19 issue).
37. Tanaka, K.-I., and Ohnishi, S.I. (1976): Biochim. Biophys. Acta, 426:218-231.
38. Untracht, S.H., and Shipley, G.G. (1977): J. Biol. Chem., 252:4449-4457.
39. van Dijck, P.W.M., de Kruijff, B., van Deenen, L.L.M., de Gier, J., and Demel, R.A. (1976): Biochim. Biophys. Acta, 455:576-587.
40. Williamson, P., Bateman, J., Kozarsky, K., and Mattocks, K. (1982): Cell, 30:725-733.
41. Wisnieski, B.J., and Iwata, K.K. (1977): Biochemistry, 16:1321-1326.

42. Wood, W.G., and Schroeder, F. This volume.
43. Zachowski, A., Favre, E., Cribier, S., Herve, P., and
    Devaux, P.F. (1986): Biochemistry, 25:2585-2590.

Central Nervous System Disorders of Aging:
Clinical Intervention and Research, edited by
Randy Strong et al. Raven Press, New York
© 1988.

DOLICHOLS: THEIR ROLE IN NEURONAL MEMBRANE AGING

Grace Y. Sun,*[†] Friedhelm Schroeder,[+]
Lisa S. Williamson,** Chris Gorka,[++]
Albert Y. Sun,*[†] and W. Gibson Wood[++][§]

*Sinclair Research Farm; University of Missouri
Schools of [†]Medicine and **Veterinary Medicine,
Columbia, Missouri 65203;
[+]University of Cincinnati Colleges of Pharmacy
and Medicine, Cincinnati, Ohio 45267-0004;
[++]Veterans Administration Medical Center; and
[§]St. Louis University School of Medicine,
St. Louis, Missouri 63125

Because neurons are postmitotic cells and lack the ability
to multiply, intricate biochemical mechanisms must exist to
maintain their functional integrity and metabolic activities
throughout the life span of those cells. It is not surprising
to find that neurons possess unusual plasticity in order to
cope with injuries and adaptation to environmental challenges.
In this regard, aging in brain can be envisaged as a gradual
decline in its capacity to maintain various neuronal membrane
functions. There are a few identifiable biological markers to
define the aging process in brain, although some biochemical
events may be more affected by age than others. Among these, a
characteristic feature of the aged neurons as compared to the
younger ones is the accumulation of lipofuscin pigments in the
aged. Brizzee and Ordy (5) observed that the decline in
hippocampal functions (e.g., learning, short-term memory, and
arousal) correlated significantly with the loss of neurons and
an increase in the lipofuscin pigments. In fact, these age
pigments (or lipofuscin pigments) are ubiquitous in different
body organs. Recently, a subcellular fraction enriched in
these lipofuscin pigments was isolated and their chemical
composition analyzed (21). There is also evidence that like
the lysosomal bodies, a high proportion of dolichols is also
present in these lipofuscin pigments. This chapter will review
the biochemistry of dolichols, and describe its role in aging

223

and lipopigment formation and its effects on membrane structure and functions.

BIOCHEMISTRY OF DOLICHOLS

Dolichols are long chain polyisoprenols ranging from 85 to 105 carbons in length, although C-90 and C-95 are generally the most abundant species (Fig. 1). They are synthesized from acetate and share part of the biosynthetic pathway for cholesterol. Breckenridge et al. (4) attempted to isolate these long chain polyisoprenols from brain and to identify their characteristic structures. Dolichols are ubiquitous among body organs, but higher levels are found in testis, kidney, liver, brain, and various exocrine glands (8,26,30). In human tissue, it has been shown that the pituitary gland and testis are particularly enriched in these compounds (8).

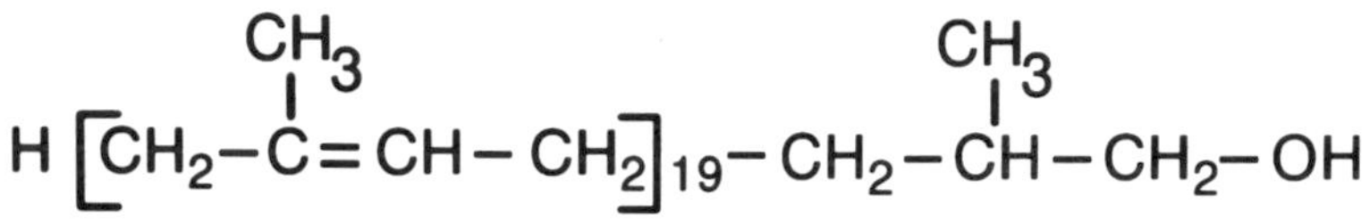

$$H \left[CH_2 - \underset{\underset{CH_3}{|}}{C} = CH - CH_2 \right]_{19} - CH_2 - \underset{\underset{CH_3}{|}}{CH} - CH_2 - OH$$

DOLICHOL [C80 - 105]

Characteristic Features

1. **Accumulate with normal and pathological aging**

2. **Concentrated in ceroid lipofuscin pigments**

Function: For Glycoprotein Assembly

FIG. 1. The molecular form of dolichols.

Dolichols are known to exist in three forms: 1) free dolichols; 2) dolichyl phosphate or pyrophosphate; and 3) dolichyl ester. In the phosphorylated form, dolichols are important as an eukaryotic glycosyl carrier in the biosynthesis of asparagine-linked oligosaccharides (22). Therefore, some dolichyl phosphates are linked to polysaccharides in various forms. Studies with brain membranes indicated that dolichyl monophosphate is formed by a CTP-dependent kinase (6), and Zn^{2+} was a potent effector for activation of this enzyme (32). The phosphorylated dolichol is rapidly glycosylated in the presence of GDP-mannose or UDP-N-acetylaglucosamine to form diphosphodolichyl polysaccharides (10). More recent study by

Scher et al. (34) indicated that while dolichol kinase is highly enriched in the heavy microsomal fraction, the phosphatase is recovered largely in the light microsomal fraction. It is interesting to note that high dolichyl phosphate phosphatase activity is also found in the axon plasma membrane fraction (34). In rat liver, dolichyl phosphate is synthesized in the microsomes (2) as well as in other cytoplasmic surfaces (1). Although both dolichol and cholesterol are known to share a common initial biosynthetic pathway, different nutritional conditions were found to affect cholesterol biosynthesis more than the synthesis of dolichyl phosphate (14). Wong and Lennarz (43) demonstrated that after synthesis in the microsomal fraction, dolichols were transferred to the mitochondria-lysosome fraction. Accumulation of dolichols with age may be occurring primarily in this fraction. Rossignol et al. (29) further reported that synthesis of dolichyl phosphate from acetate is very slow (t 1/2 = 40 to 70 hours), but the rate of hydrolysis in the phosphate head groups is more rapid (t 1/2 = 5.7 to 7.7 hours). This equilibrium may be important in maintaining a critical level of the dolichyl phosphate for glycoprotein biosynthesis. Therefore, it is reasonable to speculate that the phosphate group of dolichyl phosphate is maintained in a dynamic state of metabolism and that both dolichol kinase and dolichyl phosphate phosphatase may play a key role in regulating the cellular level of dolichol and its phosphorylated form. A disturbance of the equilibrium would result in the accumulation of one form or the other. Since dolichyl phosphate phosphatase activity is found enriched in rat liver plasma membranes (28), this leads to the possibility that significant amounts of dolichols may also be present in the plasma membranes.

Less is known about the acylation and deacylation pathways related to biosynthesis of dolichyl esters. Dolichyl esters are thought to be formed by a transesterification reaction with phosphatidylcholine as the acyl donor (12). On the other hand, Scher and Waechter (35) observed a dolichyl ester hydrolase activity in calf brain membranes. Based on the pH profile, dolichyl ester hydrolase (pH 7.5) is different from the cholesteryl ester hydrolase (pH 5.0 to 5.5) and triolein hydrolase (pH 5.0). Dolichyl palmitate esterase was found in the cell-free extracts of both pancreas and intestinal mucosa (13). The role of this enzyme was thought to promote the absorption of dolichol from the dietary source.

When labeled dolichol was injected into rats, most of the radioactivity was recovered in the liver (27). The brain did not appear to absorb any of the label. The half-life for turnover of labeled dolichol in liver was estimated to be around 17 days.

DOLICHOLS AND AGE

Recent studies have indicated that high levels of dolichols were found in human as well as animal brain during aging (17,24,25). In human brain gray matter, dolichol level increased more than tenfold from 18 µg/g (6-year-old) to 263 µg/g (68-year-old) (25). Although there is also a steady increase in dolichol level in rat brain with age, the rat brain normally contains less dolichol per gram tissue weight than human brain (17). Whether this difference is related to the shorter life span of rodents is not known.

In general, dolichol increases with age, although the rate of increase varies widely among different body organs (26). For example, testis shows a greater age-related increase than liver, but the rapid increase in dolichol in testis is actually more profound during the developmental period (14 to 60 days of age) and not thereafter (19). Sakakihara and Volpe (31) showed two distinctive phases of rapid dolichol deposition in rat brain; the first phase is during development and the second is during aging. Furthermore, the rate of increase of dolichols in the developing brain, showing a peak around 25 days, is different from that for cholesterol which indicates a peak at 18 days. The major developmental processes occurring during this time are myelination and synaptogenesis. Dolichols are unevenly distributed in different brain regions and are normally higher in the cortical gray matter than in the subcortical white matter (33). Furthermore, dolichol in the thalamic region showed a more precipitous increase with age than in any other brain regions (33). High levels of dolichols in brain have also been found in patients with Alzheimer's disease (41) and in various forms of neuronal ceroid lipofuscinosis (Batten disease) (15,17). Abnormally high levels of urinary excretion of dolichols were also observed in patients with Batten disease (18) and with metastatic cancer (24). Thus, there is abundant evidence indicating that dolichols or their derivatives may play an important role in normal and pathological aging processes. In fact, establishing a direct relationship between the level of dolichol and the lipofuscin pigments in brain with age will undoubtedly be a useful biochemical index for assessing the aging process.

DOLICHOLS IN SUBCELLULAR MEMBRANES

Dolichols are unevenly distributed among different subcellular membranes. Eggens et al. (8) reported the presence of high dolichol levels in mitochondria (especially the outer membrane), Golgi, lysosomes and plasma membranes, whereas, microsomes, peroxisomes and nuclei contain only very low levels of the compound. Using differential centrifugation, Wong and Lennarz (43) found that the majority of dolichols in rat liver are associated with the lysosome-rich fraction. Examination of

the dolichol distribution in testicular fractions also revealed
a large enrichment in the Golgi apparatus within the Sertoli-
rich tubular fragments (19). Although the lysosomes and Golgi
were not separately isolated, a determination of dolichols in
8-month-old mouse brain subcellular fractions indicated an
enrichment in mitochondria and myelin; and relatively low levels
were found in microsomes and synaptic plasma membranes (SPM)
(Fig. 2). Except for the microsomes, almost all subcellular
fractions showed an increase in dolichol level with age.
However, it is surprising that the increase was most dramatic
in the myelin fraction. In order to test whether the dolichols
in myelin are actually present in the myelin sheath and not in
the mitochondrial contaminant within the axon, myelin isolated
from mouse cerebral cortex was subjected to osmotic shock and
further purification by layering on a discontinuous sucrose
gradient. The recovered purified myelin showed a similar level
of dolichols, indicating that this compound is indeed an
integral part of the myelin membrane. When the amount of
dolichols in myelin of C57BL/6NNIA mice is plotted against age
(results of several preparations), the increase with age is
nearly linear up to 30 months (Fig. 3). Thus, this is the first
time in which dolichol is detected in significant quantity in
the myelin membranes. Further studies are needed to explore
its functional role in the membrane and whether its progressive
increase with age may be altered in pathological aging.

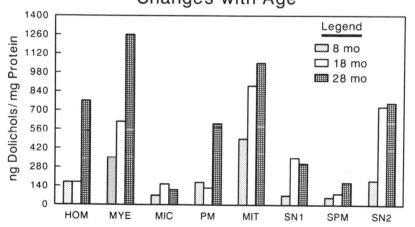

Dolichols in Mouse Brain Subcellular Fractions: Changes with Age

FIG. 2. Dolichol content in brain subcellular fractions of
C57BL/6NNIA mice and with respect to age. Brain subcellular
fractions were isolated by differential and sucrose gradient
centrifugation. Results are average values from two
preparations.

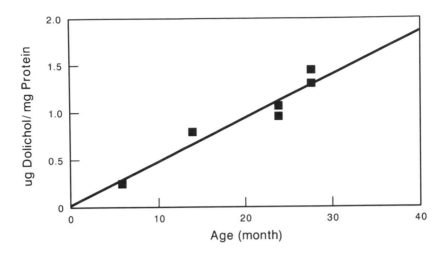

FIG. 3. Level of dolichols in purified myelin of
C57BL/6NNIA mice. Myelin from various age mouse groups were
purified through osmotic shock and used for analysis of
dolichols.

The distribution of dolichols among different cell types in
brain has not been assessed; nevertheless, their presence in
high level in the gray matter seems to favor a neuronal
localization.
    Abnormally high dolichol levels were reported in brains of
Alzheimer patients (41). In fact, dolichol levels are found
elevated in metastatic brain tumors (24), in urine of alcoholics
(23), and in urine of newborns whose mothers were heavy alcohol
users (40).
    A number of studies have reported the presence of abnormally
high levels of dolichols in patients with Batten disease (17).
It has also been proposed that these patients show an increase
in dolichol level in the urinary sediment (18). However, this
contention was argued by Bennett et al. (3) who were not able
to observe an increase in dolichol level in urinary sediment of
patients with Batten disease or those with other storage and
neurodegenerative disorders. Nevertheless, a more recent
sampling of Batten disease patients from different locations
showed a significant increase in dolichols in all forms of
neuronal ceroid lipofuscinosis (42).

DOLICHOLS AND LIPOFUSCIN PIGMENTS

    Lipofuscin pigments are found to accumulate in various body
tissues with age. However, they are especially prominent in
patients with Batten disease (or ceroid lipofuscinosis). There
are several forms of Batten disease, and Goebel et al. (9)
observed ultrastructural diversity in the appearance of these

residual bodies with respect to cell types and tissues. These curvilinear profiles are always contained in a membrane-bound cytosome (7). In primate brain, the increase of lipofuscin pigment with age is especially prevalent in the hippocampus CA1 area and in visual area 17 (5).

A number of hypotheses have been generated to explain the etiology of these autofluorescent bodies that accumulate in Batten disease and with age. Extraction of the lipofuscin pigments yielded fluorescent compounds having spectral properties typical of Schiff base conjugates. Thus, they are thought to be products resulting from peroxidation of polyunsaturated long-chain fatty acids which give rise to malondialdehyde. This hypothesis, however, has not been well-supported. Studies of glutathione peroxidase activity and peroxidation of polyunsaturated fatty acids in leukocytes from patients with Batten disease did not reveal obvious differences (11,37). When Drosophilia melanogaster flies were given either a linoleic acid supplement or a fat-free diet, the age-related increase in lipofuscin pigments was found regardless of the diet given (38).

Recently, some animal models are available for the study of the lipofuscin pigments accumulation. Examining the ceroid lipofuscin pigments in English setters, Keller et al. (15) found that while levels of dolichol in brain increase with age, the dolichol level in these dogs afflicted with ceroid lipofuscinosis was surprisingly similar to that in controls. On the other hand, there was a large increase (three- to fivefold) in dolichyl phosphate levels in the affected dogs as well as in human brain tissue from a 5-year-old with late infantile ceroid lipofuscinosis (15). Thus, whether dolichol is a major component of the lipofuscin pigment is still debatable. Very recently, the lipofuscin pigments in liver obtained from sheep afflicted by ceroid lipofuscinosis were isolated and its chemical constituents examined (21). The lipid constituents of the lipofuscin pigments resembled that of lysosomal lipids. In the neutral lipid fraction, an obvious enrichment in dolichol, dolichyl esters, ubiquinone and free fatty acids was observed. Again, an enrichment of these "lysosomal" lipids in the liver of affected species was not evident. Furthermore, no obvious difference in acyl group composition of the major phospholipids was found in liver between the affected and unaffected species. Surprisingly, the protein portion of the lipofuscin pigments showed the unique presence of some low molecular weight proteins, especially one with molecular weight around 3500 daltons (20). These proteins are not found in normal lysosomes. Their results suggest that ceroid lipofuscinosis may result from an inherited defect in lysosomal protein catabolism.

DOLICHOL EFFECT ON MEMBRANE STRUCTURE AND FUNCTION

Because of the gradual increase in dolichol with age, a
pertinent question to ask is whether the accumulation of these
highly nonpolar compounds in cells may affect neuronal membrane
structure and function. Studies measuring 1,6–diphenyl–1,3,5–
hexatriene (DPH) fluorescence polarization in phospholipid
model membranes have reported dolichol at 1:1000 molar ratio
which significantly increased the fluidity (39) and permeability
(16) of phosphatidylethanolamine containing membranes. The
above–mentioned studies used model membranes. Effects of
dolichol on membrane structure of biological membranes have not
been examined until recently (44). Dolichol in mouse brain SPM
both fluidized and rigidified SPM detected by DPH and trans–
parinaric acid, respectively. The rigidifying effect of
dolichol was confirmed by electron spin resonance using 5–doxyl
and 16–doxyl stearic acid spin labels incorporated into SPM.
Dolichol does affect the physical properties of the membrane.
The discrepancy between DPH and the fluorescent fatty acid and
spin label probes was subsequently shown to result from the use
of bovine serum albumin (BSA) (36).
    Two types of studies were carried out to examine effects of
dolichol on membrane function. In the first study, the effect
of dolichol on Na^+,K^+–ATPase activity in SPM was examined.

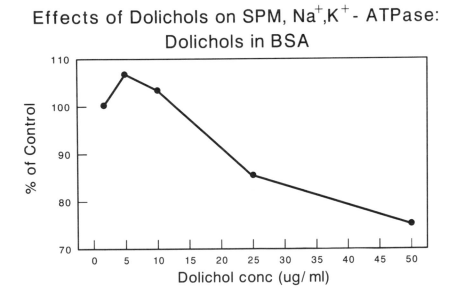

FIG. 4. Effects of dolichols on Na^+,K^+–ATPase activity
in mouse SPM. Dolichols were introduced into the membrane
using BSA (1%).

Dolichols were incorporated into the membrane by preincubation with BSA. As shown in Fig. 4, dolichol exerted a biphasic effect on the enzyme enhancing it at the low concentration range (1 to 5 μg/ml) and inhibiting it at higher concentrations. In the second experiment, dolichols were dissolved in dimethyl sulfoxide (DMSO) prior to delivering to the SPM and assay of Na^+,K^+-ATPase activity. Again, low concentrations of dolichols (1 to 5 pg/ml) indicated a slight stimulation of the Na^+,K^+-ATPase activity, and inhibition was observed at high concentrations (Fig. 5).

Effects of Dolichols on SPM, Na^+,K^+ - ATPase: Dolichols in DMSO

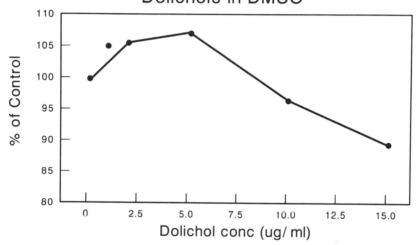

FIG. 5. Effects of dolichols on Na^+,K^+-ATPase activity in mouse SPM. Dolichols were dissolved in DMSO and introduced to the incubation medium to make the final concentration of DMSO to 1%. There is no effect of DMSO on Na^+,K^+-ATPase activity at 1% level.

Two experiments were carried out to examine the effect of dolichols on the incorporation of arachidonic acid into membrane phospholipids (Table 1). The addition of dolichol alone did not seem to affect the uptake activity. However, in the presence of BSA, which is used as a vehicle for incorporating the dolichols into membranes, dolichols resulted in an increase in labeling of phosphatidylinositol, but the labeling of other phospholipids and triacylglycerols was not altered. In the second experiment, dolichol and plasma membranes were incubated at 23°C for 1 hour and in the presence of BSA. After preincubation, the plasma membranes were sedimented and aliquots were taken for the assay of arachidonyl transfer activity. Results again indicated an increased uptake of labeled arachidonate into phosphatidylinositol but not phosphatidylcholine. Under this condition, an increase in incorporation into triacylglycerols was also observed. The results thus indicate that dolichol exerted a small but discernible effect on the acyltransferase activity.

TABLE 1. Lipid ratios of PM after incubation with

[1-^{14}C]-20:4 under different conditions

Conditions	PI/PC	TG/PC
(A) PM at 4°C	2.95 ± 0.13	2.14 ± 0.23
(B) PM at 23°C	2.41 ± 0.17	2.48 ± 0.18
(C) PM + BSA at 23°C	1.52 ± 0.01	0.69 ± 0.04
(D) PM + BSA + dolichols at 23°C	1.94 ± 0.11	1.00 ± 0.06

Abbreviations: BSA, bovine serum albumin; PC, phosphatidyl-choline; PI, phosphatidylinositol; PM, plasma membrane; TG, triglyceride.

Results indicated an increase in labeling of PI and TG with respect to PC due to the presence of dolichols in the preincubation mixture.

Dolichols are long-chain polyisoprenols that are ubiquitous among body organs with higher levels shown in brain and various exocrine glands. Increasing evidence has shown that dolichol levels not only increase with age, they also play an important role in pathological aging. Dolichols have an effect on membrane structure and function. An increase in dolichols in membranes with age may be an important factor in the decline in neuronal membrane functions.

ACKNOWLEDGEMENT

The excellent editorial assistance of Sandy Melliere and Sharon Smith was much appreciated.

REFERENCES

1. Adair, W., and Cafmeyer, N. (1983): Biochim. Biophys. Acta, 751:21-26.
2. Adair, W., and Keller, R. (1982): J. Biol. Chem., 257:8990-8996.
3. Bennett, M., Mathers, N., Hemming, F., Zweije-Hofman, I., and Hosking, G. (1985): Pediatr. Res., 19:213-216.
4. Breckenridge, W., Wolfe, L., and Ng Ying Kin, N. (1973): J. Neurochem., 21:1311-1318.
5. Brizzee, K., and Ordy, J. (1979): Mech. Ageing Dev., 9:143-162.

6. Burton, W., Scher, M., and Waechter, C. (1979): J. Biol. Chem., 254:7129–7136.
7. Carpenter, S., Karpati, G., Andermann, F., Jacob, J., and Andermann, E. (1977): Brain, 100:137–156.
8. Eggens, I., Chojnacki, T., Kenne, L., and Dallner, G. (1983): Biochim. Biophys. Acta, 751:355–368.
9. Goebel, H., Zeman, W., Patel, V., Pullarkat, R., and Lenard, H. (1979): Mech. Ageing. Dev., 10:53–70.
10. Hemming, F. (1983): In: Biosynthesis of Isoprenoid Compounds, edited by J.W. Porter and S.L. Spurgeon, pp. 306–354. John Wiley and Sons, New York.
11. Jensen, G.E., and Clausen, J. (1983): Scand. J. Clin. Lab. Invest., 43:187–196.
12. Keenan, R., and Kruczek, H. (1975): Anal. Biochem., 69:504–509.
13. Keenan, R., Rice, N., and Adrian, G. (1982): Biochim. Biophys. Acta, 711:490–493.
14. Keller, R. (1986): J. Biol. Chem., 261:12053–12059.
15. Keller, R., Armstrong, D., Crum, F., and Koppang, N. (1984): J. Neurochem., 42:1040–1047.
16. Lai, C., and Schutzbach, J. (1986): FEBS Lett., 203:153–156.
17. Ng Ying Kin, N.M.K., Palo, J., Haltia, M., and Wolfe, L.S. (1983): J. Neurochem., 40:1465–1473.
18. Ng Ying Kin, N.M.K., and Wolfe, L.S. (1982): Pediatr. Res., 16:530–532.
19. Nyquist, S.E., and Holt, S. (1986): Biol. Reprod., 34:89–95.
20. Palmer, D.N., Barns, G., Husbands, D.R., and Jolly, R.D. (1986): J. Biol. Chem., 261:1773–1777.
21. Palmer, D.N., Husbands, D.R., Winter, P.J., Blunt, J.W., and Jolly, R.D. (1986): J. Biol. Chem., 261:1766–1772.
22. Parodi, A.J., and Leloir, L.F. (1979): Biochim. Biophys. Acta, 559:1–37.
23. Pullarkat, R., and Raguthu, S. (1985): Alcoholism: Clin. Exp. Res., 9:28–30.
24. Pullarkat, R.K., Raguthu, S., and Pachchagiri, S. (1984): Trans. Am. Soc. Neurochem., 15:171.
25. Pullarkat, R.K., and Reha, H. (1982): J. Biol. Chem., 257:5991–5993.
26. Pullarkat, R.K., Reha, H., and Pullarkat, P.S. (1984): Biochim. Biophys. Acta, 793:494–496.
27. Rip, J., and Carroll, K. (1985): Biochem. J., 227:705–710.
28. Rip, J., Rupar, C., Chaudhary, N., and Carroll, K. (1981): J. Biol. Chem., 256:1929–1934.
29. Rossignol, D., Scher, M., Waechter, C., and Lennarz, W. (1983): J. Biol. Chem., 258:9122–9127.
30. Rupar, C.A., and Carroll, K.K. (1978): Lipids, 13:291–293.

31. Sakakihara, Y., and Volpe, J.J. (1984): Dev. Brain Res., 14:255-262.
32. Sakakihara, Y., and Volpe, J.J. (1985): J. Biol. Chem., 260:15413-15419.
33. Sakakihara, Y., and Volpe, J.J. (1985): J. Neurochem., 44:1535-1540.
34. Scher, M., Devries, G., and Waechter, C. (1984): Arch. Biochem. Biophys., 231:293-302.
35. Scher, M., and Waechter, C. (1981): Biochem. Biophys. Res. Commun., 99:675-681.
36. Schroeder, F., Gorka, C., Williamson, L.S., and Wood, W.G. (Unpublished manuscript)
37. Schwerer, B., and Bernheimer, H. (1978): J. Neurochem., 31:457-460.
38. Sohal, R., Bridges, R., and Howes, E. (1984): Mech. Ageing Dev., 25:355-363.
39. Valtersson, C., van Duyn, G., Verkleij, A.M., Chojnacki, T., de Kruijff, B., and Dallner, G. (1985): J. Biol. Chem., 260:2742-2751.
40. Wisniewski, K.E., Pullarkat, R.K., Harin, A., and Vartola, M. (1983): Ann. Neurol., 14:382.
41. Wolfe, L.S., Ng Ying Kin, N.M.K., Palo, J., and Haltia, M. (1982): Lancet, ii:99.
42. Wolfe, L., Palo, J., Santavuori, P., Andermann, F., Andermann, E., Jacob, J., and Kolodny, E. (1986): Ann. Neurol., 19:270-274.
43. Wong, T.K., and Lennarz, W.J. (1982): J. Biol. Chem., 257:6619-6624.
44. Wood, W.G., Gorka, C., Williamson, L.S., Strong, R., Sun, A.Y., Sun, G.Y., and Schroeder, F. (1986): FEBS Lett., 205:25-28.

Subject Index

A

Actin, 191–96
Adrenergic system, 6–7
Age, brain function and
  cholinergic systems, 72
  compared to Alzheimer's, 11–13,72
  dolichols, 223,226,227–228,229,232
  gene expression, 189–96
  membrane changes, 200,201–6,
    214–216,218,232
  in the very old, 2
Aluminum, 9
Alzheimer's disease (AD), *see also*
    Neuritic plaques;
    Neurofibrillary tangles
  aluminum, 9
  autotoxins, 60,67
  axonal transport, 56–60
  blood flow, 100–1
  and depression, 107–14
  diagnosis, 41,48,97,101,107–108,
    110–112,114
  dolichols, 226,228
  focal sensitivity, 4
  gene expression in, 182
  histology, 17
  imaging, 6,96–97,100–103
  incidence, 1,107
  and infarcts, 51
  neuronal loss, 21,22,28–29,41,50,
    52–65,181
  neurotransmitter systems, 42
    catecholamine, 21,46,49–63,67,183
    cholinergic, 21,71–72,80,83–85,99,
      101–02
  and normal aging, 11–13
  plasticity and repair, 10–11
  symptoms, 64–67,72
  therapies, 66–67,71–73,80–86
  threshold for, 8
  and trophic factors, 29–30,66–67

Amyotrophic lateral sclerosis (ALS)
  on Guam, 18–19,22
  incidence, 31
  neurofibrillary tangles, 19,22–23
  neuroreceptors, 99
  pathology, 17–18,31–32
  and trophic factors, 32–33
Apnea, sleep
  causes, 131–135,141–143
  consequences, 127,136–41
  and snoring, 129–30
  treatment, 143–44
Axonal transport, 56–60

B

Batten disease, 226,228–29
Blood flow, cerebral, 100–1;
    see also Infarction
Brain function, changes in
  age vs disease, 1–2
  gene expression, 195–96
Brain structure changes, 3,102–3;
    see also Neurons; White matter

C

Calcium
  and Alzheimer's, 9
  channels, 163–64
  and neuronal loss, 8
Catecholamines, *see also* Dopamine;
    Epinephrine; PNMT
  in Alzheimer's, 21,46,49–52,60–63,
    67,183
  biosynthesis, 43,183–84
  distribution and assays, 6–7,43–47
  gene expression, 183–86
  in Parkinson's, 183
  in tardive dyskinesia, 124–25

235